HOSTILES

AND

HORSE SOLDIERS

HOSTILES AN[

Indian Battles and

With a FOREWORD *by*

MERRILL J. MATTES

THE BATTLE OF BEECHER ISLAND

*This painting, depicting a scene of the famous fight, was made by Robert Lindneux.
It is reproduced here through the courtesy of the State Historical Society
of Colorado, Denver.*

ORSE SOLDIERS:
...igns in the West

y **LONNIE J. WHITE** *with contributions by*
**JERRY KEENAN, STANLEY R. DAVISON,
JAMES T. KING,** *and* **JOE A. STOUT, Jr.**

PUBLISHED BY
PRUETT PUBLISHING COMPANY
BOULDER, COLORADO
1972

TO THOSE WHO FOUGHT

Foreword

THE INDIAN WARS of the Western Plains seem to have endless fascination for scholars as well as for the general public. The Indians wars east of the Mississippi were on a larger scale and they covered a greater period of time, yet they do not engage our attention today nearly as much as those of the trans-Mississippi West. The explanation of this lies in part with the fact that action in the Western theater was more recent and thus fresher in memory. But there is another psychological factor that accounts for this phenomenal pre-occupation with Western Indian fights.

Except for the prologue of the 1851 clash between the Sioux and General Harney's troopers near Ash Hollow on the Great Platte Road, and the epilogue of the Wounded Knee disaster in 1890, the period of warfare on the Plains is essentially that spanned by events described in this book. This would be roughly from the Sioux and Cheyenne uprising of 1864 during the Civil War, dramatized by the Sand Creek Massacre, and 1886, the time of the Apache's moment of truth. During this span of about twenty-five years there were hundreds of remote skirmishes, battles and campaigns, but they involved altogether only a few thousant combatants. Any one of a dozen Civil War battles fought in hours involved far greater numbers. Why the fascination with these scattered small-scale events in far-away places wherein the ultimate outcome was inevitable?

The explanation lies in our psychic roots. The Indian wars of the West have the same elements found in the ancient classics — the epic struggle of sacrificial heroes against a seemingly grotesque and inhuman foe in the setting of a vast, rugged and colorful wilderness.

After the Civil War, the Indian wars provided professional occupation for soldiers accustomed to the military life. The news of battles from the Far West provided an emotional outlet for a citizenry somewhat bored by peace after the holocaust of the Civil War. The elemental clash of blue-clad soldiers and red men, either near-naked or robed in barbaric splendor, was a continuing morality play with bloody overtones that intrigue modern man as it did his forebears. Scholarly treatment of these violent encounters does not obscure the dramatic syndrome, in which the reader may imagine himself the weary sun-burned cavalry officer scanning the horizon for savage smoke-signals.

Today the young descendants of Indian warriors seem intent on proving the error of white man's history. To them their ancestors were

Foreword

the heroes defending their homeland against the ruthless paleface invaders. For them the confrontations leading to the Little Big Horn are also a morality play, but with the roles of heroes and villains reversed.

The measure of true scholarship is objectivity. The scholarly contributions to this volume are objective in such degree that Indians and whites alike can read these pages and feel the excitement of distant tomtom or bugle call, whichever sound they are tuned to!

— MERRILL J. MATTES,
Chief, History and Historic Architecture,
National Park Service, Denver, Colorado

April, 1972

A Word from the Publisher

THE HISTORY OF THE INDIAN WARS in this country certainly does not represent America's finest hour. Yet to ignore this episode of our past, no matter how unjust it may have been, is to disregard the history and the forces which have shaped this nation.

From that moment when the first Europeans set foot on the North American Continent until that tragic day at Wounded Knee, South Dakota, they were years marked by misunderstandings, avarice, and deceit. The White American, motivated by a combination of Manifest Destiny, "get rich quick," and just the simple promise of a chance to start fresh in a big, new country, pushed ever deeper into the Indians' sanctuary. The latter responded with violence and was, in turn, met with violence.

As the public's guardian, the U. S. Army was given the unenviable task of subjugating the Indian. It was a bitter, relentless struggle with an inevitable outcome.

From a publisher's point of view it may be rash to set forth another book on the subject of the Indian wars; so much has already been written. And yet, it is our belief that the several studies presented herein offer sufficient new material and fresh analysis to make this collection a significant contribution to the history of the American West.

I wish to take this opportunity to extend my thanks to the staff of Pruett Publishing Company; to the authors for their excellent contributions; to Lonnie J. White of Memphis State University for serving as guest editor, and especially to Mr. and Mrs. Lorrin L. Morrison, editors and publishers of JOURNAL *of the* WEST, for graciously allowing us to reprint this material, and for their splendid cooperation throughout the process of bringing this book to life.

— F. A. PRUETT

Boulder Colorado
June, 1972

Table of Contents

List of Illustrations

List of Sketch Maps

Introduction

THE INDIAN WARS on the North American continent began almost with the appearance of the first Europeans on its shores and lasted until the close of the last American frontier in about 1890. The various battles and campaigns that comprised these wars have, owing to their spectacular nature and significance in the white man's conquest of the frontier, inspired the writing and publication of numerous articles and books. Of particular interest and significance were the Indian encounters during the period from 1864 to 1890, when the final removal of the hostile Indian as a barrier to settlement was at last accomplished. The scene was the trans-Mississippi West, and among the tribes and regions involved were the Cheyennes, Arapahoes, Kiowas, and Comanches on the Southern Plains; the Sioux on the Northern Plains; the Bannocks and Paiutes in the Pacific Northwest; and the Apaches in the Southwest. It is the struggles with these Indians in these regions that the nine feature articles reprinted here under nine chapter headings are concerned. Taken as a whole, these articles, by providing much fresh detail and analysis on the subjects they treat, make a worthy contribution to our knowledge of the Western Indian wars.

The first five chapters contain accounts of battles and campaigns on the Southern Plains frontier. Chapter 1 deals with one of the most notorious incidents ever to occur in the annals of Western Indian warfare — the Sand Creek, Colorado, massacre of 1864. The massacre and its background and aftermath are examined at some length. Chapter 2 is concerned mainly with a little-known but spectacular battle on the Kansas frontier in 1867, the Battle of Prairie Dog Creek. Chapter 3 treats, in scholarly fashion, a well-known encounter — the Battle of Beecher Island, Colorado, in 1868 — in which a relatively small body of scouts held off for days a large force of hostiles. Chapter 4 describes the role of the Nineteenth Kansas Volunteer Cavalry in General Phil Sheridan's celebrated winter campaign in Indian Territory and the Texas Panhandle in 1868-1869. And Chapter 5 follows the movements of the troops and describes the several actions in the Texas Panhandle during the Red River War of 1874-1875.

These articles appeared originally as part a series entitled "Warpaths on the Southern Plains" in JOURNAL of the WEST. They are reprinted here with only a few minor changes and corrections. Some slight over-lapping in Chapters 3 and 4 is attributable to the fact that the articles were not written to connect one with the other but to stand alone as separate features. The author of the first five chapters (articles), Lonnie J. White, holds the Ph.D. degree from the University of Texas, teaches Western and Indian history at Memphis State University, Memphis, Tennessee, has written or edited a number of books and articles, and is the editor of this volume. He has also edited a topical number of JOURNAL *of the* WEST (Volume XI, No. 1 — January, 1972), which was devoted to "Indian Battles and Campaigns in the West," and from which the following four chapters, with only a few minor changes, have been taken.

These four chapters deal with various aspects of the Indian wars in other Western regions. Chapter 6 provides a careful analysis of each facet of the famous Wagon Box engagement, which occurred near Fort Phil Kearny on the Bozeman Trail in 1867, and of the later controversy over the exact location of the fight. The author, Jerry Keenan, has written several articles and is currently Western and Regional History Editor for Pruett Publishing Company, the publisher of this book. Chapter 7 relates General George Crook's activities in the critical days following his celebrated engagement on the Rosebud in 1876 and while General George A. Custer's colorful career was being ingloriously terminated a relatively short distance away on the Little Big Horn. The author, James T. King, received his Ph.D. degree from the University of Nebraska, is professor of history at the University of Wisconsin, River Falls, is the author of a biography of General Eugene A. Carr, and is currently preparing a book-length study of General Crook.

Chapter 8 consists of a series of private letters written by Major Edwin C. Mason, a participant in the Bannock-Paiute War of 1878, which Professor Stanley R. Davison obtained from the family papers of Mason's grandson, Colonel Kenneth M. Moore, U. S. Army, retired. These letters afford an intimate look at the Bannock-Paiute campaign and its conduct by General O. O. Howard through the eyes of an officer who was free to say, in private correspondence to his family, precisely what was on his mind. Professor Davison, the editor of these letters, holds the Ph.D. degree from the University of California, Berkeley, teaches at Western Montana College at Dillon, and is a member of the editorial staffs of JOURNAL *of the* WEST and *Montana Magazine*. The next and last chapter of the book is an account of part of the noted Geronimo Campaign as told by a soldier, a private, who participated in it. Specifically, it tells of the unsuccessful endeavor of Captain Henry W. Lawton's command to track down the renegade Apaches under Geronimo in northern Mexico and southern Arizona in 1886 for the purpose of forcing them to surrender. The editor of this outstanding document, Joe A. Stout, Jr., earned his Ph.D. degree at Oklahoma State University at Stillwater, is currently an assistant professor of history at Missouri Southern College, Joplin, and is the author of a number of articles in scholarly journals.

Much credit for the development of this book is due to Mr. and Mrs. Lorrin L. Morrison, the editors and publishers of JOURNAL *of the* WEST,

Introduction

who graciously gave their permission to reproduce the chapters contained herein. Thanks are also due the other authors and editors for their contributions and their consent to republish their work. I am also personally indebted to Mr. and Mrs. Morrison and to Jerry Keenan for their assistance relating to editorial matters. And on behalf of the authors and editors I would like to express appreciation to the several persons, libraries, institutions, and historical organizations that supplied illustrative and research materials for the chapters in this book.

—— LONNIE J. WHITE

FROM BLOODLESS TO BLOODY:

The Third Colorado Cavalry and the Sand Creek Massacre

T HE DISCOVERY OF GOLD in the Pike's Peak region in the late 1850's brought prospectors by the thousands westward to the Rocky Mountain country. Mining camps and towns soon dotted the entire area and Colorado Territory was created in 1861. Needless to say, the advent of white civilization to Colorado did nothing to better relations between the whites and the Plains Indians. The Cheyennes and Arapahoes had even before the miner invasion been giving trouble on the Platte overland route to the Far West. The frontiersmen now did more than just pass through the Indian country; they began settling on lands set aside for the Cheyennes and Arapahoes in the Fort Laramie Treaty of 1851.

The Indians, however, though restless and unhappy, made no immediate trouble. But doubting that they would long remain docile, William Bent, agent for the Upper Arkansas Indians, pressed hard for a treaty that would place them on a reservation where they would have little contact with the pioneers. Bent was convinced that such a treaty would prevent a war that could mean disaster to the Indians. Bent's views prevailed, and in the Treaty of Fort Wise in 1861 the Southern Cheyennes and Arapahoes ceded their claim to all their former lands, which embraced the larger part of eastern Colorado, except for a relatively small reservation on the Upper Arkansas River. The treaty was defective, however, because the Cheyenne Dog Soldiers, the largest and most hostile of all Cheyenne bands, refused to sign it.

During the ensuing years the Indians manifested considerable restlessness. The Upper Arkansas Cheyennes and Arapahoes were unhappy with their reservation because it afforded only a limited supply of buffalo and other game. And they often fought the Utes of the mountains and stole and killed stock as they passed through the white settlements.

More troublesome were the Indians of the Upper Platte Agency who raided along the South Platte until they were eventually driven eastward to the Republican River by a company of Second Colorado Cavalry. Since the Cheyennes and Arapahoes of this agency were not signers of the Fort Wise treaty, John Evans, governor of Colorado Territory and ex-officio superintendent of Indian affairs, urged an extension of its terms to them. Until they relinquished their claim to the lands set aside for them in the Fort Laramie treaty, as their kinsmen on the Upper Arkansas had done in the Fort Wise treaty, there would be no

1

peace and the mining country of Colorado would remain subject to Indian title. The Arkansas River reservation was, Evans believed, large enough to accommodate all the Cheyennes and Arapahoes.

Despite threats of war by the Indians and a number of isolated raids apparently involving warriors of both the Upper Arkansas and Upper Platte Agencies, the year 1863 opened on the Colorado frontier in relative peace. Indian activity increased during the year, however, on the overland trails. On the Santa Fé (Arkansas) road, Colonel Jesse H. Leavenworth of the Second Colorado Cavalry and Samuel G. Colley, Indian agent on the Upper Arkansas since 1861, sought diligently to pacify the restless Indians. The Comanches and Kiowas as well as the Cheyennes and Arapahoes gave trouble on this route. Active on the Platte road were the Sioux and the Upper Platte Cheyennes and Arapahoes. Although Governor Evans worked hard to bring both divisions of the Cheyennes and Arapahoes together apparently for a new treaty, he was unsuccessful.

Professor Donald J. Berthrong asserts that Governor Evans now "moved systematically to prove that the Plains Indians were hostile" because he wished "to force a situation which would enable him to clear Indians from all settled regions of Colorado territory." This explains, Berthrong implies, Evans' acceptance of reports that the Indians planned a general outbreak for 1864. One of the governor's sources was Robert North, a squaw-man who had lived with the Arapahoes since his youth, who told Evans that he witnessed a medicine dance fifty-five miles from Fort Lyon at which the Kiowas, Comanches, Kiowa-Apaches, the Northern Arapahoes, the Cheyennes, and the Sioux agreed to take to the warpath in the spring of 1864.[1] Evans' acceptance of such reports, however, may simply have been the result of the Indians' refusal to meet him even to talk about a treaty. Since they would not treat with him and they were committing sporadic raids, it was easy for Evans to believe what North and other informants told him, that the Plains Indians planned a major uprising.

An Indian war did indeed come to Colorado in 1864. It was not, however, initiated by a concerted attack against the frontier; instead, it began inconspicuously with an Indian raid on a herd of cattle owned by two government contractors, Irwin and Jackman, who were "engaged in transporting army stores" to military posts in Colorado, New Mexico, and "other portions of the plains." The raiders, Cheyennes, struck the herd while it was on the headwaters of Sand Creek (Big Sandy) on April 5 and drove one hundred seventy-five head eastward toward the headwaters of the Smoky Hill River.[2]

Learning of the raid, Colonel John M. Chivington, commander of the First Colorado Cavalry and the District of Colorado, sent Lieutenant George S. Eayre and eighty men with two howitzers and ten supply wagons in pursuit. Leaving Camp Weld, located just outside Denver, on

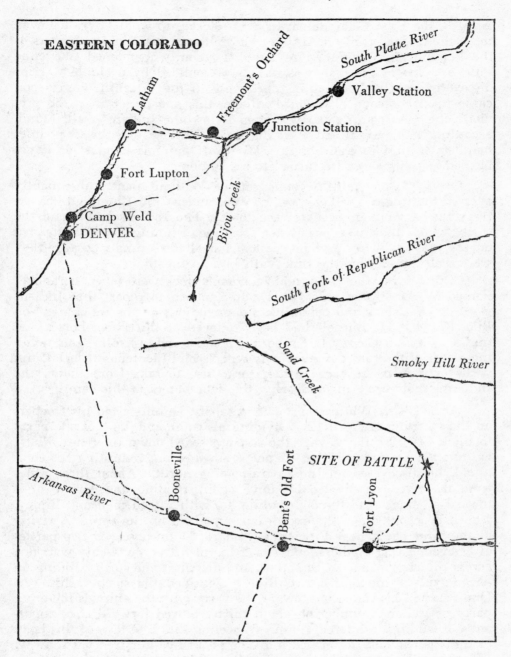

APPROXIMATE SITE OF THE SAND CREEK MASSACRE

April 8, the First Colorado cavalrymen picked up what Eayre believed to be the raiders' trail on April 14 and followed it to the headwaters of the Republican. There Eayre found a recently-abandoned Cheyenne village. One of his men was seriously wounded by a single warrior discovered nearby. Marching northwest on the fifteenth, Eayre soon came upon a second abandoned village, this one larger than the previous one. A scouting party sent to follow the Indians' trail, found, according to Eayre, nineteen of the stolen cattle which the Cheyennes had left behind in their flight. His draft animals exhausted, Eayre burned the village and returned to his station.[3]

George Bent, half-Cheyenne son of William Bent, subsequently averred that the two villages, which were under Crow Chief and Beaver, respectively, were innocent of the theft. The Indians had found the stock, which they were accused of stealing, running loose unattended on the prairie. They had no reason to steal the animals because they were well-supplied at the time with buffalo meat.[4]

A few days after Irwin and Jackman's stock were taken, a rancher named W. D. Ripley rode into Camp Sanborn to report that Indians were "taking stock and committing depredations on the ranchmen" on Bijou Creek. He himself had been relieved of thirty-five horses and mules. Captain George L. Sanborn, First Colorado Cavalry, commanding officer of the camp, immediately sent Second Lieutenant Clark Dunn with forty men "to recover the stock, also to take from them [the Indians] their fire-arms and bring the depredators to this camp."[5]

Armed with Whitney pistols and sabers, Dunn started his troopers on the morning of April 12. Dividing his command, he sent one party to Bijou Creek while he with the rest proceeded down the South Platte to Junction Station. Riding thence southward and reuniting his command, he discovered an Indian trail going north. About three miles from the river, he divided his force again, sending one portion of it toward a "smoke" to the right while he, with fifteen men and Ripley, who had accompanied the expedition, remained on the trail. Arriving at the river bank, near Fremont's Orchard, Dunn observed two parties of Cheyenne Dog Soldiers, one, consisting of fifteen or twenty warriors, across the river ahead of the other, and driving some stock. Riding on ahead with a one-man escort, Ripley identified the stock as his. As Dunn started his command toward the party with the animals the other party of Indians, numbering about thirty, moved forward also, apparently intending to intercept him. Wheeling into line toward this body of Indians, which also formed into line about five hundred yards away, Dunn sent Ripley and four men on after the stock while he himself advanced alone toward the Indians facing him for the purpose of talking to the chief. As he and the chief talked, warriors began coming up with their bows strung. Breaking off the conversation Dunn apparently retreated with the Indians right behind him. Since the chief refused his demand that the Indians surrender the stock, Dunn ordered his men to disarm them. As they started to obey his order, the warriors, according to Dunn, opened fire.[6]

For over thirty minutes the two forces battled it out at close range, until the Indians retired to a nearby bluff, carrying with them, if we may believe Dunn, "some 8 or 10" dead and "about 12 or 15" wounded warriors. Both the Ripley party and the Indians driving the stock participated in the fight. The soldiers drove the Indians a half-mile or more during the fray. Dunn's losses were four men wounded, two mortally. Reuniting his command, Dunn chased the warriors for about fifteen miles. Returning during the night to Camp Sanborn for fresh horses and a guide, Dunn the next day pursued the Indian trail until it was finally obliterated by a snowstorm.[7]

The Cheyennes' account of the incident differed somewhat from that of Dunn's. As Black Kettle later told it, if we may believe Lieutenant Joseph A. Cramer, First Colorado Cavalry, the Indians Dunn fought picked up some lost stock on the prairie while traveling north, intending to leave it at Elbridge Gerry's ranch. Finding no one at the ranch, they took the animals with them. Accosted by Dunn, they agreed to surrender the stock except for one animal which they told him they could not hand over until one of their party, who had taken it on a hunt, returned. Dunn's men then began taking the Indians' arms. But when one of the warriors refused to let go his weapon the soldiers tried to take it by force, the Indians began firing, and in the ensuing battle three warriors were killed or wounded.[8]

George B. Grinnell, who received his information from Indian participants, states that the Dog Soldiers were en route north to join the Northern Cheyennes in an expedition against the Crows. They picked up four stray mules on the prairie. A man, presumably Ripley, came into their camp and claimed the mules, but they would not give them up without a present to pay "for their trouble." Ripley then reported the loss of his animals to Captain Sanborn and he sent Dunn after them. The soldiers, when they found the Indians, charged them without warning. In the fight, the soldiers retreated and three warriors were wounded.[9]

Dunn's fight near Fremont's Orchard signaled the real beginning of the Indian War of 1864. Whether the Indians or the soldiers were the aggressors depends upon who the investigator wishes to believe. Either side could very well have been the guilty party, for as the Denver *Daily Rocky Mountains News* commented:

> It requires men of much sagacity and common cautious sense, with arms or without them, to fool around [with] Indians. They [the Indians] have to judge of us as we have to do them, when we see them advancing, by the "looks of things"; and other things being unsettled, the first opportunity is generally seized, by both the red and white skins.[10]

The military authorities were not at the time, of course, aware of the Indian side of the incidents. Had they been, although they would probably have chosen to believe their commanders in the field, they might have pursued a less aggressive policy. As it was, Major General Samuel R. Curtis, commander of the Department of Kansas, ordered Colonel Chivington to pursue and punish the depredators without reference to district lines, and Chivington, in turn, instructed his commanders, in essence, to "kill them" on sight.[11]

The war was soon escalated by another engagement on the South Platte. As the result of several raids by Indians identified as Cheyennes upon Morrison's and other ranches, Major Jacob Downing, First Colorado Cavalry, who was now in charge of military operations on the Platte road in Chivington's district, stationed two detachments of soldiers, one under Lieutenant Dunn and the other under Lieutenant George H. Chase, at ranches near Junction Station. It was Downing's intention to punish all Cheyennes that his command came across even though he understood that the Cheyennes as a tribe "discountenanced" the depredations committed by a few of them.[12]

Presently, the Cheyennes drove off a number of horses from Moore and Kelly's Ranch. Both Dunn's and Chase's detachments were nearby at the time and they trailed the raiders southward toward the Republican River. Twenty-five miles from the Platte, they found eleven abandoned lodges and destroyed them.[13]

A few days later, Major Downing with forty men left Camp Sanborn to search for a camp of hostile Cheyennes reported to be in the vicinity. On May 1 he captured a half-Cheyenne-half-Sioux who, in return for his life, agreed to lead him to the village. At 6:00 o'clock a. m., on May 3, Downing found the Indians near Cedar Bluffs about sixty miles north of the South Platte. After securing the pony-herd and leaving ten men to guard it, Downing dismounted his command, detailed several men to hold the horses, and attacked the village. The surprised Indians quickly retreated to the protection of a canyon. For about three hours the two forces shot it out with neither side giving ground. Running low on ammunition, Downing destroyed the Indian lodges and headed home.

Downing reported his losses as one killed and one wounded, the Indians' as twenty-five killed and thirty or forty wounded. Major Edward W. Wynkoop, First Colorado Cavalry, subsequently stated, however, that the Cheyennes told him they lost only two squaws and two papooses evidently killed. The captured ponies Downing "distributed among the boys"; later, however, because General Curtis disapproved of his doing so, Downing turned them over to the government. Downing believed the Cedar Canyon fight was the beginning of an Indian war "which must result in exterminating" the red men. Although Down-

ing was certain that the Cheyennes he fought were guilty of depredations, Grinnell avers that they were not even aware of "any trouble with
[the] whites."[14]

In the meantime, Lieutenant Eayre had left Denver on another
punitive expedition. Eayre returned from his earlier expedition convinced that the hostile Cheyennes were camped on the Republican
River, some two hundred miles east of Denver. Obtaining permission
from Chivington to go after them, Eayre with eighty-four men, two
howitzers, and a supply train started for the Republican on April 24.
A week later, he reported that he was on a branch of the Smoky Hill
River and following a large, fresh Indian trail. Unknown to him two
large Indian camps, one Sioux, the other Cheyenne, were on either side
of him. On May 16 he came upon an estimated four hundred Cheyennes heading north about three miles from the Smoky Hill and less
than a day's march from Fort Larned, Kansas. According to Eayre, the
Cheyennes attacked him, "and after a persistent fight of seven and one-
half hours [he] succeeded in driving them from the field," killing three
chiefs and twenty-five warriors. His own losses were four men killed
and three wounded and "a number" of horses killed, wounded, and
stampeded. After the fight he took his exhausted command on to Fort
Larned.[15]

Grinnell and Indian Trader John S. Smith tell us that the Indians,
under Black Kettle and Lean Bear, were unaware of the difficulties on
the Platte, and Lean Bear was shot down in cold blood by the soldiers
as he and others rode out to talk to them.[16] And William Bent stated
that the Cheyennes were leaving the vicinity of Fort Larned to go on
a hunt when they saw the soldiers. Lean Bear rode up to them, pro-
fessed friendship, and was shot by a trooper for his trouble. For ten
or fifteen miles the Indians pressed the attack against the retreating
cavalrymen, losing two warriors in addition to Lean Bear.[17]

Major T. I. McKenny of Curtis' staff, who received his information
from one of Eayre's officers, also reported the fight as less than a victory
for the Army though he named the Indians as the aggressors. Eayre
"wandered off out of his district" — actually, as noticed above, General
Curtis' orders permitted the crossing of district lines — and about fifty
miles from Fort Larned while his command was "well scattered" over
the prairie, he was attacked and forced to retreat.[18]

If the Arkansas Cheyennes were peaceful before Eayre's fight, such
was no longer the case, for they and the Platte Cheyennes struck the
Central Plains frontier as it had never been struck before. They were
presently joined on the warpath by at least portions of the Sioux, Kiowas,
Comanches, and Arapahoes. While Cheyennes and Sioux raided on the
Platte in Nebraska and Colorado, Cheyennes, Kiowas, Comanches, and
Arapahoes depredated on the Santa Fé road in Kansas, Colorado, and

New Mexico. Throughout the remainder of the year and on into 1865 the Indians remained on the warpath, prepetrating some of the most destructive raids ever committed on the Central Plains. Perhaps as many as one hundred or more frontiersmen "bit the dust" in the raids during the summer and fall alone.[19]

One significant raid occurred thirty miles southeast of Denver on June 11. After running off forty-nine mules from Coal Creek thirteen miles from the capital, a party of Indians proceeded to Box Elder Creek where they burned a ranch house belonging to Isaac P. Van Wormer, murdered the occupants, Nathan W. Hungate, his wife and two children, and drove off thirty horses and mules. According to the statement of one who was at the scene shortly after the massacre, Mrs. Hungate was found about one hundred yards from the house "stabbed in several places and scalped, and the body bore evidences of having been violated. The two children had their throats cut, their heads being nearly severed from the bodies." The body of the man, according to other witnesses, was discovered some distance from the house "horribly mutilated and the scalp torn off." The bodies of the entire family were brought to Denver in a wagon by Van Wormer and placed on public display.

First Colorado cavalrymen with orders from Colonel Chivington not to take Indian prisoners proceeded immediately to the scene of the raids, but they were unable to pick up the Indians' trail. Needless to say, the Hungate massacre and the exhibiting of the mangled bodies in Denver served only to increase the people's hatred of the Indians. "From the throats of thousands," wrote one contemporary, "went up the cry of redress." Presumably the whites' anger was directed at the Cheyennes, who were at the time believed to be the culprits. They were later identified by Arapaho Chief Neva as four Northern Arapahoes.[20]

General Curtis was hard pressed to meet the emergency. Although he had some sixty-five hundred men in his department in June, most of them were engaged in the Civil War immediately east of the Plains. Curtis augmented the strength of the frontier garrisons as much as he could and stationed troops along the overland trails. In July, he established the District of the Upper Arkansas for the better defense of the Kansas frontier. Two new posts — Fort Ellsworth (later Fort Harker) and Fort Zarah — were erected in the district. Supplementing the federal troops were Kansas Colorado, and Nebraska militiamen. And, as the reader will notice below, a regiment of Colorado volunteers was raised for federal service. In one instance, in July, Curtis led one hundred federals and three hundred Kansas militiamen on an Indian-hunting expedition in Kansas only to find the Indians "scattered."[21]

Another expedition led by Major General James G. Blunt, commandant of the District of the Upper Arkansas, in September, encountered a large concentration of Indians northwest of Fort Larned,

Kansas, and after a fight pursued them for some distance.[22] Despite the widespread attacks, which threw the frontier into considerable turmoil and put Curtis to much trouble in providing defense, Curtis did not agree with Governor Evans that the Plains tribes had, in accordance with a preärranged plan, formed a "powerful combination" and embarked on an all-out war for the purpose of driving out the white man; as Curtis apparently saw it, the Indian war was no more than a series of spontaneous, isolated raids for the purpose of acquiring stock.

While General Curtis labored to protect the entire Central Plains, Governor Evans sought to obtain greater protection for the Colorado frontier. Although Colorado had two volunteer regiments in federal service, one — the Second Colorado Cavalry — was on duty in Missouri while part of the other — the First Colorado Cavalry — was, in the spring of 1864, ordered to Kansas. The removal of Colorado troops by Curtis was vigorously protested by Evans on the grounds that it left Colorado poorly defended against the Indians.[23]

On June 14, Evans telegraphed Secretary of War E. M. Stanton asking authority to organize a regiment of volunteers to serve as federal troops for one hundred days. Evidently anticipating that Stanton might urge the use of territorial militia, Evans stated that it could not "be made useful unless in U. S. service to coöperate with [federal] troops." One notices that this request was made on the heels of the Hungate massacre near Denver. A week later, Evans telegraphed Curtis proposing that Curtis station additional men on the Platte. "I could furnish you two or three companies of Militia with their own horses if required." But the territorial militia law was "so defective that I cannot subsist or send in pursuit; and I doubt the expediency of any troops being in active service not under your command." Three days later, Evans wrote Delegate H. P. Bennet in Washington requesting help in obtaining a "favorable response" to the proposal he made to Stanton.[24]

Believing the war had commenced "in earnest," Evans on June 27 issued a proclamation "to the friendly Indians of the Plains," which was evidently designed to keep them peaceful. If they should join their fellow-tribesmen on the warpath there would be no "nucleus for peace" and the war might last longer than it would otherwise. Evans' proclamation called for agents, interpreters, and traders to instruct the friendly Indians to "keep away" from the hostiles and to "go to places of safety." Fort Lyon, Fort Larned, Fort Laramie, and Camp Collins were designated as points of rendezvous where the friendlies would be given provisions and assigned to places of safety by their agents.[25]

With the Indians raiding across the entire Central Plains frontier, especially in Kansas and Nebraska, and interrupting mail and travel into Denver, Evans on August 10 issued an appeal to the "patriotic citizens of Colorado" beseeching them "to organize for the defense of your homes and families against the merciless savages." Every settlement should "organize its volunteer militia company for its defense, arming themselves as far as practicable, and I will supply the deficiency until my supply of arms is exhausted." Any person who killed a hostile was "a patriot; but there are Indians who are friendly, and to kill one of these will involve us in greater difficulty. It is important therefore to fight only the hostile . . ." Evans' appeal was heartily endorsed by the *Daily Rocky Mountain News*:

> Self preservation demands decisive action, and the only way to secure it is to fight them [the Indians] in their own way. A few months of active extermination against the red devils will bring quiet, and nothing else will."[26]

Despite Evans' call for the organization of the militia, Evans still had little faith in its effectiveness, for he wired Commissioner of Indian Affairs W. P. Dole on the same day as his appeal asking him to "Please bring all the force of your department to bear in favor of speedy re-enforcement of our troops, and get me authority to raise a regiment of 100-days' mounted men." The Territory's "militia law is inoperative, and unless this authority is given we will be destroyed." Evans' long-sought authority to raise a regiment of volunteers was forthcoming a day or two later. "Your Governor," stated the departmental assistant adjutant general to Colonel Chivington on August 13, "has been authorized to raise a mounted 100-days' regiment. The ordnance, quartermaster, and commissary officers in your district will furnish the necessary supplies upon proper requisitions."[27]

On August 11, Evans issued another proclamation, which went beyond his appeal in urging Coloradans to action against the hostile Indians. His special messengers, whom he had sent among the Indians directing the friendlies to report in at the military posts named in his June proclamation, had "now returned" and most of the Indians had refused to come in. Consequently, he now authorized "all citizens of Colorado, either individually or in . . . parties . . . to go in pursuit of all hostile Indians on the plains, scrupulously avoiding those who have responded to my . . . call to rendezvous at the points indicated, also to kill and destroy . . . wherever they may be found, all such hostile Indians." Furthermore, they had his permission to retain any property which they might capture. To those citizens who would "organize under the militia law" he would issue arms and ammunition and "present their accounts for pay as regular soldiers for themselves, their horses, their subsistence and transportation, to Congress . . ." Slowly militia companies were enrolled and at least three of them served near Russellville, at Fort Lupton, and on the South Platte.[28]

Why did Governor Evans take these seemingly urgent measures? The answer may be that he hoped to force a military solution to the Indian war which would result in the Cheyennes and Arapahoes' giving up their claims to Colorado mining lands. He may also have been motivated simply by a desire to protect the settlements and to keep open the lines of communication with the outside world. And they may have been taken, at least in part, as the result of political pressures arising from the statehood movement.

Colorado's first struggle for statehood began in earnest at about the same time as the initial events of the Indian war. During the winter a territorial convention memorialized Congress asking for an enabling act. Because the admission of Colorado would mean additional, needed political strength to the national party in power, Congress authorized the territory to frame a state constitution and to elect state officials. Statehood was strongly endorsed by Governor Evans, Henry M. Teller, Colonel Chivington, and the Colorado press, especially the *News*, edited by William N. Byers and John L. Dailey. In general, the men who supported statehood were members of the territorial Union Administration (Republican) Party, the majority party, while those who opposed it belonged to the Democratic Party.

The Union Administration Party named a slate of candidates that included Chivington's name as a candidate for Congress. It was also evidently understood that, if statehood carried, Teller and Evans would be sent to the U. S. Senate. The party argued that statehood would give Colorado a greater voice in Washington in such matters as the route of a transcontinental railroad, protection against the Indians, and mining laws, and that it would terminate the tenure of certain territorial judges, one of them Stephen S. Harding, whose court decisions regarding Indian lands and mining claims were most unpopular.

Among those in opposition to statehood were Dr. Thomas D. Worrall, Judge Charles Lee Armour, Allen A. Bradford, Rodney French, and U. S. Marshal A. C. Hunt. The spokesman for the anti-state faction was the *Black Hawk Daily Mining Journal*, edited by Frank Hall and Ovando J. Hollister. The anti-state men objected to statehood partly because they believed it would increase the cost of government and impose a higher tax burden on Colorado mines and citizens. They charged, also, that the movement had been got up by territorial officials solely for the purpose of furthering their own political ambitions. Among their targets were Governor Evans and Colonel Chivington.

Perhaps one of their most telling charges was that Evans and Chivington were guilty of mismanagement of Indian affairs. It was suggested that Evans and Chivington deliberately provoked the Indian war because they saw in it an opportunity to enhance their own personal reputations. And they were responsible for the territory's poor state of defense. They, especially Evans, not General Curtis, were responsible for the removal of the Colorado troops from the territory. Had they wished it, the volunteers would never have been sent away. Their

11

failure to prevent their "withdrawal . . . was a criminal neglect of the life and property of citizens." Chivington was out stumping the territory in behalf of statehood and his candidacy for Congress when he should be trying to keep open the overland routes. Of the two, Evans received much the greater amount of attention in the anti-state press.

At first glance, it would appear, since the majority of the Indian raids were being committed on the overland trails in Nebraska and Kansas, that Colorado should have felt the Indian war less than her two neighbors to the east. The following statement, which appeared in the *Journal* on August 20, would indicate, however, that perhaps such was not the case:

> Our communication with the States is cut off, so that machinery, merchandise, provisions, passengers, the mails, etc., have ceased to come forward. Gold cannot be shipped East, or currency West, and the supply of the latter in the banks is nearly exhausted. Work, therefore, must soon generally cease because the money to pay the workmen cannot be obtained. The crops in the Territory are unusually abundant, and we are in the midst of harvest. Indian massacres, however, are alarming the ranchemen [sic], and they may be driven to rendezvous for protection before securing their crops. So leaving out of view the inhuman cruelties practiced upon the defenceless people of the outer settlements, the prospect, not only of an absolute cessation of business, but also of utter starvation or abandonment of the country, stares us in the face.

The state forces labored valiantly to counter their opponents' charges. The *News* denied that Evans and Chivington were guilty as charged, and Evans issued his appeal and proclamations and successfully sought authority to raise a third regiment of volunteers. On August 25 and 26, the *News* printed official correspondence dating back to 1863 showing that the governor had tried to treat with the Indians, had warned higher authorities that he expected an outbreak, and had protested the removal of Colorado troops. Evidently realizing that he had become a serious liability to the statehood movement, Evans announced early in September that he would not be a candidate for the U. S. Senate. But the anti-state men had done their work well, for on September 13 the people went to the polls and rejected the proposed constitution and, at the same time, the candidates for state offices.[29]

While the statehood struggle of 1864 was coming to a close, significant events were taking place on the territory's southeastern frontier. Early in September, three Indians — One-Eye, Minimic and a squaw — were captured by three soldiers near Fort Lyon. In their possession were two letters similar in content, one addressed to Major Edward W. Wynkoop, First Colorado Cavalry, post commandant, and the other to Agent Colley. They had been written by Edmund Guerrier and George Bent for Black Kettle "and other Chiefs." In them the chiefs admitted that their people were on the warpath and that they were holding seven white prisoners. They were now willing to make peace, however, "pro-

12

From Bloodless to Bloody

— Courtesy, Western Collection,
Denver Public Library

THE HON. JOHN EVANS
Colorado Territorial Governor

— Courtesy, Library, State Historical Society
of Colorado

WILLIAM N. BYERS
Editor, Rocky Mountain News

— Courtesy, Library, State Historical Society of Colorado

PARTICIPANTS IN THE CAMP WELD CONFERENCE, SEPTEMBER 28, 1864

*Identifiable participants in the Camp Weld Conference are, from left to right, standing
in the back row: John Smith, interpreter (third from left), White Wolf, Kiowa(?),
(fourth from left), Bosse, Arapaho; Middle row, seated: Neva, Arapaho, Bull
Bear, Cheyenne, Black Kettle, Cheyenne, One-Eye, Cheyenne; kneeling,
front row: Major Edward W. Wynkoop and Silas S. Soule,
provost marshal.*

STEPHEN S. HARDING
Territorial Judge

WILLIAM BENT
Indian Agent and Trader

GATHERING FOR THE CAMP WELD CONFERENCE

*This view, looking toward the South Platte River from the intersection of Fourteenth
and Arapahoe Streets, was made on September 28, 1864. The occasion was the arrival
in Denver of Black Kettle and other Indian chieftains to treat with Governor
John Evans, according to Jerome C. Smiley, photographer.*

14

— *Courtesy, Library, State Historical Society
of Colorado*

COL. JOHN M. CHIVINGTON
Commander, District of Colorado

— *Courtesy, Library, State Historical Society
of Colorado*

COL. SAMUEL F. TAPPAN
Photo by Brady

— *Courtesy, Library, State Historical Society
of Colorado*

COL. GEORGE L. SHOUP
Photo by George D. Wakeley, Denver

— *Courtesy, Western Collection,
Denver Public Library*

MAJOR SCOTT J. ANTHONY
First Colorado Cavalry

15

— Courtesy, Library, State Historical Society of Colorado

OFFICERS OF THE THIRD COLORADO CAVALRY

Identifiable officers are, left to right: Captain Theodore G. Cree, Company A (left);
Captain John MacCannon, Company I (middle); J. J. Johnson (far right).

viding you make peace with the Kiowas, Comanches, Apaches, Arapahoes, and Sioux." Major Wynkoop, to whom the couriers were taken
by the soldiers, learned also, upon questioning them, that about three
thousand Cheyennes, Arapahoes, and Sioux were encamped together on
the headwaters of the Smoky Hill River near the Kansas line.

Wynkoop decided to go to the Indian village for a talk, despite the
possibility that he might be falling into a trap. If nothing else he hoped
to secure the release of the white captives. With one hundred thirty
men, one section of artillery, and the three Indian messengers Wynkoop
left Fort Lyon on September 6. Early in the morning of the tenth, as
the command was approaching a branch of the Smoky Hill, it came
upon some six to eight hundred well-armed hostile-looking warriors
"drawn up" in battle formation. Halting his command, Wynkoop
formed the cavalry in line, corralled the supply train, and sent One-Eye
forward to request a council with the chiefs.

No doubt to the relief of the badly outnumbered soldiers, the Indians agreed to talk, whereupon Wynkoop moved the command to a
strong position several miles from the village. At about 9:00 o'clock
a.m. Black Kettle and other principal chiefs of the Cheyennes and
Arapahoes arrived at the camp and seated themselves in a circle for the
conference. Assisting Wynkoop in the proceedings were Captain Silas
S. Soule, Lieutenant Cramer, and Lieutenant Charles E. Phillips. John
S. Smith and George Bent served as interpreters.

Wynkoop told the chiefs that he himself did not possess the authority to make a peace treaty, but if they would surrender their captives to him as evidence of their desire for peace, he would take them
to a white chief who could make a treaty. The white chief he evidently
had in mind was Governor Evans, for he next read to them Evans'
proclamation of June 27.

Several of the chiefs, however, seemed reluctant to accept Wynkoop's proposition. Bull Bear, a Dog Soldier chief, blamed the whites
for the Indian war and expressed doubt that peace was possible. His
brother, Lean Bear, who had favored peace, had been killed by soldiers.
Little Raven, though he wished to shake hands with the whites, also
doubted that a peace could be effected. Of the group, only Black Kettle
was in favor of accepting the offer. He did so even though he believed
the whites had started the war.

During the council, a number of warriors slipped past the guards
and amused themselves by inspecting Wynkoop's camp, almost causing
an incident between them and the soldiers. Black Kettle, however,
finally talked them into leaving, and as soon as the council was over,
Wynkoop moved the command some twelve miles back down the stream.
Fearing Indian treachery, some of the soldiers began talking mutiny
and demanding that Wynkoop take them back to Fort Lyon immedi-

ately. Wynkoop, a persuasive talker, managed, however, to allay their fears, and the crisis passed.

The next day, September 11, a party of Indians galloped in with one of the captives and a message from Black Kettle stating that he would bring in the others on the twelfth. Black Kettle, however, brought with him only three of the remaining prisoners. The others, two women and a baby, were not in his camp, but he hoped they could be produced later. One woman, Mrs. John Snyder, whom the Indians were supposed to be holding, they could not hand over because she had killed herself soon after her capture on the Arkansas.[30]

With Black Kettle and six other chiefs and the four captives, Wynkoop's command returned to Fort Lyon. On September 18, Wynkoop wrote Governor Evans telling him about his recent expedition and that he was bringing the delegation of head men to Denver for a conference. It seems clear enough, in light of future events, that Wynkoop made a serious mistake in acting on his own in going to the Indian village and in by-passing regular army channels to take the chiefs to Denver. Had he followed standard military procedure he would have handled the matter through the commanding officers of the District of the Upper Arkansas and the Department of Kansas.[31]

Wynkoop and the white captives arrived in Denver ahead of the chiefs and their military escort. In conference with Evans, Wynkoop found the governor displeased with what he had done. The Indians had declared war against the United States, the governor told him, and the matter of war or peace was now in the hands of the Army. That General Curtis also considered it his problem there can be no doubt, since he telegraphed Chivington on the twenty-eighth that it "is better to chastise [the Indians] before giving anything but a little tobacco to talk over. No peace must be made without my directions." Chivington's views were similar to those of Curtis. Wynkoop insisted, however, despite Evans' objection, that Evans talk to the chiefs and the governor finally consented to do so.

That Wynkoop was unusually persuasive with words is suggested by the fact that he apparently convinced Editor Byers, who had been "opposed to anything which looks like a treaty of peace" because he doubted the Indians' sincerity, that "compromise" was the only solution to the Indian war. The Indians, the editor said in the *News*, after talking to Wynkoop, "unquestionably had great provocation for hostilities, and were not the first to violate friendly relations." Since Wyncoop was "very familiar with all the circumstances" and he believed that the chiefs could "control all the warriors of their tribes and that a treaty with them will be faithfully and honorably kept on their part," Byers was willing "to defer his judgment."

The *Journal*, however, saw things in much the same light as had

18

Byers before he talked to the major. The chiefs Wynkoop brought to Denver had "little or no authority" over their tribes as a whole. These chiefs, whose warriors had been "murdering our people and stealing our stock," now wanted peace solely because "winter is approaching." No peace should be made, the editor intimated, until the Indians were punished.[32]

Evans met with the chiefs at Camp Weld on September 28. Present, among others, were Wynkoop, Chivington, Shoup, Soule, Cramer, and Smith. The Cheyennes were represented by Black Kettle, Bull Bear, and White Antelope, the Arapahoes by Neva, Bosse, Heaps-of-Buffalo, and No-ta-nee. Ute Agent Simeon Whiteley acted as secretary.

Black Kettle told the governor that after seeing his proclamation of June 27, he had taken "hold of the matter" and, as soon as he could do so, had assembled his people for a council. The Indians decided to comply with his wishes and sent word of their decision to Fort Lyon. Wynkoop came to their camp and they returned with him to see the governor. "We have come with our eyes shut," the chief declared, "following his handful of men, like coming through the fire." The chiefs wished "to hold you by the hand. You are our father."

Evans, in reply, stated that he was "sorry you did not respond to my appeal at once." The Indians had been given two opportunities to make peace, one by his terms of June 27 and the other in 1863 when he had asked them to meet with him on the Republican. Instead of treating with him the previous year they entered into an alliance with the Sioux and went on the warpath. Even if he possessed the power to make a treaty, which he did not now have, Evans doubted that the chiefs present in council could control their warriors beyond the winter. Although his June proclamation remained in force, the power to make peace was now in the hands of the "great war chief." ". . . I hand you over to the military, one of the chiefs [Chivington] of which is here today, and can speak for himself to them, if he chooses."

The Indians denied that they had made an alliance with the Sioux, though it was true they had gone on the warpath. They did so after they were attacked by soldiers near Fremont's Orchard. It seemed to Neva, who claimed that he had always favored peace and had "received good counsel" on a visit to Washington in 1863, that the whites now, "when I shake hands with them, they seem to pull away."

The conference adjourned after the following remarks by Chivington:

> I am not a big war chief, but all the soldiers in this country are at my command. My rule of fighting white men or Indians is to fight them until they lay down their arms and submit to military authority. They are nearer Major Wynkoop than any one else, and they can go to him when they get ready to do that.

As the *News* interpreted it,

>   Colonel Chivington told them [the Indians] that an unconditional surrender and laying down of their arms was the first step for them to take, after which, such arrangements as might be deemed proper would be made. He referred the whole matter to Major Wynkoop, in command at Fort Lyon, who was much nearer to their reservation and hunting grounds, and more familiar with their disposition, wants and necessities.

The *News* also stated:

>   Every one present seemed to be satisfied with the course taken in this important and critical interview, and the council broke up with the belief that these chiefs will use their utmost influence to induce their tribes to lay down their arms; a consummation devoutly to be wished for.[33]

Although the meaning of Chivington's statement is not entirely clear, he evidently meant to say that there might be peace after *all* the Cheyennes and Arapahoes laid down their arms.

It is impossible to ascertain precisely why Evans refused to accept the Indians' bid for a peace treaty at Camp Weld. It may be that he was sincere in his belief that the matter of war or peace was indeed no longer in his hands. One suspects, however, that a peace made by him would have been sustained in Washington. Professor Berthrong suggests that Evans wished to keep the war boiling until "a land cession" could be obtained "from the Cheyennes and Arapahoes." "Clearing Indian title to Colorado territory would give additional justification for the Republican political faction seeking statehood."[34] This explanation seems a little shallow in view of the fact that statehood had recently been defeated at the polls. It is entirely possible, however, that Evans saw continued war and a land cession as a means of restoring political prestige lost as the result of the failure of the state movement. Leaving the land-cession theory out of it, he may simply have, with an eye to his political future, followed the policy which he believed would be most popular with a majority of Coloradans. Another possible explanation is that given by Major Wynkoop. The Third Colorado Cavalry was at the time of the conference organizing to fight Indians, and if Evans made peace with the Indians, it would appear to Washington authorities that he had misrepresented the Indian danger and had caused the government needless expense. Certainly a peace treaty would have disappointed the volunteers for they were evidently spoiling for a fight (see discussion below). Whatever the reason for Evan's attitude, the conference ended without a treaty, and the chiefs returned with the Wynkoop party to Fort Lyon.[35]

The Third Colorado Cavalry began organizing in about mid-August. Recruiting, however, proceeded slowly, and in Arapahoe County, which included Denver, the major center of population, Chivington declared martial law in an effort to speed up enlistments evidently in both the "Hundred Day Service" and the militia. Both the *News* and the *Journal*

20

gave their blessings to the cause, and mining superintendents, plagued by lack of supplies and soaring prices as the result of the interruption of overland traffic, "suspended work so that their hands may go on the warpath."

Six companies — four in Denver and one each in Central City and Boulder — were raised before the end of August. By about mid-September six more companies had been organized. The total number of men enrolled was 1,149, which was somewhat short of the authorized 1,200. Of over eight hundred men whose occupations are known, more than five hundred were farmers and miners and about two hundred were laborers, clerks, teamsters and freighters, carpenters, mechanics and engineers, printers, and merchants. Among the printers was John L. Dailey of the *News*. Thanks to the "serious effort" of Evans and Chivington to secure capable officers, one-half of the officers at the company command level and above had seen military service of some sort before. There is evidence to suggest that politics may have played at least a minor role in the selection of officers.

The point of rendezvous for the "Thirdsters" was Camp Evans, which was located just north of Denver. Majors William F. Wilder and Samuel M. Logan successively commanded the regiment and camp until Colonel George L. Shoup assumed command on September 21. Late in August and early in September, Chivington stationed six companies on the frontier, two south of Denver and four at Fort Lupton, Latham, Junction Station and Valley Station on the South Platte.

Apparently a more difficult problem than organizing the regiment was supplying and equipping it. Since the district quartermaster had only a limited stock on hand, it was necessary to obtain arms, equipment, and other stores mainly at Fort Leavenworth. An ordnance train arrived on about August 30; others presumably came in later. According to Lieutenant Charles C. Hawley, acting district ordnance officer, the regiment was issued two howitzers, 1,103 used rifles, muskets, and carbines — mainly old .54 caliber rifles, and 103 used revolvers. The regiment was even more deficient in horses, since it was issued eight hundred or less, some in good condition and others barely serviceable. More difficult to procure than horses, since these items were in scant supply locally, were saddles and other horse-equipments. It was not until after a shipment of saddles and bridles arrived that the regiment was able to take the field.[36]

The volunteers at Camp Evans, while they waited for equipment and supplies, drilled, paraded, listened to speeches, and played. Editor Hollister, who observed them on parade, stated in the *Journal* that they were "a magnificent set and as well drilled and soldierly as could be expected under the circumstances." He also noticed that the "gambling halls" of Denver were "very lively, and they and the streets are full of men and boys covered with lemon stripes 'sashaying' gaily round on their dignity just as if it twasn't their business to get killed immediately." On September 26 Colonel Chivington, "in the name of the ladies of Denver," presented the regiment with a "very handsome Regimental flag and guidons for the companies . . ." Colonel Shoup, who received the items in behalf of the command, replied

> . . . in a neat, appropriate speech, thanking the ladies for the interest they had manifested, promising never to surrender the colors into the hands of foes of any color or race, and then he explained to the men the difficulty in procuring an outfit, and assured them they would not be detained in camp a moment after that outfit was obtained, etc. With three cheers for the ladies, three for the Governor [presumably the principal speaker for the occasion] and Colonel commanding, and three for their Regimental Colonel, the boys marched back to camp . . .[37]

But all was not well with the volunteers, for the populace of Colorado was anxious for them to go after the Indians. When the volunteers were not immediately supplied and equipped, Coloradans began "grumbling that nothing was likely to be done, hounding the authorities, and taunting the officers and soldiers in camp. . . ." As the days turned into weeks and the weeks into months and the regiment still did not embark on a campaign, the taunting presumably became sharper and harder to endure. The "Bloodless Third" was still in camp and its one hundred days of life was rapidly expiring. As the *Journal* subsequently put it, "It was the old 'On to Richmond' [cry], repeated."

The derisive references to the volunteers by their fellow-Coloradans undoubtedly explain in part why those at Camp Evans reäcted the way they did to a rumor that the Camp Weld conference of September 28 had resulted in a peace treaty. According to Editor Byers, this false report almost caused the Thirdsters to "mutiny." Noticing the events and commenting on their eagerness to get into action, Byers assured the soldiers that there would "probably be enough" fighting "to satisfy the most ambitious." Fifteen bands of Sioux remained on the warpath, "leaving out the question of the Kiowas and Comanches. None talk of laying down their arms except the Arapahoes and Cheyennes."[38]

Camp life and heckling, however, was not the fare of the entire regiment. One of the companies sent to the Platte was D Company under Captain David H. Nichols, which arrived at Valley Station, about one hundred fifteen miles from Denver, on September 23. Learning in the evening of October 9 that a lone, painted warrior had appeared at the Wisconsin Ranch and boasted of a "heap Cheyenne" camp about a dozen miles away, Captain Nichols, a lieutenant, twenty-nine men, and two guides proceeded to the ranch where they were joined by eleven soldiers and another guide. Approaching near some springs shortly after sunrise the next morning, October 10, Nichols halted his command and sent a scouting party on ahead "to prospect" for Indians. The Cheyennes were there but their camp numbered only two lodges.

Leaving every fourth man to hold the horses, Nichols advanced behind the cover of a hill, got between the Indians and their ponies, and commenced firing into the lodges. The surprised Indians, numbering six warriors, three squaws, a youngster about fifteen years old who "shot an arrow well," and two papooses, ran from their tipis and took up a position under a bank near the springs. But the soldiers "went for them in earnest, and in a very short time they raised the white flag, but too late. They went under, one and all . . ." The women and children were evidently killed in cold blood, after the men had fallen, despite the objection of several of the troopers. One of the volunteers, Morse H. Coffin, excused the atrocity on the grounds that "the idea was very general that a war of extermination should be waged" against the Indians without regard to age or sex.

After the massacre, the men burned the camp, scalped their victims, and took the pony-herd. From papers found in the lodges, it was learned that one of the warriors, presumably the chief, was named Big Wolf. That the Indians were hostile there is little doubt, for among their belongings the troopers found "the scalp of some white lady and her shoes, covered with blood, and some articles of underclothing. We also found bills of lading . . . from parties in Saint Joseph to Denver merchants, and signed by one Peter Dolan, who no doubt went under."[39] But despite the violent nature of this affair, it was a small event, and it was not enough to satisfy the citizens of Colorado who were calling on the Third Colorado Volunteer Cavalry for action.

One of those persons severely criticized for the Third's inaction was the district commander, Colonel Chivington. Chivington was forty-three years old, a big man physically, and a Methodist minister. At the organization of the First Colorado Cavalry, he declined the chaplainship in favor of a regular commission. In 1862 Major Chivington turned in an outstanding performance against a Confederate invasion force at Apache Canyon, New Mexico Territory. The same year "the fighting preacher" was made a colonel and placed in command of the District of Colorado. He subsequently incurred the enmity of a number of officers in the First Colorado, among them Lieutenant Colonel Samuel F. Tappan, and Colonel Jesse H. Leavenworth of the Second Colorado. In 1864 the anti-state opposition apparently succeeded in making it appear that Chivington had not acted vigorously enough in protecting the territory against the Indians. Chivington's candidacy for representative to Congress died with the defeat of statehood in the September election and he was in the same election defeated decisively by Allen A. Bradford in the race for territorial delegate to Congress.[40] Chivington probably now looked for some means to restore his waning popularity. An expedition against the Indians was certain to elevate him in the eyes of his fellow-citizens! It seems possible, too, that Chivington

23

was simply spurred to action by the pressure of the citizenry and the discontent of the volunteers.

Chivington may have had another reason for planning an expedition. On October 16, Brigadier General Patrick E. Connor, commandant of the District of Utah, a noted Indian fighter, was ordered to take charge of protecting the overland route between Salt Lake City and Fort Kearny without regard to departmental lines. Chivington undoubtedly regarded Connor, who had influence with the Chief of Staff, as a threat to his authority, though Connor did not have the power to commandeer Chivington's troops. Connor's "invasion" of Chivington's district certainly did nothing to enhance Chivington's standing with the citizens of Colorado. A successful expedition led by Chivington would restore the people's confidence in him and thwart any future encroachment on his jurisdiction by Connor. It may be, also, that Chivington aimed at a brigadier generalship. Connor had won his star by surprise-attacking an encampment of Shoshoni and Bannocks on Bear River, Idaho, in 1863, killing two-hundred twenty-four Indians.[41]

Whatever the reasons for Chivington's actions in the fall and winter of 1864, Chivington in about mid-October commenced preparations for a major campaign against the Indians. The six companies at Camp Evans and one stationed at Fort Lupton were dispatched to the Bijou Basin. On October 16, Chivington wrote Wynkoop from Denver that he was collecting the Third at a point sixty miles from the capital and that he was going after the Indians, whom he believed to be concentrated on the Republican River. But he could not easily do so because the regiment was armed with nothing "but our muskets." He wished Wynkoop would send him a shipment of Starr carbines that had evidently been sent to Fort Lyon.[42]

But, for reasons that have not been ascertained, he did not take the Third to the Republican. In about mid-November he ordered Companies A, B, E, H, I, and M in the Bijou Basin encampment — known as Camp Elbert — to proceed to Fort Lyon via Booneville on the Arkansas. Company A had arrived at Camp Elbert since its establishment and Companies K and L had been sent from there to relieve Companies C, D, and a detachment of H on the South Platte. Chivington's orders also applied to the relieved troops who had just arrived in Denver. "Heavy snows" prevented them from marching to the Bijou Basin; instead, they met the column at Booneville. The command was also joined by Company G from Camp Baxter south of Denver and by parts of Companies C, E, and H of the First Colorado. Two companies, K and L, and a number of horseless men from other companies were left behind. Chivington himself arrived to take command of the expedition on November 23. Major Hal Sayr noticed in his diary that Chivington's assumption of command "gives pretty general dissatisfaction," an observation supported by another contemporary who declared that at the time "a more unpopular commander could hardly be found."[43]

That Coloradans were still complaining loudly about the Third's failure to subdue the Indians even as the colonel was forming his expedition on the Arkansas is suggested by the following editorial in the *Journal* of November 28:

> We learn from reliable sources that a large portion of the 3d Regiment has been moved to Fort Lyon, though for what purpose we know not unless it be to permit the Indians to resume their pastime of throat cutting and scalping without fear of interruption. Every mounted man has been sent away out of their reach, and now we may look forward to lively times on the Platte. On the 13th of next month, the term of their enlistment will have expired, and our brave mountain boys will be sent home to enjoy the reputation of "Bloodless Hundred Dazers." What a brilliant administration we are living under to be sure.[44]

Presumably because he wished to surprise the Indians, Chivington gave no advance notice of his intended destination, not even to the officers at Fort Lyon. The statement quoted immediately above was the first in either the *News* or the *Journal* to give it, and it did not appear until it no longer mattered. On about November 24 Chivington moved his command eastward from Booneville toward Fort Lyon. At Bent's ranch, fourteen miles above Fort Lyon, Chivington left a guard with instructions for it to prevent anyone leaving to warn the Indians of his coming.

Several significant events had taken place at Fort Lyon since Wynkoop's return from the Camp Weld conference. Wynkoop told the chiefs who had accompanied him to Denver that they could bring in their villages to a point near the post. There they would be safe from attack by the army. On about October 18, a large body of Arapahoes under Left Hand and Little Raven made camp about two miles away.

Early the next month General Curtis relieved Wynkoop of command in favor of Major Scott J. Anthony, First Colorado Cavalry, evidently because he was displeased with Wynkoop's "official proceedings in regard to Indians . . ." Wynkoop had undoubtedly exceeded his authority in taking the Indians to Denver and in offering them the protection of the post. His removal was promptly protested by Captain Soule, Lieutenant Cramer, and other officers at the post, who believed Wynkoop's course had been the correct one. A. G. Boone, W. Craig, Allen A. Bradford, and others also supported Wynkoop's policy because they believed it had brought an end to hostilities on the Upper Arkansas. Other citizens, however, who evidently wanted the Indians punished, did not think so kindly of it.[45]

Anthony, upon assuming his new command on November 2, told the Arapahoes that they might remain where they were as prisoners of war on condition they surrender their arms and turn in certain stolen

25

property. The Indians complied with Anthony's wishes, but because the "red-eye chief," as the Indians called him, did not have rations enough to feed them longer than ten days, he returned their weapons and told them to "go out to the buffalo country" where there was game.

Anthony had not completed his dealing with the Arapahoes when a large band of Cheyennes under Black Kettle pitched camp about thirty-five miles to the northeast on Sand Creek. These Indians were only a portion of those that had been camped on the headwaters of the Smoky Hill, since part of them had moved from that vicinity after the Camp Weld conference. Anthony told Black Kettle and other chiefs just outside the post that he "was not authorized as yet to say that any permanent peace could be established, but that no war would be waged against them" while he was waiting for instructions from General Curtis. In the meantime, they could remain on Sand Creek.[46]

The Cheyenne village on Sand Creek was the objective of the Chivington expedition, which arrived at Fort Lyon on November 28. That Chivington knew the Indians were there and that he came to Fort Lyon with the intention of striking them is to some extent substantiated by the statement of the editor of the *Journal* on November 29. He had the day before received a letter, obviously written before the command's arrival at the post, from one of the expedition's officers telling him that the Third Colorado was on its way to Fort Lyon "where a large body of *hostile* Indians have congregated."[47] The expedition's coming was a complete surprise to the men and officers of the garrison, who thought when it was first sighted that it was Indians. So that no word of its presence would be conveyed to the Cheyennes encamped nearby, Chivington stationed pickets around the post for the purpose of stopping anyone who tried to leave.

Although Wynkoop before departing had, or thought he had, secured Anthony's promise to carry out his policy and Anthony had told the Indians that they would not be molested until he heard from Curtis, Anthony expressed himself in favor of Chivington's plan to attack the Cheyenne village. According to Lieutenant Harry Richmond of Company B, Third Colorado, Anthony told him and several other officers that he was "G-d d--n glad that you have come — I have got them [the Indians] over on Sand Creek 'till *I could send for assistance to clean them out.*"[48] Learning of Chivington's intention, Captain Soule, Lieutenant Cramer, and other officers stationed at Fort Lyon tried to talk Chivington out of it because they considered the Indians friendly. But Chivington was unmoved. "D--n any man," he is said to have exclaimed, "who is in sympathy with an Indian." The Cheyennes were killers of women and children and he meant to destroy them.[49]

At about eight o'clock p.m. in the evening, November 28, the expedition broke camp and headed toward the Cheyenne village on Sand

Creek. Precisely how many troops it numbered is unknown since the estimates of contemporaries vary. Shoup stated that there were about "one hundred and seventy-five men of the First Colorado, a small detachment of the First New Mexican [Infantry], and about six hundred and fifty of my regiment." Chivington gave the number of Thirdsters as about four hundred fifty and that of the First Colorado as about two hundred fifty. The expedition picked up one hundred twenty-five troops and two howitzers at Fort Lyon. The command was divided into five battalions under Lieutenant Colonel Leavitt L. Bowen, Major Sayr, and Captain T. G. Cree of the Third and Lieutenant Luther Wilson and Major Anthony of the First. Robert Bent and old Jim Beckwourth served as guides. Beckwourth had come with the expedition from Denver; Bent had been impressed into service at Fort Lyon.[50]

Throughout the cool, clear night the volunteers marched rapidly in columns of fours until at daylight they came upon the nearly dry Sand Creek. The Indian camp stood to their front on the north side of the creek where the stream made an east-west bend. It numbered one hundred thirty Cheyenne and eight Arapaho lodges.

Chivington began the attack immediately by sending Wilson's battalion across the creek to cut the Indians off from one of their two pony-herds. The other herd, which was southwest of the village below the creek, was subsequently secured by two companies of the Third. As the result of this stratagem, the surprised Indians were forced either to stand and fight or to run on foot. Wilson's troopers, after accomplishing their objective, dismounted and began pouring in a galling fire upon the village from the northeast. The two companies of the Third, after capturing the other herd, also turned and began firing on the village from the south.

Meanwhile, Anthony's battalion crossed the stream, dismounted, and opened fire from the southeast. The Third, which was to make the main attack between Anthony and Wilson, was the last to enter the fray. Halting the men briefly in the bed of the stream, Chivington ordered them to "throw off all superfluous luggage." "I don't tell you to kill all ages and sex," he is reported as saying, but "remember our slaughtered women and children." The command then advanced on foot to a position behind Anthony's. For a short time the Thirdsters shot through and over their comrades of the First, but Anthony presently corrected the situation by moving to the left. Pressing forward under a cover of artillery fire, the volunteers were soon moving westward through the village and along the stream.

The Indians thought when they first heard the soldiers coming that the noise was that of a buffalo herd. Pro-Indian sources would have us believe that Black Kettle tried unsuccessfully to stop the attack by displaying both an American flag and a white flag over his tipi. The Thirdsters generally denied that he did so, which may not mean that there were no flags but that in the confusion and from where they were they may not have seen them. We are told that White Antelope also attempted to halt the assault by running toward the troopers with his hands up and shouting to them not to fire. When they did not stop, he stood steady with his arms folded over his chest as a gesture of friendship. But he was shot down for his trouble.

In camp was trader John S. Smith, a soldier of the First Colorado, and a teamster, who had recently come from Fort Lyon. Smith was almost shot by some of the volunteers who considered him "no better than an Indian" before he, the two men, and Charles Bent, another of the half-Cheyenne Bent brothers, were directed by Chivington to a place of relative safety.

Fleeing from the village, a large number of Indians, many of them women and children, formed a battle line of sorts a short distance above where the creek made its eastward bend. Digging holes in the loose sand, they fought for their lives. Chivington and others later claimed that these holes were rifle pits which the warriors prepared before the fight, though it was not the custom of the Plains Indians to fortify a village. Although the Indians suffered heavy losses in this combat, a number of them survived, and they and others gathered after dark in a ravine about ten miles above the village.[51]

One surmises from the conflicting accounts of the battle, that the soldiers, after the initial advance, fought in considerable disorder and without much direction from their officers. The fighting spread to include a wide area and much of it was at close range, in some instances hand-to-hand with knives and rifles. Apparently, vicious atrocities were committed. First Lieutenant James D. Cannon of the First New Mexico Volunteers, who allegedly came along only because he was ordered to by Anthony, subsequently stated:

> . . . I did not see a body of man, woman, or child but was scalped, and in many instances their bodies were mutilated in the most horrible manner — men, women, and children's privates cut out . . .[52]

There seems little doubt that the soldiers scalped and mutilated bodies Indian fashion, though it may be that the extent of it was, in the aftermath of the affair, which will be discussed below, exaggerated somewhat. Even had Chivington tried to stop the carnage, and the evidence seems to indicate that he did not, it is doubtful that he would have been successful, for the record indicates that western volunteers were not inclined to show mercy to Indians in any instance.[53]

The battle ended about mid-afternoon and in the evening the expedition went into camp on the battleground, the men sleeping on their arms. There Colonel Chivington evidently wrote two reports, one to General Curtis and the other to the acting assistant adjutant general of the District of Colorado in Denver, each giving essentially the same account of the fight. He had struck a Cheyenne village containing some "900 to 1,000 warriors," killing "between 400 and 500" Indians and capturing about 500 ponies and mules. Several of the Indian dead were chiefs, one of whom he mistakedly identified as Black Kettle. That he had struck a hostile band Chivington did not doubt for he was shown "by my Chief Surgeon, the scalp of a white man taken from the lodge of one of the Chiefs, which could not have been more than two or three days taken; and I could mention many more things to show how these Indians, who have been drawing Government rations at Fort Lyon, are and have been acting." His own losses were nine men killed and thirty-eight wounded.[54]

Other sources indicate that Chivington grossly exaggerated the number of Indians in the village and that of those killed. There were only about five hundred Indians in the village, of which probably some one hundred fifty were killed. Precisely how many of the killed were women and children is unknown since the sources are in disagreement. One of the Thirdsters, Morse H. Coffin, set the number as about one-third of the total while John Smith estimated it at about two-thirds. Among the chiefs killed were, according to Grinnell, White Antelope, One-Eye, War Bonnet, Yellow Shield, and Yellow Wolf. Chivington stated in a report on December 16 that he took no prisoners, and according to Major Anthony, Chivington had told the men he did not want to take prisoners; nevertheless several women and children were, according to George Bent, captured.[55]

"Some skirmishing" took place the next day, November 30, between parties of soldiers and some Indians still remaining in the vicinity. According to Major Sayr, about a dozen more Indians were killed "and one or two of our men" were "brought in badly mutilated" during the day. Also killed on the thirtieth was Jack Smith, half-blood son of John Smith. Jack was allegedly shot to death through an opening in the lodge where he was being held. Coffin attributes this killing to the unhappiness of the soldiers with Smith for his having fought against them the day before. The same day the command's transportation arrived from Fort Lyon and the troopers burned the village.

Although Chivington stated on November 29 that he planned to go "for the villages of the Sioux, . . . reported about eighty miles from here on the Smoky Hill," he did not do so; instead, on December 1, he marched southward toward the Arkansas where he evidently hoped to strike Little Raven's band of Arapahoes. Fifteen miles south of the Sand Creek battlefield, he was met by the supply train under Major Anthony and Captain Soule, which he had sent to Fort Lyon for supplies after the fight. Reaching the Arkansas River, the command turned and proceeded down-stream. It crossed the Kansas-Colorado border on December 3 hot on the Arapahoes' trail. But on December 5 Chivington decided, because his horses were exhausted and the Third's period of enlistment was "nearly out," to abandon the pursuit and return to Fort Lyon.[56]

News of the fight at Sand Creek reached Denver on December 7. The next day the *News* printed two private letters giving its details. One was from Colonel Shoup to a Denverite. Shoup estimated the Indian losses at "about 300" killed. "Our men," he said, "fought with great enthusiasm and *bravery*, but with some disorder." There was no truth in the "story" that "Indians are our equals in warfare." The other letter was from Major Anthony to his brother, also of Denver. "I never saw more bravery displayed by any set of people on the face of the earth than by those Indians," he declared. "They would charge on a whole company singly, determined to kill some one before being killed themselves. We, of course, took no prisoners, except John Smith's son, and he was taken suddenly ill in the night and died before morning." (Anthony evidently did not know Jack Smith's true fate.) Commenting on the battle, as reported in these letters, the *News* declared that "the Third, and First, and the First New Mexico . . . have won for themselves and their commanders, from colonel down to corporal, the eternal gratitude of dwellers on these plains." The remaining hostiles probably would now ask for peace.

The *Journal*, which learned of the battle from a letter of Captain H. M. Orahood to his wife at Black Hawk, expressed similar sentiments. "It is impossible to estimate the value of this occurrence to Colorado." The *Journal* did not care who got the "credit" for the victory — Connor, Chivington, Shoup, "even Gov. Evans — some one deserves credit and they shall have it. . . ." The territory had been saved "from ruin." In subsequent issues both the *Journal* and the *News* printed the official reports of a number of the ranking officers who had participated in the battle. One notices that in none of them was there more than a hint of the atrocities committed by the soldiers upon the Indians.[57]

On December 22 the Third Colorado arrived in Denver from Fort Lyon amidst the plaudits of the multitude. Its "return" was, declared the *News*, "the grand feature of to-day."

> Those ten companies, (the Eleventh and Twelfth of the regiment being stationed at the Junction Valley Station, on the Platte, protecting that route, and for a few months past) who have stood the severity of the season, the snowstorms of Bijou Basin, the fatigues of forced marches, and the deprivation of all comforts both by day and night — camping where the hostile savage was expected to be met, or following the red assasins [sic] to their strongholds in the interior of the desert — were the admired of all observers, on their entry into town this morning.
>
> Headed by the First regiment Band, and by Colonels Chivington and Shoup, Lieut. Col. Bowen and Major Sayr, the rank and file of the "bloody Thirdsters" made a most imposing procession, extending, with the transportation trains, from the upper end of Ferry street through Larimer, G and Blake, almost back to Ferry street again. As the "bold

sojer boys" passed along, the sidewalks and the corner stands were thronged with citizens saluting their old friends and the fair sex took the advantage of the opportunity, wherever they could get it, of expressing their admiration for the gallant boys who donned the regimentals for the purpose of protecting the women of the country, by ridding it of red-skins. Although covered o'er with dust, and suffering from the hardships of the tented field, the boys looked bully, and the general appearance of the whole was soldierly and service-like.[58]

Soon after the Third's arrival, Denver's "streets, hotels, saloons and stores" were "thronged with strangers, chiefly 'Indian killers'." And a "high old time there was" during the ensuing night. According to the *News*, the volunteers, happy to be home, talked freely and with considerable exaggeration about their experiences. And "no two men give the same version of the big battle, and, of the stories of a score of them, there ain't three alike, respecting the minutiae of the great glorious victory."

The soldiers also exhibited and sold trophies of the fight. A number of Sand Creek "trappings, beaded garments, scalps, and so forth" were hung "as curiosities" in "some of the bars." A "Navajoe blanket" taken from a "defunct Indian" was "rafled off" for $150.00. And on several occasions during the ensuing weeks "striking trophies" were displayed at the Denver Theater.[59]

The troopers remained in Denver until December 28, when they were finally mustered out. But some of them presumably did not soon go home, for the "sudden" death of the district paymaster officer just before the muster-out prevented the regiment's being paid off. This situation worked "a great hardship" on the men, according to the *News*, because they could not "immediately procure employment" in Denver and they could not "well leave — even if they had the means — until their accounts are settled up." Evidently a number of them solved the problem by giving other persons the power of attorney to act for them, thus enabling them to leave town. Not until March, 1865, did the former soldiers receive their money.[60]

Except for the mention of scalps and trophies, the *News*, while the volunteers were waiting to be let out of service, printed nothing to indicate that Sand Creek might have been more of a massacre than a battle. The *Journal*, however, made no effort to conceal the fact that the victory at Sand Creek might have been a tainted one. On December 30, it commented that some of the ex-soldiers, who had just come in from Denver, "do not scruple to say that the big battle of Sand Creek was a cold-blooded massacre." Many stories they were telling "are too sickening to repeat." Presently, the *Journal* concluded that rumors of a massacre and that the Indians were friendly were false because "no quibble" was to be found in the official reports "respecting the propriety" of the attack, Major Anthony, whose post — Fort Lyon — was outside

Chivington's district, had accompanied the expedition voluntarily, and the command had suffered considerable losses.[61]

Word reached Washington that Sand Creek was not entirely what Chivington and some of his subordinates indicated it was even before the *Journal* made mention of it in Colorado. On December 29, there appeared in the columns of the *News* the following item, dated Washington, D. C., December 28, 1864:

> The affair at Fort Lyon, Colorado, in which Colonel Chivington destroyed a large Indian village, and all its inhabitants, is to be made the subject of Congressional investigation. Letters received from high officials in Colorado say that the Indians were killed after surrendering, and that a large portion of them were women and children.

This item, needless to say, "created considerable of a sensation" among the former troopers and caused them to wonder who the "high officials" responsible for the adverse story of Sand Creek were. Their purpose in telling such a story as they had told was, the *News* declared flatly, intended to discredit "two or three men" in the territory out of "personal animosity."[62]

On December 31, the *News* charged that Indian traders at Fort Lyon were behind the "chatter" about "peaceful Indians" at Sand Creek. Their trade had been destroyed as the result of the battle. Who were these traders? In August, 1865, the *News* asserted that Agent Colley "received Indian goods for annuities through the front door of the agency storehouses in day time, and delivered them through the back door in the night time, whence they were hauled in wagons to convenient trading points, and bartered to the Indians. . . ." John S. Smith was "also interested in the Colley Indian trade. . . ." William Bent accused not only Agent Colley and Smith, but also the agent's son, Dexter D. Colley, of being involved in this illicit trade. And if we may believe Captain Presley Talbot of the Third Colorado, Agent Colley and Smith told him at Fort Lyon after the battle that they "had lost at least six thousand dollars each by the Sand Creek fight" and they planned to represent Sand Creek to Washington "as nothing more than a massacre."[63]

Officers at Fort Lyon also criticized Sand Creek. These officers were, if we may believe the assertion of one unidentified correspondent in the *Journal*, bitter because, until Chivington's arrival at the post, they had been "making 'a good thing' out of the camp on Sand Creek" by trading the Indians government "stores." The "whole difficulty," however, originated in "personal spite" against Chivington and perhaps professional rivalry between the First and Third regiments.[64]

Precisely who the "high officials" were that touched off a furor in the East and thus precipitated an investigation is not known. If we may rely on the evidence in the *News*, it probably was not several officials but one Stephen S. Harding, territorial chief justice. On January 30, 1865, the *News* reprinted an article from an Auburn, New York, paper of December 28, 1864, containing a brief notice which it had taken from a Washington, D. C., paper stating that a high official in Colorado had written a letter to someone in the East asserting that Sand Creek "was a massacre of helpless savages, a large portion of whom were women and children." The Auburn paper named the Coloradan as "doubtless the present Chief Justice of the Territory — Hon. Ste. S. Harding. . . ." In still another article, reprinted in the *News*, the Auburn paper stated that one of Auburn's citizens and a former Colorado judge, Benjamin F. Hall, was "acquainted" with the Indians Chivington had struck and he "authorizes us to state that those Indians are entirely pacific." Hall had recently conferred with "his successor," Judge Harding, and "they both agreed that Chivington was getting up this Indian fuss without any adequate cause, merely to keep up [Tom] Pollock's (his son-in-law) exhorbitant contracts for supplies in that quarter." The *News* branded the statements of both Harding and Hall as lies.[65]

Harding denied in the *News* that he and Hall had discussed the Indian war as Hall recalled it, though he had seen Hall in Denver during the previous spring. As to the Sand Creek affair, he had never at any time written about it to Hall or to any "person holding office under the Government of the United States." An unidentified former Thirdster quickly pointed out, however, that Harding's denial was not all-inclusive. Would he deny that he had written "to persons of influence at Washington, who have, either with or without his instructions, represented his statements to the powers that be?"

Harding made no reply to the query. The *Journal*, however, leaped to Harding's defense, asserting that it "was not on Judge Harding's representations that an investigation was ordered. It was at the instigation of men who were actors in these affairs." But the *Journal* admitted that Harding had written a letter "without any idea of its being publicly used" to a friend in the East about Sand Creek. The editor regretted "exceedingly that the thing should be bruited abroad and run clear through the press of the country before the actual facts are known, because they may not have been so bad as represented by some."[66]

What were the contents of the Harding letter and where was it first printed? Presently, the *News* reprinted an extract of the letter from a Boston paper which it had taken from the *New York Herald*. The letter is reproduced below as it appeared in the *Herald* on December 26, 1864. A number of the statements were not entirely true.

33

THE BATTLE BETWEEN THE INDIANS AND COLONEL CHIVINGTON NEAR FORT LYON, COLORADO TERRITORY

Washington, December 26, 1864

The following extract from a letter written from Colorado Territory, under date of December 9, puts a different aspect upon the reported achievement of Colonel Chivington and his command near Fort Lyon, in that Territory, where five hundred Indians were reported killed. The writer occupies a highly respectable position in this Territory, and his statement may be relied upon.

He says:

You have heard, or will hear before this reaches you, of the great Indian battle near Fort Lyon between the scattered bands of Indians to and about there and the command under Colonel Chivington. It is said that five hundred Indians were killed and some nine of our troops. It may be of interest to you to know something more about the matter.

The truth will doubtless show that the attack on the defenceless savages was one of the most monstrous in history. The Indians claimed to be quiet and at peace, yet the command pitched into a village of lodges, and the most of these victims were women and papooses. None were spared. All were killed who could not escape. These Indians, I am assured, molested no travelers who passed among them. The most of them had given up their firearms before the attack was made. If such is military glory, God deliver me from all such. Yet this man, Col. Chivington, will attempt to make reputation as a military commander out of this massacre, which should cause a shudder of horror through the whole country, if it shall prove true, as I have no doubt will appear in good time.[67]

Who was the Washington correspondent to whom Harding wrote the letter and who had it printed in the *Herald*? The *News* subsequently named him, by inference, as Jack W. Wright, an employee in the Interior Department who had in 1863 surveyed the Cheyenne and Arapaho Reservation on the Arkansas River. Wright's ultimate purpose had been to hang the responsibility for Sand Creek on his old enemy, Governor Evans.[68] Whether the letter was entirely responsible for the adverse reaction to Sand Creek in the East, whether Harding actually wrote it, and whether Wright was indeed "the channel" through which it reached the *Herald*, on the basis of the scant newspaper evidence, cannot be established with certainty, but the story in general may at least provide another piece in the big puzzle of Sand Creek.

The *Journal* in the weeks immediately following Sand Creek, as noticed above, defended the attack, though it continued to blame the territorial administration for causing the Indian war. As the editor saw it, Chivington was being abused for "the only decent thing he has done for a year." What happened at Sand Creek had been happening on the frontier ever since "the landing on Plymouth Rock." But with the attack on Judge Harding, presumably a political ally, the *Journal* seemingly altered its stance. The soldiers had been the aggressors at Frémont's Orchard. The Third Colorado had been raised because the state-hood leaders had believed it would somehow help them "to carry the state." It probably would have been disbanded if statehood had succeeded. Afterward, because "Something must be done to prove that there was a military necessity for its being raised," Chivington took it to Sand Creek and struck a friendly band of Indians.[69]

Major Anthony, seemingly, also did an about face on Sand Creek. Presumably for his role in attacking Indians to whom he apparently had promised protection, at least temporarily, Anthony was in January replaced as commandant of Fort Lyon by Major Wynkoop. With the howl of rage against Chivington's action in the East, Wynkoop's star had risen, and he was restored to his old command. A few days later, Anthony resigned from the service because of "my connection" with Sand Creek. His official report, he averred in his letter announcing his decision, which had implied whole-hearted approval of the fight "was wrong in many particulars." And he now believed that one hundred fifty men could have "captured or killed the entire camp at Sand Creek, without the loss of ten men, if the troops had been properly handled." Chivington was also "greatly at fault" for not going after and subduing other Indians after the fight. As it was, Chivington had only "enraged" the hostiles, thereby causing a "new outbreak." The *News* attributed Anthony's "change of sentiment" to "the influence of public sentiment in and about Fort Lyon since Col. Chivington's command returned from that post."[70]

That the Indians were very much on the warpath in the ensuing months after Sand Creek there is no doubt. But whether the Indian war worsened as the result of Chivington's attack was evidently a matter of some disagreement among contemporaries. One of those who denied that Sand Creek made any difference was General Curtis. On January 11, 1865, Major General Henry W. Halleck, U. S. Army Chief of Staff, wired Curtis at Fort Leavenworth instructing him to investigate Chivington's alleged massacre of friendly Indians at Sand Creek.

> Statements from respectable sources have been received here that the conduct of Colonel Chivington's command toward the friendly Indians has been a series of outrages calculated to make them all hostile. You will inquire into and report on this matter, and will take measures to have preserved and accounted for all plunder taken from the Indians at Fort Lyon and other places.

In the same letter, as Curtis acknowledged the receipt of Halleck's orders, Curtis gave his own views of the Chivington affair. Chivington "acted very much against my views of propriety in his assault at Sand Creek," but "still it is not true, as Indian agents and Indian traders are representing, that such extra severity is increasing [the] Indian war." Rather, "it tends to reduce their numbers and bring them to terms." The Indians were "more united" now than previously because they "are in a destitute condition, and must at this season of the year resort to desperate measures to procure horses and provisions." Curtis would in the future do all he could to spare friendlies and to prevent "the slaughter of women and children," but "the popular cry of settlers and soldiers on the frontier favors an indiscriminate slaughter, which is very difficult to restrain." There was no doubt in Curtis' mind that a portion of the "tribes" Chivington struck "were occupied in making assaults on our stages and trains, and the tribes well know that we have to hold the whole community responsible for acts that they could restrain if they would . . ." Wynkoop had erred in establishing a "city of refuge" near Fort Lyon; nevertheless, Chivington should have "respected" it.

To Governor Evans, who was in Washington trying to secure additional defense for Colorado, Curtis had even more to say on the subject. The military had been known to treat the Indians roughly before, but Chivington's attack "may have been a kind of betrayal, accidental or otherwise, of a confidence which had improperly been given to the Indians" at Fort Lyon. Indian traders were "no doubt . . . down on Chivington" because he had disturbed their trading operations. "I suppose, too, that district attorney [S. E. Browne] who seems anxious to keep up a fuss with the military of Colorado is also sending forward his appeals for his sort of adjustment of the wrongs of rebels and savages." And finally, Curtis hoped Evans would "'explain" to Washington officials that the "clamor" about Chivington's "military conduct has considerable to do with his political operations, which are no doubt likely to interfere with other men's hopes in this regard."[71] No more objective appraisal of Sand Creek, Chivington's conduct, and the motives behind the "clamor" of the anti-Sand Creek forces than Curtis' was ever made by contemporaries.

On February 1 Colonel Thomas Moonlight, Chivington's successor as district commandant, in accordance with Curtis's instructions, appointed a military commission to investigate Chivington's "conduct" and to ascertain the disposition of the property captured by his expedition. Since Chivington had left the service in January, trial by a military court was not considered feasible. Three officers of the First Colorado constituted the commission. Its president was none other than Chivington's old enemy, Lieutenant Colonel Samuel F. Tappan! Despite a vigorous protest by Chivington that Tappan was incapable in this case of conducting "an impartial" hearing, Tappan refused to remove himself from the commission. Chivington also protested in vain against a decision by the commission not to open the hearings to the public.

Thirty-three witnesses testified before the commission, which sat in Denver and at Fort Lyon during February, March, April, and May, 1865. Among the nineteen persons who testified against Chivington and Sand Creek were Major Wynkoop, Captain Soule, Lieutenants Cramer,

Cannon, W. P. Minton, and C. M. Cossitt, and Jim Beckwourth. Several of those testifying in his behalf were Captains Cree and Talbot and Lieutenants Dunn and Richmond. Most of the anti-Sand Creek witnesses were members of the First Colorado Cavalry and the First New Mexico Infantry. They, in general, subscribed to the Indian version of the pre-Sand Creek events and considered Chivington's attack completely unwarranted. A majority of the defenders of Chivington were former Thirdsters. They gave the military view of the pre-Sand Creek incidents, denied that the Indians Chivington struck were peaceful because their lodges had contained white scalps and other spoils of war, and generally avoided references to alleged atrocities. As to the captured property — mainly ponies and buffalo robes — the commission learned that much of it had been retained by the soldiers.[72]

While the commission was still in session, Captain Soule, its first witness, was assassinated. Three attempts were made on his life during the winter and spring. The third, which occurred in the evening of April 23, succeeded. The alleged assassin, Charles W. Squiers of the Second Colorado Cavalry, and a partner named Morrow confronted Soule, the provost marshal of Denver, while he was investigating pistol shots in the upper end of town. In the ensuing exchange of shots, Soule was struck in the head and Squiers was hit in the hand. Squiers and Morrow fled town, but Squiers was subsequently apprehended in Las Vegas, New Mexico. Returned to Denver by Lieutenant James D. Cannon, Squiers was allegedly court-martialed in August, 1865, but the results, if the trial was completed, have not been ascertained. According to historian Stan Hoig, Squiers escaped and fled in the direction of California.

The *Journal*, upon learning of Soule's violent death, asserted that Soule was murdered to prevent his testifying before the military commission. The reader will recall that Soule had at Fort Lyon objected to Chivington's design to attack the Indians on Sand Creek. During the fight he had refused to order his men to fire. Learning that Soule had already testified before the commission, the editor admitted that he now had "no ground for the suspicion that the foul act was instituted by high and responsible parties" but he was nevertheless "satisfied that there was some deeper cause for this murder than the one assigned." The murder was attributed in Denver to a grudge against Soule for his having once thrown Squiers in the guard house.[73]

Another death, which may have had some connection with Soule's, was that of Lieutenant Cannon. Three days after he arrived in Denver with Squiers he was found dead in bed at the Tremont House. According to the *News*, his death supposedly resulted from an overdose of morphine, which followed two days of heavy drinking and gambling. An autopsy showed that the "brain and membranes were conjested." But the doctors were unable to determine whether the "conjestion" was caused by poison, morphine, alcoholic stimulant, or "apoplexy." The coroner's jury concluded simply that Cannon had died "from conjestion of the brain."[74] Whether the lieutenant's death in fact had anything to do with his bringing Squier's back to Denver, as its mysterious nature might suggest, it is now impossible to ascertain.

Soon after Soule's death, Chivington attempted to introduce before the commission the deposition of a freighter named Lipman Meyer which was presumably intended to discredit Soule and, in doing so, his testimony. Meyer had accompanied a detachment of men under Soule on a scout while the Chivington expedition was on the Arkansas following Sand Creek. Meyer charged that Soule had been so drunk in one instance that he had not known "which was up or down the river." He had also refused to investigate a suspected Indian camp because he was afraid of Indians. And either he or Lieutenant Cannon had stolen some of Meyer's blankets.

Colonel Tappan promptly objected to the commission's accepting the deposition as "evidence" because he believed it was intended "for the purpose of blackening the character" of a man who had never given Tappan any reason "to suspect" him as capable of doing the things of which he was charged. He objected, too, because Soule, before his death, had anticipated an assault on his "character" as the result of his Sand Creek testimony. In support of the latter assertion, Tappan submitted a statement by Captain George F. Price, Second California Cavalry, dated May 3, 1865, alleging that in March Soule had told Price that he "fully expected to be killed" on account of his testimony and that afterwards "his character would be assailed." Although Chivington asserted that Meyer's deposition had been taken before Soule's death and with Soule's knowledge, Tappan's objection was sustained.[75] It would appear, in this instance, that Chivington was correct in doubting that Tappan could conduct an objective investigation, for whether Soule was killed because of his Sand Creek testimony was then, as it is now, questionable to say the least.

An investigation less thorough than that conducted by the military commission was made by the Joint Committee on the Conduct of the War. This body was on January 10, 1865, instructed by the U. S. House of Representatives "to inquire into and report all the facts connected with the late attack . . . under Colonel Chivington . . ." Sitting in Washington, the committee heard the testimony of Jesse H. Leavenworth, John S. Smith, Captain S. M. Robbins of the First Colorado, Major Anthony, Agent Colley, Dexter D. Colley, Governor Evans, and U. S. Marshal Hunt. Several of these men could hardly be classified as first-hand witnesses. And nearly all of them gave the Indian side of events.

The committee also compiled numerous affidavits, correspondence, and official reports. Several of the statements were those of Major Wynkoop's supporters at Fort Lyon. In compliance with orders from higher headquarters, Wynkoop had collected at least part, probably all, of these after his reässumption of command at Fort Lyon in January. Excluding the official reports of the battle by the Third Colorado officers, the committee did not obtain the statement of a single member of the Third Regiment.[76]

The committee questioned Chivington, who was in Denver, by letter. In his reply Chivington stated that he attacked the Cheyennes on Sand Creek because he "had every reason to believe that these Indians were either directly or indirectly concerned in the [recent] outrages" on the Central Plains. He was at the time supported in his decision to attack them by Major Anthony and Agent Colley who "were more competent to judge of their disposition towards the whites than myself." As Chivington had understood it, the "protection" extended to the Indians by Wynkoop had subsequently been withdrawn by Anthony. Chivington deliberately surprised the village because unless Plains Indians were surprised they could not be caught and engaged. Nineteen white scalps, one of them "not more than four days" old, were "found in the camp" after the fight. Chivington did not comment on the extent of the atrocities committed by his men.[77]

Anthony testified before the committee that he had told the Cheyennes he "could make no offers of peace to them until I heard from district headquarters." But he had also told them that "they might go out and camp on Sand Creek" and as soon as he received the "authority to make peace with them I would go out and let them know it." Asked if he did not "feel" he had been "bound in good faith not to attack those Indians after they had surrendered to you, and after they had taken up a position which you yourself had indicated," Anthony replied that he

> . . . did not consider that they had surrendered to me . . . My instructions were such that I felt in duty bound to fight them wherever I found them; provided I considered it good policy to do so. I did not consider it good policy to attack this party of Indians . . . unless I was strong enough to go on and fight the main band at the Smoke Hills [*sic*] . . .

Anthony claimed that at Fort Lyon he was against Chivington's plan to attack the village on Sand Creek unless Chivington would also strike the main village on the ground that an attack upon a single village would merely "open up the war in that whole country again, which was quiet for the time." Chivington was agreeable to Anthony's condition and Anthony willingly accompanied the expedition to Sand Creek. But one notices that Anthony in a letter of November 28, 1864, reporting Chivington's arrival at Fort Lyon, makes no mention of any reservation on his part about joining the expedition. A large force as Chivington's "has been required for some time," he declared, "and is appreciated by me now, as I believe the Indians will be properly punished — what they have for some time deserved. I go out . . . to join his [Chivington's] command." Whatever the truth about his condition for supporting Chivington's proposed attack, there seems no doubt that he considered the Cheyennes on Sand Creek as hostile though he apparently had granted them sanctuary. It seems possible, in view of Anthony's complicated reasoning, that Chivington may indeed have understood from Anthony that the Indians were not under the protection of the military, though one may criticize him for not taking into consideration the alleged opposition to his proposed attack by several of Anthony's officers.[78]

In its report, dated May 4, 1865, the committee was extremely censorious of Sand Creek, Chivington, Anthony, and Evans. Sand Creek was a brutal slaughter of unsuspecting "friendly Indians." It was "difficult to believe" that soldiers "could commit or countenance the commission of such acts of cruelty and barbarity" as were attributed to them in this instance. Although the Indians "in every way conducted themselves properly and peaceably," Anthony "made haste to accompany" Chivington "on his mission of murder and barbarity." Chivington "deliberately planned and executed a foul and dastardly massacre which would have disgraced the veriest savage. . . ." And both Evans and Anthony, "though evidently willing to convey to your committee a false impression of the character of those Indians, were forced, in spite of their prevarication, to admit that they knew of nothing that they had done which rendered them deserving of punishment." All "those who have thus disgraced the government by whom they are employed" should be removed from office and punished "as their crimes deserve." Clearly the committee accepted the extreme views of the anti-Sand Creek forces. Senator Ben Wade signed the report, though by his own admission he did not attend the hearings.[79]

Both Chivington and Evans took exception to the report in separate communications published in the *News*. Chivington's letter also protested the proceedings of the military commission. Chivington did not undertake to defend himself, except in general terms; rather, he offered selected official military correspondence, private letters, and statements, which were evidently designed to show that the Cheyenne village was hostile, that Anthony considered the Indians hostile and favored the attack, and that Indian traders, embittered by their losses in trade goods, schemed at Fort Lyon after the battle to represent the attack to Washington as a massacre. One witness remembered seeing in the village not only "a number of scalps of white men, women and children," but also "a number of daguerreotypes, children's wearing apparel, and part of a lady's toilet." He did not see the white flag allegedly displayed by the Indians and the soldiers killed "comparatively few women and children."[80]

Governor Evans complained that the committee's "partial," "unfair," "erroneous," and misleading statements did him "great injustice." In a sober, methodical manner, Evans reviewed the events of 1864, noticed numerous errors of fact made by the committee, and submitted evidence to support his views and assertions. He attributed the committee's "slanderous" references to him to the efforts of a number of his political enemies in Colorado who urged his removal in Washington during the previous winter. "For this purpose, they conspired to connect my name with the Sand Creek battle, although they knew that I was in no way connected with it." The committee was *"Culpably negligent* in not examining the public documents" for the facts, "which would have exonerated me," and it was *"Culpably hasty* in concluding that I had prevaricated, because my statement did not agree with the falsehoods they had embraced."[81]

Still another congressional committee investigated Sand Creek. On March 3, 1865, Congress established a Joint Special Committee for the purpose of inquiring "into the conditions of the Indian tribes and their treatment by the civil and military authorities . . ." It was divided into three geographical subdivisions for investigative purposes. Three members, headed by Senator James R. Doolittle of Wisconsin, were assigned to an area which included the Central Plains. An investigation of Sand Creek was conducted by this group.

In Washington the three men heard testimony from Agent Colley, Leavenworth, Smith, and Evans. Traveling west in the summer of 1865 they took affidavits at Fort Riley, Fort Larned, Fort Lyon, Denver, and Santa Fé. Several affidavits were taken from civilians and servicemen who possessed second-hand information only. Most of the statements from eye-witnesses were those of First Colorado cavalrymen. The legislators were also provided with copies of the affidavits collected by Wynkoop. One "witness" highly critical of Sand Creek was Kit Carson of New Mexico Territory who had "heard it publicly stated that the authorities of Colorado, expecting that their troops would be sent to the Potomac, determined to get up an Indian war, so that the troops would be compelled to remain." Thus the investigation of this committee was hardly, if any, more satisfactory than that of the Committee on the Conduct of the War.

At Fort Lyon the investigators visited the Sand Creek battleground. There, according to Doolittle, "We ourselves picked up the skulls of infants whose milk teeth had not been shed — perforated with pistol or rifle shots." An unidentified person at Fort Lyon reported, however, that they found the site nearly "obliterated" by recent heavy rains and cave-ins of the banks. At the opera house in Denver, Doolittle attempted "to present the true Indian policy of the government" to a hostile audience. Doolittle himself subsequently described the occasion:

> When I had referred in a cool and matter of fact way to the occasion
> of conflict between the whites and Indians, growing out of the decrease

of the Buffalo and the increase of the herds of cattle upon the plains of Kansas and Colorado and said: the question had arisen whether we should place the Indians upon reservations and teach them to raise cattle and corn and to support themselves or whether we should exterminate them, there suddenly arose such a shout as is never heard unless upon some battle field; — a shout almost loud enough to raise the roof of the Opera House. — "Exterminate them! Exterminate them!"

Needless to say, the committee's report was highly condemnatory of the "wholesale massacre" of peaceful Indians on Sand Creek.[82]

Throughout 1865 Sand Creek played a prominent role in Colorado politics. In January, the *News* reported that several territorial lawmakers planned to introduce a resolution in the legislature calling for an investigation of Chivington's, Evans', and the territorial secretary's official conduct. Presently, however, the *News* announced that the plan had been dropped because Chivington and Evans' friends proposed to add the names of Judge Harding, District Attorney Browne, and Marshal Hunt to the list of those to be investigated.[83]

In mid-June the *News* reported the circulation of a rumor that Evans had been removed from office. The editor attributed his alleged removal to the efforts of "a combination" which had formed in February. The leading spirits in the "conspiracy" were Jack W. Wright of Indiana, ex-Delegate Bennet, Delegate Allen A. Bradford and "opponents to the Union Party and of the [recent] State movement." These presumably were the men Evans had reference to in his reply to the report of the Committee on the Conduct of the War. Sand Creek was the vehicle which they had used to bring about Evans' removal. Wright, an employee in the Interior Department, became Evans' enemy in 1863 when Evans objected to Wright's "anticipated surveys" of the Cheyenne and Arapaho Reservation on the Arkansas as "unnecessary" and a "waste of the public monies as proposed." Evans' incurred Bennet's wrath when he opposed the ex-delegate's endeavors to secure congressional passage of a certain mining law. Bradford was under the influence of Bennet. The rumor that Evans had been removed, however, which prompted the *News* to offer the above explanation as to why, turned out to be false. But soon thereafter Evans did indeed resign, at the request of President Andrew Johnson. Sand Creek was undoubtedly responsible for his resignation.[84]

Sand Creek was an issue in a new statehood movement. In the spring of 1865 both political parties called for a convention to frame a state constitution, though congressional authority to do so did not exist. Surprisingly enough, former anti-state men were among the leading promoters of the movement. A convention was held, a constitution was framed, and the statehood question was submitted to the voters. Supported enthusiastically by the press, including the *Journal*, statehood carried the territory.

Both the Union Administration and the Democratic Parties now entered candidates for state offices. Meeting in Denver, the delegates to the Union Administration convention approved resolutions calling for "more Sand Creek battles" and endorsing the battle already fought by a vote of fifty-four to nineteen. Soon afterwards, Chivington announced himself as an independent candidate for Congress. But he subsequently withdrew in favor of the Union Administration candidate, George M. Chilcott. Chivington explained that he entered the contest only because he doubted Chilcott's position on Sand Creek. Since Chilcott was now standing firmly on the matter and Chivington was an old supporter of the Union Administration Party he did not wish to endanger the election of its candidate.

A third party called the Sand Creek Vindication Party was formed because its members, soldiers and former soldiers of the First, Second, and Third Regiments, doubted that several of the Union Administration candidates favored the Sand Creek plank of the platform. Most of the candidates the new party put forward were the same as those of the Union Administration Party. Two names not among the Union Administration list of candidates were Edwin Scudder for governor and George L. Shoup for lieutenant governor. Shoup, who was said by the *News* to be "the idol of the Colorado troops, and one of the Territory's best citizens," declared in a statement accepting his nomination that "I always have, and do still think that the chastisement inflicted on the Indians at Sand Creek, was justly merited."

In the election, the Union Administration candidates were generally successful. The lieutenant governorship, however, was won by Shoup. Meeting soon thereafter, the new state legislature selected former Governor Evans and Jerome B. Chaffee as U. S. Senators. Although Congress initially rejected a bill to admit Colorado as a state, that body later approved it only to have both it and a new bill vetoed by President Johnson.

The success of the Union Administration Party, which stood on Sand Creek, and that of Shoup and Evans in the elections would seem to indicate that a majority of Coloradans attached no opprobium to Sand Creek, to the men who were there, or to those who supported it. One notices, however, that neither of the Sand Creek parties chose to nominate John M. Chivington. Chivington as the commander at Sand Creek undoubtedly had been stigmatized even in Colorado by the Eastern press, the investigations, and his enemies locally; presumably, therefore, he was considered a political liability to both Sand Creek parties and their cause. It is also possible that the statehood leaders may have feared that his election to a post under the state constitution as proposed would have jeopardized the success of statehood in Washington. Whatever the reason for the exclusion of Chivington's name from a party ticket, Chivington evidently did not consider his career in

Colorado a promising one, for he left the territory in 1865 and he did not return for nearly two decades.[85]

The battle or massacre at Sand Creek was thus controversial almost from the moment it occurred. This might not have been so had it not been for the political and personal animosities in Colorado at the time and had Chivington not struck a village that seemingly had been granted temporary immunity from attack. Wynkoop, Curtis, Anthony, Evans, the officers and men of the Chivington expedition, and the white inhabitants of Colorado, must share the blame, if Sand Creek is to be condemned, with Chivington, upon whom most of the "fall out" has descended, for Sand Creek. None of the investigations was entirely thorough or objective. And there is no evidence that federal authorities recognized that such atrocities as were presumably committed in the battle were probably to be expected when the government permitted the use of local, relatively untrained, emotionally involved volunteers to serve against Indians who were terrorizing the frontier. As to the effect of the massacre on the Indian situation, it is unnecessary to say that it did nothing to better relations with the Cheyennes and their confederates, the Arapahoes, but one finds it difficult to accept the suggestion that Sand Creek may have been the primary cause of all subsequent troubles with those tribes.[86] The basic cause of future conflict between the Indians and whites on the Central Plains was the rapid advance of white civilization into that area in the years immediately following the Civil War.

NOTES

1. Donald J. Berthrong, THE SOUTHERN CHEYENNES (Norman: 1963), pp. 121-172; Stan Hoig, THE SAND CREEK MASSACRE (Norman: 1961), pp. 3-35. William E. Unrau examines the problem of the Indian land titles in Colorado Territory in "A Prelude to War," *Colorado Magazine*, Vol. XLI (Fall, 1964), pp. 299-313. Professor Unrau apparently considers the failure to solve the problem by treaty or otherwise as an important cause of the ensuing Indian war of 1864. He does not, however, contend, as Berthrong does, that Evans deliberately sought an Indian war as a solution to the matter.
2. Chivington to AAG, Department of Kansas, April 9, 1864, WAR OF THE REBELLION: *A Compilation of the Official Records of the Union and Confederate Armies*, Series I, Vol. XXXIV, Pt. III, p. 113; *Daily Rocky Mountain News* (Denver, Colorado), March 2, 1865. (*Official Records* hereafter cited O. R.)
3. Eayre to Chivington, April 23, 1864, O. R., Series I, Vol. XXXIV, Pt. I, pp. 880-882.
4. George B. Grinnell, THE FIGHTING CHEYENNES (Norman: 1958), pp. 137-140; Berthrong, *Southern Cheyennes*, pp. 177-178.
5. Sanborn's report, April 12, 1864, O. R., Series I, Vol. XXXIV, Pt. I, p. 883; *News*, March 2, 1865.
6. There are some minor irreconcilable discrepancies in detail between the two accounts Dunn gave of this incident. In his relatively short official report, he states that he "walked forward" to meet the Indians. In a later detailed statement, he says he rode out to meet them and was called back by his men.
7. Dunn's report, April 18, 1864, O. R., Series I, Vol. XXXIV, Pt. I, pp. 884-885; *News*, March 2, 1865; Dunn's testimony, Report of the Secretary of War communicating in compliance with a resolution of the Senate of February 4, 1867, a copy of the evidence taken . . . by a military commission, ordered to inquire into the Sand Creek massacre, November, 1864, *Senate Executive Document* No. 26, 39th Congress, 2nd Session, pp. 180-181. (The latter source hereafter cited Military Commission report.)
8. Cramer's testimony, Military Commission report, p. 32.
9. Grinnell, FIGHTING CHEYENNES, pp. 140-142. For other accounts of the affair see, "The

Chivington Massacre," Report of the Joint Special Committee appointed to investigate the condition of the Indian tribes and their treatment by the civil and military authorities of the United States, *Senate Reports*, 39th Congress, 2nd Session, Report 156, pp. 72-73, 93. (Hereafter cited The Chivington Massacre.)

10. *News*, April 14, 1864.
11. See *O. R.*, Series I, Vol. XXXIV, Pt. III, pp. 85, 98, 149-151, 303-304.
12. Downing to Chivington, April 20, 21, 1864, *O. R.*, Series I, Vol. XXXIV, Pt. III, pp. 242, 250-252.
13. Downing to Chivington, April 27, 1864, *O. R.*, Series I, Vol. XXXIV, Pt. III, p. 314.
14. Downing to Chivington, May 2, 3, 1864, *O. R.*, Series I, Vol. XXXIV, Pt. I, pp. 907-908, Pt. III, p. 407; Downing's statement, Wynkoop's statement, The Chivington Massacre, pp. 69, 75; Grinnell, *Fighting Cheyennes*, p. 143. See also Military Commission report, pp. 32, 126.
15. Eayre to Chivington, April 23, May 19, 1864, Wynkoop to Maynard, May 27, 1864, Series I, Vol. XXXIV, Pt. I, pp. 882, 934-935; Chivington to Charlot, May 28, 1864, Eayre to Chivington, May 1, 1864, Series I, Vol. XXXIV, Pt. IV, p. 101; Grinnell, *Fighting Cheyennes*, p. 144.
16. Smith's statement, The Chivington Massacre, p. 59; Grinnell, *Fighting Cheyennes*, pp. 145-146.
17. Bent's statement, The Chivington Massacre, p. 93.
18. McKenny to Charlot, June 15, 1864, *O. R.*, Series I, Vol. XXXIV, Pt. IV, p. 403.
19. Berthrong, *Southern Cheyennes*, pp. 187-206, 213, 224ff.; Eugene F. Ware, THE INDIAN WAR OF 1864 (Lincoln, Nebraska: 1960). Detailed accounts of these raids may be found in the *News*, the Lawrence *Kansas Daily Tribune*, and the *O. R.* Many of the newspaper accounts are telegraphic reports from the scene of action. The *News*, September 29, 1864, stated that "near one hundred persons have been killed by the Indians along the Platte and Arkansas Rivers" during the last three months.
20. Brown, Corbin, and Darrah to Maynard, June 13, 1864, Maynard to Davidson, June 11, 1864, Chivington to Davidson, June 12, 1864, Davidson to Maynard, June 19, 1864, *O. R.*, Series I, Vol. XXXIV, Pt. IV, pp. 320-321, 330, 354-355, 462; *Black Hawk Daily Mining Journal* (Colorado), June 15, 1864; Letter of Lt. Richard, May 5, 1865 to *Missouri Democrat* in *News*, May 29, 1865; Statement of Robert North, June 15, 1864, Evans to Dole, June 15, 1864, Report of the Commissioner of Indian Affairs for 1864, *House Executive Document* No. 1, 38th Congress, 2nd Session, pp. 372, 383-384; Grinnell, *Fighting Cheyennes*, p. 150; Barthrong, *Southern Cheyennes*, pp. 190-191.
21. Curtis to Governor Carney, June 6, 1864, abstract, June, 1864, *O. R.*, Series I, Vol. XXXIV, Pt. IV, pp. 250, 619; Livingston to Pratt, December 1, 1864, *O. R.*, Series I, Vol. XLI, Pt. I, pp. 883-837; Curtis to Carney, July 28, 1864, Curtis to Halleck, July 28, 1864, Curtis to Blunt, August 9, 1864, Pratt to Mitchell, August 31, 1864, Curtis to Charlot, July 23, 1864, *O. R.*, Series I, Vol. XLI, Pt. II, pp. 369, 445-446, 629-630, 965; *Kansas Daily Tribune*, July 29, August 29, 1864; *News*, August 25, 26, November 4, 1864; *Journal*, August 29, October 1, 1864; Leroy W. Hagerty, "Indian Raids Along the Platte and Little Blue Rivers, 1864-1865," *Nebraska History*, Vol. XXVIII (July-September, 1947) (October-December, 1947), pp. 176-186, 239-260; Marvin H. Garfield, "The Military Post as a Factor in the Frontier Defense of Kansas, 1865-1869," *Kansas Historical Quarterly*, Vol. I (November, 1931), pp. 54-55.
22. Hoig, *Sand Creek Massacre*, pp. 107-109; Grinnell, *Fighting Cheyennes*, pp. 161-162.
23. Evans to Curtis, May 28, 1864, Evans to Chivington, November 9, 1864, *O. R.*, Series I, Vol. XXXIV, Pt. IV, pp. 97-99; Curtis to Halleck, July 23, 1864, *O. R.*, Series I, Vol. XLI, Pt. II, p. 368; Evans to Curtis, May 28, 1864, *News*, August 25, 1864; Raymond G. Carey, "The Puzzle of Sand Creek," *Colorado Magazine*, Vol. XLI (Fall, 1964), p. 285; Hoig, *Sand Creek Massacre*, pp. 25-30, 56-57; Berthrong, *Southern Cheyennes*, pp. 188-189, 193-194.
24. Evans to Stanton, June 14, 1864, *News*, August 25, 1864; Evans to Curtis, June 21, 1864, Evans to Bennet, June 24, 1864; *ibid.*, August 26, 1864.
25. Evans to the friendly Indians of the Plains, June 27, 1864, Evans to Colley, June 16, 29, 1864, *O. R.*, Series I, Vol. XLI, Pt. I, pp. 963-964.
26. Evans to patriotic citizens of Colorado, *News*, August 10, 1864.
27. Evans to Dole, August 10, 1864, Charlot to Chivington, August 13, 1864, *O. R.*, Series I, Vol. XLI, Pt. II, pp. 644, 695.
28. Proclamation, *News*, August 11, 1864; *Journal*, August 18, 20, 29, October 1, 1864; Gill to Chivington, August 23, 1864, Browne to Evans, August 24, 1864, Browne to Chivington, August 24, 1864, *O. R.*, Series I, Vol. XLI, Pt. II, pp. 844-845.
29. *News*, April 12, 19, 21, 27, May 18, July 21, 22, 25, 30, August 3, 4, 11, 12, 16, 24, 25, 26, 27, 29, 30, September 3, 7, 8, 15, 19, 1864; *Journal*, April 8, 9, June 15, 16, 17, July 16, 22, 25, 28, 30, August 1, 2, 3, 6, 8, 11, 13, 16, 18, 20, 21, 24, 25, 29, 30, September 2, 5, 1864; *News-Extra*, August 23, 1864; Elmer Ellis, "Colorado's First Fight for Statehood, 1865-1868," *Colorado Magazine*, Vol. VIII (January, 1931), pp. 23-26.

30. Mrs. Snyder had been taken in mid-August in one of the most vicious raids of the season. She with her husband and two other men were attacked by a party of Arapahoes and perhaps Cheyennes while they were riding in an ambulance near Booneville on the Arkansas. Mrs. Snyder had just arrived in Denver from the East and Mr. Snyder was taking her to Fort Lyon where he worked as a blacksmith. Thomas Pollock, who came upon the scene shortly after the braves departed, reported finding Mrs. Snyder gone and the three men dead. Snyder's head "was scalped and part of his body shamefully mutilated. The other two bodies were so horribly disfigured as to defy identification." Another contemporary, a First Colorado cavalryman named Snyder, which suggests that he was related to the deceased, stated over a year later that the warriors removed John Snyder's testicles and placed them "in his mouth," cut off one of his legs, and tied him by the other "to the upper part of the ambulance." Mrs. Snyder escaped from the Indian village only to be chased down and recaptured. The night after her return she used her dress as a rope to hang herself from the lodge poles of her tipi. News, August 24, September 29, 1864, November 9, 1865; Military Commission report, pp. 57, 216; The Chivington Massacre, p. 89; Hoig, Sand Creek Massacre, pp. 88-89, 107, note 26. The soldier's account contains a number of obvious errors. The Snyder raid was only one of several committed in this vicinity at the time.
31. Wynkoop to Tappan, September 18, 1864, O. R., Series I, Vol. XLI, Pt. III, pp. 242-243; Wynkoop to Evans, September 18, 1864, Report of the Commissioner of Indian Affairs for 1864, House Executive Document No. 1, 38th Congress, 2nd Session, pp. 377-378; Cramer's testimony, Military Commission report, pp. 34, 44-45, 169; Guerrier's statement, The Chivington Massacre, pp. 65-66, 87; Grinnell, Fighting Cheyennes, pp. 158-160; Hoig, Sand Creek Massacre, pp. 97-107. Wynkoop himself subsequently acknowledged his mistake in going to Evans rather than to his superiors. Wynkoop to Tappan, January 15, 1865, O. R., Series I, Vol. XLI, Pt. I, p. 960.
32. Wynkoop's statement, The Chivington Massacre, p. 77; Chivington to Charlot, September 26, 1864, Curtis to Chivington, September 28, 1864, O. R., Series I, Vol. XLI, Pt. III, pp. 399, 462; News, September 27, 28, 1864; Journal, September 30, 1864.
33. Proceedings of Camp Weld conference, The Chivington Massacre, pp. 87-90; News, September 29, 1864.
34. Berthrong, Southern Cheyennes, p. 211.
35. Wynkoop's statement, The Chivington Massacre, p. 77; News, October 3, 1864.
36. Journal, August 16, 18, 19, 20, 23, September 6, 23, 26, 27, October 6, 1864; News September 15, 19, 1864; News-Extra, August 23, 1864; Military Commission report, pp. 34-37, 81-83, 175; Chivington to Curtis, August 30, 1864, O. R., Series I, Vol. XLI, Pt. II, p. 946; Raymond G. Carey, "The 'Bloodless Third' Regiment, Colorado Volunteer Cavalry," Colorado Magazine, Vol. XXXVIII (October, 1961), pp. 275-300. Dr. Carey's thoroughly researched article, cited above, is devoted almost entirely to the organization of the Third Colorado.
37. Journal, September 23, 26, 29, 1864; News, September 27, 1864.
38. News, September 29, 1864; Journal, January 5, 10, 1865.
39. Nichols to Shoup, October 10, 1864, News, October 10, 1864; Nichols to Chivington, October 11, 1864, O. R., Series I, Vol. XLI, Pt. III, pp. 798-799; Chivington to Curtis, October 10, 1864, O. R., Series I, Vol. XLI, Pt. I, p. 883; Morse H. Coffin, THE BATTLE OF SAND CREEK (W. M. Morrison: Waco, Texas, 1965), pp. 5-9. Coffin states that there were four squaws and two papooses. Nichols himself saw only ten Indians, but he was told there were also small children in the group.
40. See Journal, September 3, 7, 1864; News, May 6, 1864; Hoig, Sand Creek Massacre, pp. 19-20, note 1, 26-29.
41. Carey, "The Puzzle of Sand Creek," Colorado Magazine, Vol. XLI, pp. 292-293; Raymond G. Carey, "Colonel Chivington, Brigadier General Connor, and Sand Creek," DENVER WESTERNERS BRAND BOOK, Vol. XVI (1960), pp. 105-136; Janet Lecompte, "Sand Creek," Colorado Magazine, Vol. XLI, p. 316; Communication of D., News, February 4, 1865; Journal, August 24, 1864, January 10, 1865.
42. Chivington to Wynkoop, October 16, 1864, O. R., Series I, Vol. XLI, Pt. IV, pp. 23-24.
43. Lynn I. Perrigo, "Major Hal Sayr's Diary of the Sand Creek Campaign," Colorado Magazine, Vol. XV (March, 1938), p. 54; Communication of D., News, February 4, 1865; Carey, "The 'Bloodless Third' Regiment," Colorado Magazine, Vol. XXXVIII, p. 297.
44. Journal, November 28, 1864.
45. Letters of Soule, Cramer and others, November 25, 1864, Military Commission report, pp. 93-94; Communication of P., October 12, 1864, News, October 20, 1864.
46. Anthony to AAAG, District of the Upper Arkansas, November 6, 16, 1864, O. R., Series I, Vol. XLI, Pt. I, pp. 912-914; Anthony's testimony, "Massacre of Cheyenne Indians," House of Representatives, Report of the Joint Committee on the Conduct of the War, 38th Congress, 2nd Session, 1865, pp. 16-20; Berthrong, Southern Cheyennes, p. 213. (Report of the Joint Committee on the Conduct of the War hereafter cited Massacre of Cheyenne Indians.)

47. *Journal,* November 29, 1864. The italics are mine.
48. See Communication of Lt. Richmond, *News,* February 6, 1865. Lieutenant Dunn subsequently recalled that Anthony told him that he "was d---d glad we had come, and the only thing that he was surprised at was that we had not come long before, knowing how he was situated." Dunn's testimony, Military Commission report, p. 182.
49. Soule's testimony, Cramer's testimony, Cossitt's testimony, Minton's testimony, Military Commission report, pp. 11, 21, 47, 147, 152-153, 156; Cossitt and Minton's statement, Agent Colley's statement, The Chivington Massacre, pp. 54, 61-62.
50. Chivington to Curtis, December 16, 1864, *O. R.,* Series I, Vol. XLI, Pt. I, pp. 948-950; *News,* December 8, 1864, January 3, 1865; *Journal,* January 5, 1865; George Bent to Hyde, March 9, 1905, Coe Collection, Yale University Library, microfilm copy, Kansas State Historical Society; Hoig, *Sand Creek Massacre,* pp. 143-144.
51. Chivington to Curtis, December 16, 1864, *O. R.,* Series I, Vol. XLI, Pt. I, pp. 948-950; *News,* December 17, 1864; reports of Shoup, Bowen, Anthony, and others, *ibid.,* January 3, 1865; Military Commission report, pp. 10, 13, 60, 66-69; Grinnell, *Fighting Cheyennes,* p. 171; Coffin, *Sand Creek,* pp. 18-40; Bent to Hyde, March 15, 1905, Coe Collection, microfilm, Kansas State Historical Society; Hoig, *San Creek Massacre,* pp. 145-162.
52. Cannon's statement, January 16, 1865, The Chivington Massacre, p. 53.
53. This view is shared to some extent by Carey, " 'Bloodless Third' Regiment," *Colorado Magazine,* Vol. XXXVIII, p. 299.
54. Chivington to Curtis, November 29, 1864, *O. R.,* Series I, Vol. XLI, Pt. I, pp. 948-950; Chivington to Wheeler, November 29, 1864, *News,* December 8, 1864. All told ten men were killed on the field or died of wounds soon afterwards. Chivington's account of November 29 to AAAG Wheeler is shown as addressed to the *News* in *O. R.,* Series I, Vol. XLI, Pt. I, pp. 950-951, but the letter, which is identical to that in the *O. R.,* is shown in the *News,* December 8, 1864, as addressed to Wheeler.
55. Chivington to Curtis, December 16, 1864, Smith's statement, *O. R.,* Series I, Vol. XLI, Pt. I, pp. 948-950, 968; Coffin, *Sand Creek,* p. 34; Anthony's testimony, Massacre of Cheyenne Indians, pp. 22-23; Grinnell, *Fighting Cheyennes,* p. 173; George Bent, "Sand Creek: An Eyewitness Account," *Denver Westerners Brand Book,* Vol. XIX (1964), p. 59; Bent to Hyde, March 15, 1905, Coe Collection, microfilm, Kansas State Historical Society.
56. Perrigo, "Sayr's Diary," *Colorado Magazine,* Vol. XV, pp. 55-56; Chivington to Curtis, December 16, 1864, *O. R.,* Series I, Vol. XLI, Pt. I, pp. 948-951; *News,* December 12, 1864; Chivington's report, December 16, 1864, Shoup to Maynard, December 6, 1864, *ibid.,* January 3, 1865; Coffin, *Sand Creek,* p. 28; Military Commission report, pp. 71, 136; Massacre of Cheyenne Indians, pp. 49, 53; Hoig, *Sand Creek Massacre,* pp. 155-160.
57. *News,* December 7, 13, 1864; January 3, 1865; Shoup to Sopris, December 3, 1864, Anthony to brother, December 1, 1864, *ibid.,* December 8, 1864; *Journal,* December 9, 1864, January 4, 1865.
58. *News,* December 22, 1864.
59. *Ibid.,* December 22, 23, 24, 28, 29, 1864, March 9, 1865.
60. *Ibid.,* December 29, 1864, February 23, March 1, 13, 1865.
61. *Journal,* December 30, 1864, January 5, 1865.
62. *News,* December 29, 30, 31, 1864.
63. *Ibid.,* December 31, 1864, August 14, 1865; Communication, January 3, 1865, *Journal,* January 3, 1865; William Bent's statement, The Chivington Massacre, p. 95; Talbot's testimony, Military Commission report, pp. 208-209; Hoig, *Sand Creek,* pp. 24-25, n. 12.
64. Letter of January 3, 1865, *Journal,* January 5, 1865.
65. Articles reprinted from Auburn (New York) *Advertiser & Union,* December 28, 2[?], 1864, in *News,* January 30, 31, 1865.
66. Communication of Harding, January 31, 1865, *ibid.,* January 31, 1865; "A Thirdster" to editors, February 1, 1865, *ibid.,* February 6, 1865; *Journal,* February 2, 1865.
67. *New York Herald,* December 26, 1864; Extract from *Boston Journal* in *News,* February 4, 1865. See also communication of Junius, *News,* February 6, 1865. The only notice about the Sand Creek fight to appear in the *Herald* before the letter printed December 26 was that in the issue of December 9, 1864. It gave an account probably based on Chivington's report of November 29.
68. *News,* June 19, 1865; Unrau. "Prelude to War," *Colorado Magazine,* XLI, p. 313.
69. *Journal,* January 5, 10, 11, 16, February 18, 24, March 2, 1865.
70. Anthony to Moonlight, January 21, 1865, *News,* February 1, 1865. See also communication of D., *ibid.,* February 4, 1865.
71. Halleck to Curtis, January 11, 1865, Curtis to Halleck, January 12, 1865, Curtis to Evans, January 12, 1865, *O. R.,* Series I, Vol. XLVIII, Pt. I, pp. 489, 502-504.
72. Military Commission report; *News,* February 16, March 11, May 30, 31, 1865; *Journal,* February 1, April 25, 1865; Hoig, *Sand Creek Massacre,* p. 169; Wm. J. Mellor, "Military Investigation of Colonel John M. Chivington Following the Sand Creek Massacre," *Chronicles of Oklahoma,* Vol. XVI (September, 1938), pp. 451, n. 22, 462-463.

73. *Journal*, March 11, April 25, 26, 28, 1865; *News*, April 24, 25, 27, 28, June 13, August 2, 1865; Hoig, *Sand Creek Massacre*, p. 172. Morrow is supposed to have fled down the Platte immediately after the shooting. In a statement given by Squiers and published in the *Santa Fe Gazette* Squiers claimed that he and Morrow had been drinking and firing shots in the street when Soule came up and fired at Squiers, who had his gun in hand, after asking if they were soldiers, wounding Squiers in the hand. Morrow shot the captain and he and Squiers ran back to camp and then left town going in different directions. See article from *Santa Fe Gazette* reprinted in *News*, June 13, 1865.
74. *News*, July 11, 14, 15, 18, 1865.
75. Military Commission report, pp. 183-190.
76. See Massacre of Cheyenne Indians, pp. 81-93; *O. R.*, Series I, Vol. XLI, Pt. I, pp. 959-972, Pt. IV, p. 976.
77. Massacre of Cheyenne Indians, pp. 104-108.
78. Anthony to Helliwell, November 28, 1864, *O. R.*, Series I, Vol. XLI, Pt. IV, p. 708; Massacre of Cheyenne Indians, pp. 18, 27-29.
79. Massacre of Cheyenne Indians, pp. i-vi; Carey, "The Puzzle of Sand Creek," *Colorado Magazine*, Vol. XLI, p. 298.
80. Communication of Chivington, *News*, June 24, 1856.
81. Evans to the public, August 6, 1865, *News*, September 12, 1865; The Chivington Massacre, pp. 78-93.
82. The Chivington Massacre, pp. 5-6, 26-99; Extract of a letter, June 15, 1865, *News*, June 19, 1865; Doolittle to Mrs. L. F. S. Foster, March 7, 1881, in "Notes and Documents," *New Mexico Historical Review*, Vol. XXVI (April, 1951), pp. 152, 156-157.
83. *News*, January 14, February 9, 14, 1865.
84. *News*, June 15, 19, August 1, 14, September 18, 20, October 19, 1865; *Journal*, June 6, 1864; Edgar C. McMechen, LIFE OF GOVERNOR EVANS: *Second Territorial Governor of Colorado* (Denver, 1924), pp. 139-141.
85. *News*, October 18, 19, 23, November 7, 8, 9, 11, 13, 15, 17, 30, 1865; Ellis, "Colorado's First Fight for Statehood," *Colorado Magazine*, Vol. VIII, pp. 26-28; Hoig, *Sand Creek Massacre*, p. 176; Regional S. Craig, THE FIGHTING PARSON: *The Biography of Colonel John M. Chivington* (Los Angeles: 1959), pp. 231-237.
86. See William H. Leckie, THE MILITARY CONQUEST OF THE SOUTHERN PLAINS (Norman: 1963), pp. 23-24.

THE BATTLES OF THE SALINE RIVER
and
PRAIRIE DOG CREEK

TWO SPECTACULAR INDIAN ENGAGEMENTS of the Southern Plains frontier which have attracted little attention are the battles of the Saline River and Prairie Dog Creek, a tributary of the Republican River, both in northwestern Kansas. One occurred a short distance from Fort Hays, Kansas, the other in the vicinity of the Kansas-Nebraska line near the Republican River. They are significant mainly as examples of Plains Indian warfare and the U. S. Army's efforts to subdue the hostile nomadic Indians. Both battles originated in the post-Civil War Indian troubles on the Kansas frontier.

As the result of Indian restlessness in the Department of the Missouri, Major General Winfield S. Hancock, the departmental commander, led a large expedition to the Plains in the spring of 1867 to admonish the Southern Plains tribes against future violations of the treaty of 1865 and to show them by a display of strength that he possessed the means with which to punish them if they did not heed his warnings. Hancock's plans went awry, however, when a large concentration of Sioux from the Northern Plains and Dog Soldier Cheyennes, camped on the Pawnee Fork of the Arkansas River west of Fort Larned, fled upon the approach of his troops. They committed depredations on the Smoky Hill stage route to Denver as they traveled north. Many moons would pass before peace returned to the Kansas frontier.

Several weeks after the outbreak, Cheyenne and Sioux war parties returned to the Smoky Hill from their villages to the north, attacking stage stations, overland coaches, wagon trains, surveying parties, and railroad workers in the vicinities of Forts Wallace and Harker. To the south, a band of Kiowas under Satanta and a portion of Black Kettle's Cheyennes raided on the Santa Fe Trail. The Kiowas also depredated on the Smoky Hill. Because the attacks were spread over a large area, General Hancock was forced to disperse his forces and fight mainly on the defensive. An expedition from the Smoky Hill to the Platte River in Nebraska and back by part of the Seventh United States Cavalry under Lieutenant Colonel (brevet Major General) George A. Custer in June and July failed to lessen appreciably the pressure against the two great overland routes of travel through Kansas.[1]

One of the vicinities hit hardest by the hostiles during the summer was that between Forts Harker and Hays. Fort Harker was the headquarters of Colonel (Brevet Major General) Andrew J. Smith, com-

49

mandant of the District of the Upper Arkansas. It was located on the Smoky Hill River near the town of Ellsworth at the crossing of the Santa Fe stage road. The Union Pacific Railroad, Eastern Division, which ran parallel to the Smoky Hill stage road,[2] was completed as far west as Fort Harker by mid-summer and under construction for many miles beyond. Fort Hays was situated on the railroad nearly seventy miles west of Fort Harker.

On June 22, 1867, parties of warriors, identified as Kiowas, made simultaneous attacks along twenty miles of the railroad and stage route west of Bunker Hill station, killing and scalping two laborers and one stage company employee and driving off the livestock from Bunker Hill and Fossil Creek stations. Fearing for their lives, some one thousand railroad workers west of Wilson Creek station left their posts for the safety of the nearest forts or settlements. A few days later the Indians struck again, killing, wounding, and scalping several frontiersmen. The *Junction City Weekly Union* stated on June 29 that about twenty persons had been reported killed west of Ellsworth during the previous week and that eleven Mexicans had been killed in one day on the Santa Fe road southwest of Fort Harker. The raids brought travel on the Smoky Hill road and work on the railroad almost to a standstill. Although the Kiowas and Sioux were the only Plains tribes mentioned in the reports of atrocities — most of them referred to the raiders merely as "Indians" — it seems reasonable to assume, in view of their later activities in the area, that the Cheyennes were also involved in these attacks.[3]

In response to the reports of depredations and the appeals of railroad officials for help, Governor Samuel J. Crawford ordered arms and ammunition placed in the hands of the construction crews and telegraphed the Secretary of War asking for authority to raise a regiment of volunteers for service on the frontier. Unless prompt and decisive measures were taken, the governor declared, the routes of travel and the frontier settlements would have to be abandoned. Crawford's request was passed on to Lieutenant General William T. Sherman, commander of the Division of the Missouri, who after some indecision wired Crawford his permission to raise a battalion. On July 15, four companies of Kansas Volunteers were mustered into federal service at Fort Harker as the Eighteenth Kansas Cavalry, Major Horace L. Moore, of Lawrence, commanding. But by that time the attacks on the Smoky Hill had stopped. Consequently, the new battalion was sent forth to look for the raiders disturbing the peace along the Arkansas. However, as will be noticed below, it would soon be recalled to the Smoky Hill.[4]

Late in July, the Indians renewed their raids on the line of the railroad with two unsuccessful night assaults against a guard of Negro soldiers stationed nearly thirty miles west of Fort Hays. Two, more significant, attacks occurred a few miles east of Fort Hays on August 1. Early in the afternoon about thirty Cheyennes swooped down upon several unarmed workers employed by Contractors Campbell and Clinton, causing them to panic and run "in all directions." Needless to say, the entire crew was killed and scalped. The braves then started to charge another group of laborers working some distance to the west, but as they came close enough to see that the men were armed they wheeled around and retreated. The other attack, which occurred almost simultaneously and in the same vicinity, was made by a large party of Cheyennes against Big Creek station. Notwithstanding a vigorous fire from the stage company employees and a guard of Thirty-eighth United States (Negro) Infantry, they succeeded in running off twenty-six horses and mules and mortally wounding one of the defenders. The raiders lost two killed for their trouble. The leader of the attack was identified by an "old citizen" as Roman Nose, one of the Dog Soldier Cheyennes' most outstanding warriors.[5]

Upon learning of the attacks, Captain (Brevet Lieutenant Colonel) Henry C. Corbin, commandant of Fort Hays, took part of his garrison of Thirty-Eighth Infantry to Big Creek station and sent Captain (Brevet Major) George A. Armes, commander of F Company, Tenth United States (Negro) Cavalry, bivouacked near the post, to Campbell and Clinton's railroad camp. Picking up the trail of the raiders at Big Creek station, Corbin followed it northward toward the Saline River until dark and thence returned to the fort. At the same time, Armes was tracking the perpetrators of the depredation near Campbell and Clinton's camp up the north branch of Big Creek. Since the trail widened after it left the site of the massacre, Armes concluded that he was pursuing more Indians than his command, numbering forty Negro troopers, two white officers (including himself), and two guides, could handle. Consequently, he returned to Campbell and Clinton's camp, reaching there shortly after midnight, and sent six soldiers to Fort Hays for thirty additional men and a piece of artillery.

When after four hours of waiting the reinforcements did not show up, Armes apparently concluded that none were coming and he struck out again to look for the Indians on the Saline, leaving four men, sick with cholera, behind. Thirty minutes after his departure the reinforcements arrived, and although they followed Armes' trail for some distance in an effort to catch up with him, they were forced to turn back when the lieutenant in charge became sick with stomach cramps. (Armes subsequently intimated that he might have been sick with fear of Indians.) Returning to the fort, the troops were sent out again, this time under a sergeant. While searching for Armes on a branch of the Saline, they virtually stumbled into a camp of about fifty Indians. Three shots were enough to scatter the surprised nomads in every direction. Unable to find any sign of Armes, the soldiers returned to Fort Hays.

In the meantime, Armes' command had come on the Saline directly north of the contractors' camp and had been attacked, about twelve miles up-stream from that point by about seventy-five Cheyennes. Within a few minutes the soldiers were surrounded by a fast-moving ring of well-mounted, hard-riding Indians. Dismounting his men, Armes formed them into a wide, hollow square and placed the horses in the center. Several men, sick with cholera, were assigned to leading the animals. Armes then resumed the march in the hope that he might find the Indians' camp and recover the livestock stolen from Big Creek station. The appearance of a larger body of warriors, summoned by means of signal fires, however, prompted Armes to discontinue the advance and retreat towards Fort Hays.

For eight hours the warriors, numbering upwards of four hundred, kept up the attack. During that time the fight moved fifteen miles from the place where Armes began his retreat. In the open country the Indians employed the circling tactic; in the rough, they dodged from rock-to-rock and gully-to-gully firing "at every chance." They were armed with Spencer repeating carbines, rifles, revolvers, and bows and arrows. Occasionally, several of the more bold would collect and charge through the square. Six Indians were killed and several wounded while making these daring dashes. In each case, the dead or injured brave was picked up and carried away to prevent his falling into the hands of the enemy. Two of the most active warriors, Armes noticed, were white men or half-breeds. (One suspects they were the latter.)

Armes coolly directed the defense, at first on foot, then upon being shot in the hip, from his horse. With the command's supply of ammunition dwindling rapidly, Armes instructed the flankers to hold their fire to a minimum. Several of the troopers, however, became panicky at seeing Armes wounded and not only "fired all their ammunition away at random," but also sought refuge in the center of the square. Fearing that the Indians might suspect from their actions that the command was running low on ammunition, Armes, with the help of his fellow-officer, Second Lieutenant John A. Bodamer, and the guides, succeeded in persuading the fearful troopers to return with their empty carbines to the square. Armes thenceforth had no more trouble with his troops wasting their meagre supply of ammunition.

Some ten or fifteen miles from Fort Hays the Indians withdrew, presumably because they were reluctant to carry the fight closer to the fort. Armes' casualties were one man killed and one, himself, wounded. A number of the animals were also lost. Armes attributed his relatively slight losses to the warriors' unfamiliarity with the "improved" Spencer carbine which most of them seemed to be using. (One contemporary intimates that the Plains Indians were poor shots with firearms of any kind.)[6] It would seem, however, that had they chosen to do so, the Indians might have overwhelmed the soldiers by sheer force of numbers. It was indeed, as Armes himself declared, "the greatest wonder in the world" that his command "escaped being massacred."[7]

Armes' impromptu expedition by no means discouraged the Indians who were soon back in action around Fort Hays. On the night of August 3, a small wagon train with an escort was assaulted while in camp at White Rock stage station some twenty-five miles to the west. After one and one-half hours the warriors left, apparently with no losses on either side. On August 5 a large party of Indians struck Wyck's "party of engineers" at Fort Hays station but fled upon the approach of troops from the post. In other raids a few days later several men were wounded and a considerable number of livestock were driven off.[8]

Terrified by the attacks, the railroad workers sought to bolster their sagging courage by drinking excessive amounts of "bad whiskey" furnished to them by "some evil disposed" ranchmen. The effect was, however, just the opposite of that intended. Unable to control their fear, laborers numbering into the hundreds flocked to the safety of Fort Hays, causing Colonel Corbin to worry that their lying around the post hungry, dirty, and drunk might, just as his command was getting rid of one cholera epidemic, lead to the outbreak of another. Corbin repeatedly sent them back to their camps with guards to protect them from the Indians, but in each instance they no sooner started to work again than they "broke loose" in a general stampede for the fort. Finally, in desperation, Corbin ordered the seizure of all whiskey in the vicinity. As it turned out, Corbin's action may have been unnecessary, since the Indian attacks ceased at about the same time as his order. At any rate, the laborers, with nothing to prevent their doing so, returned to work and gave no more trouble.[9]

Major Armes in his official report of the battle of the Saline recommended to his superiors the sending of a large military expedition to the Saline and Solomon Rivers for the purpose of seeking out and punishing the hostiles guilty of the raids around Fort Hays. With the continuation of the depredations after Armes' defeat, Generals Sherman, Hancock, and Smith evidently decided to act on his proposal and bring the Eighteenth Kansas Cavalry from the Arkansas to the Smoky Hill for the purpose of coöperating with Armes' company of Tenth Cavalry in a stepped-up campaign against the Indians. The Kansas Volunteers left their camp near Fort Dodge on August 9, arrived at Fort Hays on August 12, and with the Negro regulars started out to look for the hostiles the next day. Despite his wound, which was giving him some trouble, Brevet Major Armes accompanied the expedition apparently as second in command to Major Moore of the Eighteenth Kansas.[10]

Dividing into two parts, the command made a thorough search of the Saline. With Companies B and C of the Eighteenth Kansas and the Tenth Cavalry regulars, numbering about one hundred thirty-five men, Armes scouted downstream while Moore with Companies A and D of the Kansas Volunteers, numbering about one hundred twenty-five men, and an artillery piece, scouted upstream. Finding no Indians, the expedition reunited briefly, then divided again to search the North Fork of the Solomon River. Armes was supposed to strike the river "low down," Moore ten miles "above," they were then to communicate with each other by means of scouts. But Armes struck the stream above Moore and the two forces lost contact.[11] Moore's portion of the expedition found no Indians; Armes', however, was not so fortunate.

After a forty-mile march up the Solomon, Armes moved his command in a southwesterly direction almost to the Smoky Hill. Discovering a trail going northwest, Armes followed it to a point on the Saline about forty-five miles from Fort Hays and went into camp. Taking a three-man escort, Armes himself rode to Fort Hays on the evening of August 17 for supplies. While at Fort Hays Armes secured a half-way promise from Major Joel H. Elliott, who had just arrived with seven companies of Seventh Cavalry from Fort Wallace, to follow him to the Republican River, where the Indian trail seemed to be leading, for the purpose of aiding him "in bagging Indians." (Elliott, however, for some reason did not march to Armes' support.) Armes returned to his command the next morning with five wagons of rations and forage and twenty-two additional men.

Traveling mainly at night and resting in the shelter of ravines during daylight hours so as not to be seen by the Indians, Armes reached the upper Solomon on the morning of August 20. Some time after resuming the march that evening, a bright light was observed away to the east. Halting the command, Armes sent Captain George B. Jenness of the Eighteenth Kansas with two men to investigate. Jenness found the light to be a burning log where a party of Indians had camped the day before. On the way back to report its findings, the Jenness party became lost in the prairie darkness and made camp until daylight.

When Jenness did not immediately return, Armes resumed the march. As the expedition was entering the breaks of Prairie Dog Creek, one of the scouts, Allison J. Pliley, observed several signal arrows fly into the air about two miles to the front. Evidently an Indian scouting party had spotted the column and was attempting to warn other warriors nearby. Forthwith Armes ordered Lieutenant John W. Price to follow with the wagons and sixty-five men of the Eighteenth Kansas as far as Prairie Dog Creek while he with the rest of the force pushed on ahead.[12]

Arriving on Prairie Dog Creek at 9:00 a. m., August 21, Armes halted for breakfast and a rest. During the break a single Indian fired at one of the sentinels. Believing a large concentration of Indians to be nearby, Armes moved out immediately to continue his search. At about 3:00 o'clock in the afternoon Armes was struck by from two hundred to three hundred warriors as he approached near the Indians' village several miles north of the Prairie Dog. An attempt by the red men to cut off the lead detachment under Second Lieutenant Frank M. Stahl, Eighteenth Kansas, failed. Captain Edgar A. Barker, Eighteenth Kansas, with one-half the command then started a charge, but the appearance of a larger body of warriors presumably caused him to order a retreat.

Dismounting, the Negro regulars and the Kansas Volunteers took up a position in the nearest ravine. Captain Barker directed the defense in the rear which opened onto a plain to the south; Lieutenant Stahl was on the right and front; and an unidentified Tenth Cavalry officer (probably Lieutenant Bodamer) was on the left. Armes gave orders from the center of the circle. For several hours the battle raged with the Indians mounting one charge after another. Conspicuous among their leaders was Satanta of the Kiowas. Mounted on a beautiful gray horse, Satanta shouted encouragement to his braves and sounded the charge with a bugle at least a dozen times. In each instance, however, his warriors were compelled to break off and retreat with considerable losses.

At sundown, when the fighting finally subsided, the command, guided by Lieutenant Stahl (Armes had lost his directions), slipped away under the cover of night to Prairie Dog Creek. The casualties in the battle numbered eleven men badly wounded. Most of the injuries had been inflicted by arrows, which though aimed at the defenders on the near side of the gulch sometimes had fallen on the backs of the soldiers on the opposite side.[13]

In the meantime, another body of soldiers had been attacked. Captain Jenness and his two-man detail had, after daybreak on the twenty-first, found their way to the wagon train on the Prairie Dog and then started to look for Armes. They were joined during the morning by two messengers from Fort Hays, one with a small detail of Negro guards, and several stragglers from the main command, including Pliley, the scout. While following Armes' trail the little aggregation was "suddenly startled" by the "unearthly yells" of some three hundred to five hundred painted Indians "swooping down" upon it from a ridge about one-half mile away. Simultaneously, the men observed, according to Jenness, a small party of cavalrymen riding toward them at full gallop from the direction of the principal command.[14] As the warriors came within three hundred yards, the two parties of soldiers joined. Assuming command, Jenness ordered the men to follow him in a dash for the main column, supposed to be about four miles to the north. Pliley, an experienced plainsman and former officer in the Fifteenth Kansas Cavalry, objected, however, that some of the horses were incapable of out-running the Indians' lighter and faster ponies. Countermanding his own previous order, Jenness instructed the little detachment, numbering twenty-nine men, to dismount and form a hollow square around the horses. The soldiers took their places just in time to meet the Indians' assault.

Forced to break off the charge by the rapid-fire from the troopers' carbines, the warriors formed "a complete circle" around the square "just within range of the guns." In an effort to stampede the troopers' horses they whooped and yelled and shook blankets and lances with streamers attached. They were armed with rifles, revolvers, shotguns, and bows and arrows. Hanging onto the opposite sides of their ponies for protection, they fired "sometimes over the horses' backs and sometimes under their necks." Occasionally, "each alternate Indian would . . . wheel his horse inside their circle, rein up, and discharge his piece at the square."

Hoping to join forces with Armes, Jenness moved the group slowly northward. During halts in the march, "squads of Indians would dismount, creep up behind prairie-dog hills and buffalo wallows and pour in flight after flight of arrows." Sometimes a group of warriors would dash down upon the square in "full charge." Jenness met these dashes by reinforcing the threatened side of the square with every second man from the opposite side. The Indians were compelled in each instance to "break and retreat in all directions." In one dash eleven warriors were shot off their ponies. In the most daring charge of all, an unidentified warrior, mounted on a splendid white horse and brandishing a revolver, rode over a soldier, across the square, and out the opposite side. None of some fifty shots fired at him found its mark. The warrior was probably either Satanta of the Kiowas or Roman Nose of the Cheyennes, both of whom were recognized at one time or another during the battle of the Prairie Dog.

About one-half mile from the point of attack, Scout Pliley observed "through his glass," another large body of Indians on the hills in the direction of the main command. Believing it impossible to cut through to Armes, Jenness decided to return to the creek.[15] If Armes heard his firing he would surely have come to the rescue. (Armes, thanks to a south wind, had, indeed, heard the firing, but presumably since he himself was surrounded he considered it imprudent to attempt a rescue of the Jenness detachment.)

During the retreat to the creek, a number of English-speaking warriors rode in close to shout insults. One chortled that Armes' portion of the command had been massacred and that the same thing was about to happen to Jenness and his men. Another dashed by waving the scalp of a fallen Negro soldier from the tip of his lance and shouting, "This is the way we will serve you all."

The detachment under Jenness had suffered heavy casualties. One man (the Negro soldier mentioned above) had been killed and fourteen others wounded, several of them badly. Jenness himself was injured in the right thigh and Pliley was limping from wounds in the right leg. Only a few animals remained, the wounded having been destroyed and left behind. On the advice of Pliley, who knew the great value the red men placed on horses, Jenness now turned loose all but two of the remaining animals. He hoped by this stratagem to divert the Indians' attention away from the square. The scheme worked. The warriors scrambled

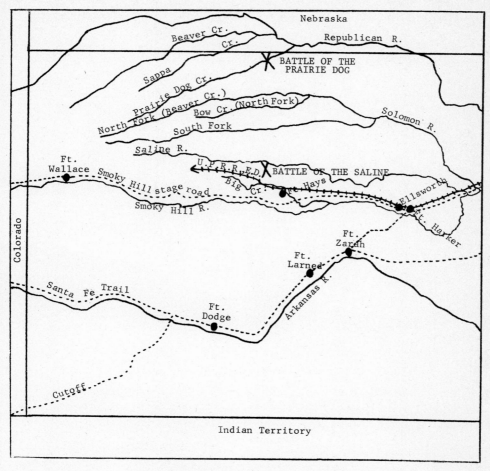

Nebraska

Beaver Cr.
Cr.
Republican R.

✗ BATTLE OF THE
PRAIRIE DOG

Sappa

Prairie Dog Cr.
North Fork (Beaver Cr.)
Bow Cr. (North Fork)
South Fork

Solomon R.

Saline R.

Ft.
Wallace
Smoky Hill stage road
U.P.R.R.E.D. ✗ BATTLE OF THE SALINE
Big Cr. Ft. Hays
Ellsworth
Ft. Harker

Smoky Hill R.

Colorado

Ft.
Zarah

Ft.
Larned

Santa Fe Trail
Arkansas R.

Ft.
Dodge

Cutoff

Indian Territory

THE KANSAS FRONTIER IN 1867

Crosses on the map indicate the general locations of the Battles of the Saline River and Prairie Dog Creek in western Kansas. The map was drawn by the author.

INDIAN RAID ON I

This illustration appeared in Harper's Weekly *on September 7, 1867. It demonstrat*

— Courtesy, The Kansas State Historical Society

MAJOR GEORGE A. ARMES

— Courtesy, The Kansas State Historical Society

SCOUT ALLISON J. PLILEY

STRUCTION CREW
by the Indians in the harassment of a railroad construction crew near Fort Hays.

KIOWA CHIEF SATANTA

ROMAN NOSE, CHEYENNE BRAVE

59

THE HOLLOW SQUARE

This illustration shows the "hollow square" method of defense used against a complete Indian encirclement. It is taken from Armes' own account of the battle in UPS AND DOWNS OF AN ARMY OFFICER.

— Courtesy, The Kansas State Historical Society

after the horses before they had gone two hundred feet. As they did so, the soldiers fairly picked them off. "It was," Pliley subsequently recalled, "like shooting into a covey of quail at close range with a shotgun." The braves who were not hit left "in a hurry," carrying their dead and wounded comrades with them.

Coming to a ravine late in the afternoon, the detachment halted and assumed a position amid "a stunted growth" of cottonwoods and willows. The surrounding terrain was so broken the braves could not charge over it. The fighting stopped as soon as it became dark, though the Indians could still be heard signaling to each other by means of animal cries. After a short rest, the group made its way slowly and quietly over an unguarded buffalo path, discovered by Pliley, to the Prairie Dog. The seriously wounded were carried on the two horses. Crossing the creek to the south side, the detachment stationed itself in the high bluffs of a canyon to await the break of day.[16]

The next morning, August 22, the Indians appeared "in full force" on the opposite bank. But before they could ride to the attack, Pliley galloped out on the better of the two horses to look for the wagon train, hoping to bring help. He found the wagons parked in a nearby ravine south of the creek and entirely surrounded by warriors collected into groups of about fifty each.[17] With some difficulty he succeeded in dodging through the Indian lines. Lieutenant Price declined, however, to send a detachment to the relief of Jenness on the grounds that he had barely enough men to defend the train.

Price had no sooner rejected Pliley's request for assistance than Armes came through the Indian encirclement with the main column. He had, as noticed above, reached the creek during the night. Upon the advent of daylight he had discovered that he was only two miles from Price. Low on ammunition, he had wasted no time in marching to join the train. Soon after Armes arrived, a force under Captain Barker proceeded to the rescue of Jenness. Breaking through the Indian enclosure, Barker formed a hollow square around Jenness' crippled and exhausted detachment and, though constantly harassed by warriors, escorted it safely back to the wagons. Armes' entire command was thus reunited.

Except for two charges, Armes remained on the defensive throughout the remainder of the day, fighting off wave after wave of Indian attackers. One of the soldiers' charges occurred when Armes sent sixteen volunteers on foot to the creek for water. As they rushed forward the braves guarding the creek scampered through the shallow water to the opposite bank. While part of the group kept the warriors under cover by means of a rapid carbine fire, the rest filled the water containers. They then returned to the wagons with only one man slightly wounded. Another charge was made in the afternoon by Armes himself with twenty mounted men — "all I could raise" — against a heavy concentration of warriors on a slope to the west. Armes drove them across the creek, but in doing so was almost cut off by "about 300 or 400" others. Returning to the train, Armes prudently refrained from any further offensive operations.

As the day was clear and still the soldiers could hear "almost every command" of the Indian chiefs. They could also hear the reds calling them names and challenging them to come out of "that hole" and "give us a fair fight." Probably in an effort to divide the command, one of the enemy shouted in plain English that "we don't want to fight the niggers; we want to fight you white sons of - - - -." It may be, however, that the Indians did not relish fighting the Negroes. The Negro soldiers not only had a good reputation as Indian fighters, but also, according to a perceptive newspaper correspondent, possessed a "penchant" for taking scalps; and the Indians believed that without their scalps they had little chance of entering the happy hunting grounds in the hereafter.[18]

During the night Armes moved his force back toward the Solomon River in the direction of Fort Hays. But if he hoped he had eluded his antagonists he was disappointed, for he found at daybreak that he was still "entirely surrounded by Indians." As "I had all I could do to fight and keep them off," Armes made no attempt to continue the retreat during the day. Presumably, the story of the fighting on August 23 was much the same as that of the previous day.[19] One notable incident occurred, however, during the afternoon when three warriors carrying a flag of truce walked from a large group of Indians towards the camp. Armes sent one of his guides, a half-breed named Charlie Cadaro, to see what they wanted. Coming within easy gun range, the peace doves suddenly became war hawks, cursing Cadaro by name and firing at him with weapons which they had concealed beneath their clothing. Dropping to the ground Cadaro also drew a gun from concealment and returned the fire, killing one and compelling the other two to retreat.[20]

The Indians withdrew during the night and Armes continued on to Fort Hays without further molestation. The wounded together with an escort under Armes himself arrived at the fort, according to General Hancock, on the twenty-fourth, apparently ahead of the rest of the column.[21] Both Majors Moore and Elliott marched their commands to the battlesite immediately upon Armes' arrival. But finding the Indians gone, they soon returned, Moore to Fort Hays, Elliott to Fort Wallace.[22]

Armes reported his total losses as three men killed and thirty-five wounded, and the Indian losses as about fifty killed and one hundred fifty wounded. His force of one hundred sixty-four men had fought off about eight hundred warriors. Besides Satanta and Roman Nose, the scouts had recognized Charles Bent, the half-Cheyenne son of the famous trader, William Bent, among the Indian leaders. One contemporary account states that Arapahoes and Sioux as well as Kiowas and Cheyennes participated in the fight, which is probably true if there were indeed eight hundred warriors.[23]

Colonel Corbin in a statement transmitting Armes' report to departmental headquarters seemed to believe the fight had been more of a victory than a defeat and that Armes had turned in a creditable performance. Armes had, he said, done "all any one could have done with the [number of] men he had." And it was the "universal testimony" of members of his command that "the Indians have been severely punished."[24] Major Moore, however, regarded the Indians as the victors and blamed Armes for the defeat. Armes had not only "shaped his march" to the Solomon after Armes and Moore had split up on the Saline so as to "avoid" reuniting with Moore, but also made the mistake of dividing his command on the Prairie Dog. Armes' "miserable failure is owing entirely to his having been too anxious for a fight of his own which led him to run away from me [Moore] and [to] his want of judgment in scattering his command all over the plains."[25]

Moore's assessment of the outcome of the fight as a victory for the Indians seems accurate enough. Though the Indians suffered heavy casualties, they nevertheless compelled the aggressor, Armes, to retreat. Armes, himself, evidently believed the fight was less than a victory, otherwise he seemingly would not have thought it necessary to state in his official report that he would not have pursued the Indian trail so far "with so small a force" had he not expected Elliott and Moore to be somewhere in the "vicinity." Moore's criticism of Armes for dividing his command also seems legitimate. And Armes' actions preceding both the fights on the Saline and the Prairie Dog would seem to indicate that he was indeed anxious for a fight, but as to whether he purposely avoided Moore on the Solomon because he wished all the glory of a battle for himself, we have only Moore's assertion that he did so.

Armes' conduct during the fight was criticized. Pliley, who turned in an excellent individual performance, believed that Armes should have gone to the rescue of Jenness on August 21. And he was presumably the source of a charge that Armes refused to send relief to Jenness after Armes got back to the train on August 22.[26] Pliley's criticisms seem at least partially justified in view of the relative ease with which Captain Barker, who allegedly acted on his own in doing so, brought Jenness in to the wagon train. But it would seem that had the Indians chosen to take advantage of their superior numbers they might have over-powered Barker while he was in the open. And that they might have given Armes considerable trouble in attempting a rescue on the twenty-first is suggested by the fact that the Indians were seemingly bolder on that day than on either of the other two; this may have been owing to the fact that the fighting on the first day took place near the Indians' village. Pliley states that his criticisms caused Armes to be court-martialed.[27] There is no concrete evidence, however, to support Pliley's assertion.

Armes was arrested on September 12; but he was released the next day, and the cause of his trouble is unknown. That he was not a model officer seems certain enough, inasmuch as he was arrested and court-martialed a number of times during his career.[28]

The exact location of the fight is unknown. Armes and Jenness both placed it on the Beaver Creek tributary of the Solomon;[29] Pliley, Stahl, and other participants placed it on the Prairie Dog.[30] But in all probability the fight occurred on the Prairie Dog. The estimates given by contemporaries, including those of Armes and Jenness, of the distance to the battlesite from Fort Hays favor, however slightly, that stream.[31] And Armes' own accounts of his movements preceding the battle seem to place him on August 21-22 not where he believed he was, but where Pliley and others said he was, on the Prairie Dog in northwestern Phillips County, Kansas.[32]

The battle of Prairie Dog Creek ended the army's offensive operations on the Kansas frontier for the year. Urged on by eastern Indian sympathizers, Congress on July 20, 1867, created an Indian Peace Commission to make new treaties with the Plains tribes. One of the members of this commission was General Sherman, who directed General Hancock to terminate all offensive movements in his department and to fight only on the defensive pending the outcome of the commission's negotiations. Among the Jenness party when it was attacked on August 21 was a messenger carrying a dispatch to Armes ordering him to return with his command to Fort Hays.[33]

Thus the fight on the Prairie Dog was the army's last opportunity to chastise the hostiles before the peace conference. But it failed and Indian raids continued on the Kansas frontier until treaties were signed with the Southern Plains tribes in the fall. Despite the treaties, however, the Indians took to the warpath again in 1868. Had the army succeeded in punishing them for their misbehavior in 1867, they might have remained at peace in 1868, and there would have been no need for Major General Philip H. Sheridan's winter campaign of 1868-69.

NOTES

1. The foregoing is based on the author's own research principally in War Department and Indian Office records in the National Archives. Secondary accounts are in Donald J. Berthrong, THE SOUTHERN CHEYENNES (Norman: 1963), pp. 266-288, and William H. Leckie, THE MILITARY CONQUEST OF THE SOUTHERN PLAINS (Norman: 1963), pp. 30-62.
2. The Smoky Hill Stage Line was owned by Wells, Fargo and Company.
3. *Junction City Weekly Union*, June 22, 29, 1867; *Leavenworth Daily Conservative*, July 3, 4, 6, 10, 1867; *Leavenworth Daily Times*, June 25, 29, 1867; *Kansas Daily Tribune*, (Lawrence), June 29 and August 4, 1867; Hart to Weir, June 18, 1867, communication of Gibbs, June 19, 1867, Fort Hays, Letter Sent, Department of the Missouri, Records of the War Department, National Archives (hereafter cited as Fort Hays, LS, DM, RWD, NA).
4. *Weekly Union*, July 20, August 3, 17, 1867, January 25, 1868; *Daily Conservative*, July 14, 1867; clipping from the *Topeka State Record* (an extra), July 5, 1868[7], in Correspondence of the Governors — Crawford, Archives, Kansas State Historical Society; Marvin H. Garfield, "Defense of the Kansas Frontier," 1866-67," *Kansas Historical Quarterly*, Vol. I, (August, 1932), pp. 332-339.

5. Corbin to McKeever, July 30, August 4, 1867, Fort Hays, LS, DM, RWD, NA; *Daily Conservative*, August 4, 6, 11, 1867; *Daily Times*, August 6, 1867; *Kansas Daily Tribune*, August 6, 1867. Although an important Cheyenne leader, Roman Nose, was not a chief. George B. Grinnell, THE FIGHTING CHEYENNES (Norman: 1958), p. 249.

6. See the article by James A. Hadley, *Indianapolis* (Indiana) *Farm and Home Sentinel*, January 1, 1906, "Indian Depredations and Battles," clippings, Vol. I, p. 79, Library, Kansas State Historical Society.

7. Diary entries, August 1, 2, 3, 1867, Armes to Corbin, August 3, 1867, Corbin to Weir, August 3, 1867, in George A. Armes, UPS AND DOWNS OF AN ARMY OFFICER (Washington: 1900), pp. 236-240; Armes to Corbin, August 3, 1867, Corbin to Weir, August 3, 1867, Fort Hays, LS, DM, RWD, NA; *Daily Conservative*, August 6, 1867.

8. Copy of statement of Sergeant Reid, enclosed in Corbin to McKeever, August 6, 1867, Corbin to Weir, August 7, 1867, Fort Hays, LS, DM, RWD, NA; *Daily Times*, August 8, 1867; *Kansas Daily Tribune*, August 9, 1867; *Daily Conservative*, August 10, 1867.

9. Corbin to Weir, August 5 (two letters), 9, 13, 1867, Corbin to McKeever, August 8, 1867, Fort Hays, LS, DM, RWD, NA; *Weekly Union*, August 24, 1867; *Kansas Daily Tribune*, August 7, 22, 1867.

10. Henderson L. Burgess, a member of the Eighteenth Kansas, subsequently stated that Armes was in command, but Moore intimates that he, not Armes, was the commander. Burgess, "The Eighteenth Kansas Volunteer Cavalry and Some Incidents Connected with Its Service on the Plains," *Kansas State Historical Society Collections*, Vol. XIII (1913-14), p. 536; Moore to Crawford, August 31, 1867, Correspondence of Governors — Crawford, Archives, Kansas State Historical Society.

11. Moore to Crawford, August 31, 1867, Correspondence of Governors — Crawford, Archives, Kansas State Historical Society; communications of Marshall, August 15, 18, 31, 1867, *Weekly Union*, August 24, September 21, 1867; Corbin to Weir, August 7, 1867, Fort Hays, LS, DM, RWD, NA.

12. Diary entries, August 18, 19, 20, 21, 1867, Armes to Corbin, August 24, 1867, in Armes, *Ups and Downs of an Army Officer*, pp. 243, 245; Hadley, *Farm and Home Sentinel*, January 1, 1906, in "Indian Depredations and Battles," Vol. I, pp. 78-79, Library, Kansas State Historical Society; George B. Jenness, "The Battle on Beaver Creek," *Kansas State Historical Society Transactions*, Vol. IX, (Topeka: 1906), p. 444. Although the accounts of the events immediately preceding the fight and of the fight itself do not entirely agree, one finds upon close examination that they in general complement one another.

13. Diary entry, August 21, 1867, Armes to Corbin, August 24, 1867, in Armes, *op. cit.*, pp. 243-246; Forrest R. Blackburn, "The Eighteenth Kansas Cavalry and the Indian War," *Trail Guide*, Vol IX, (Kansas City, Missouri, March, 1964), pp. 8-9; Frank M. Stahl to Mrs. M. A. Spaulding, November 7, 1932, and copy of Hugh M. Johnson's account of the Prairie Dog fight, Library, Kansas State Historical Society.

14. James A. Hadley, who presumably received his information from Pliley, states that the Indians were seen about one mile away while the soldiers were watering their horses on a tributary of the Prairie Dog. He does not mention a party of cavalrymen from the main column joining the detachment under Jenness at any time. Hadley, *Farm and Home Sentinel*, January 1, 1906, "Indian Depredations and Battles," Vol. I, p. 79, Library Kansas State Historical Society. Jenness' account, however, is supported by Armes' which states that he (Armes) sent two sergeants, presumably with an escort, back with instructions for the wagon train just before he (Armes) was attacked. Armes says that they met Jenness on their way to the train and intimates that they joined him, which indeed they must have, since Jenness names one of them, Sergeant George W. Carpenter, Eighteenth Kansas, as participating in the fight. Armes to Corbin, August 24, 1867, in Armes, *op. cit.*, p. 245; Jenness, "Battle on Beaver Creek," *Kansas State Historical Society Transactions*, Vol. IX, pp. 444-445. Had there been no Indians in sight it seems logical to assume that they would have continued on to the train. I have therefore chosen to accept the Jenness story of the appearance of the troopers at the same time as the appearance of the Indians.

15. According to Jenness, the Indians on the hill actually were not warriors, as he and Pliley supposed they were at the time, but old men, women, and children from the village. They were probably out watching the fight.

16. Jenness, "Battle on Beaver Creek," *Kansas State Historical Society Transactions*, Vol. IX, pp. 444-445; Allan W. Farley (ed.), "Reminiscences of Allison J. Pliley, Indian Fighter," *Trail Guide*, Vol. II (June, 1957), pp. 1-4; Hadley, *Farm and Home Sentinel*, January 1, 15, 1906, "Indian Depredations and Battles," Vol. I, pp. 79-82, Library, Kansas State Historical Society. Pliley was the main source of Hadley's account of the Prairie Dog fight. Hadley himself was a corporal in the Eighteenth Kansas, but he was with Major Moore's portion of the battalion.

17. Jenness states that the detachment did not know the whereabouts of the wagons in relation to its position while Hadley claims that it did. The truth has not been ascertained.

18. See Theodore R. Davis, "A Summer on the Plains," *Harper's New Monthly Magazine*, Vol. XXXVI (February, 1868), p. 305; *Daily Conservative*, August 23, 1867.
19. Most accounts of the Prairie Dog fight do not make clear, as Armes does in his diary and official report, that the battle lasted for three days.
20. Diary entries, August 22, 23, 1867, Armes to Corbin, August 24, 1867, in Armes, *op. cit.*, pp. 244-248; Jenness, "Battle on Beaver Creek," *Kansas State Historical Society Transactions*, Vol. IX, pp. 449-452; Hadley, *Farm and Home Sentinel*, January 15, 1906, "Indian Depredations and Battles," Vol. I, p. 82, Library, Kansas State Historical Society; Farley (ed.), "Reminiscences of Allison J. Pliley," *Trail Guide*, Vol. II, pp. 5-6; communication of Marshall, August 31, 1867, *Weekly Union*, September 21, 1867; Hancock to Sherman, August 24, 1867, *House Executive Document* No. 240, 41st Congress, Second Session, pp. 145-146; Stahl to Spaulding, November 7, 1932, Library, Kansas State Historical Society; Blackburn, "The Eighteenth Kansas Cavalry," *Trail Guide*, Vol. IX, pp. 10-11; *Daily Conservative*, August 27, 1867.
21. Hancock to Crawford, August 24, 1867, *Kansas Daily Tribune*, August 27, 1867. Hadley states that Pliley rode to Fort Harker on August 22 for ambulances with which to bring in the wounded. Pliley said that he would not have done this had Armes not taunted him, apparently when Pliley objected to the order, "with being afraid to go." Farley (ed.), "Reminiscences of Allison J. Pliley," *Trail Guide*, Vol. II, pp. 5-6; Hadley, *Farm and Home Sentinel*, January 15, 1906, "Indian Depredations and Battles," Vol. I, p. 82, Library, Kansas State Historical Society.
22. Communication of Marshall, August 31, 1867, *Weekly Union*, September 21, 1867; Moore to Crawford, August 31, 1867, Correspondence of Governors — Crawford, Archives, Kansas State Historical Sociey.
23. Armes to Corbin, August 24, 1867, in Armes, *op. cit.*, p. 246; Hancock to Sherman, August 24, 1867, *House Executive Document* No. 240, 41st Congress, Second Session, pp. 145-146; communication of Marshall, August 31, 1867, *Weekly Union*, September 21, 1867. Lieutenant Price set the number of Indians killed at about one hundred fifty. It was unusual for the Kiowas to be so far north, but they were definitely identified.
24. Corbin to McKeever, August, 1867, Fort Hays, LS, DM, RWD, NA.
25. Moore to Crawford, August 31, 1867, Correspondence of Governors — Crawford, Archives, Kansas State Historical Society.
26. See Hadley, *Farm and Home Sentinel*, January 15, 1906, "Indian Depredations and Battles," Vol. I, pp. 77-82. Library, Kansas State Historical Society. Pliley subsequently participated in the battle of the Arickaree and served as a captain in the Nineteenth Kansas Cavalry.
27. Farley (ed.), "Reminiscences of Allison J. Pliley," *Trail Guide*, Vol. II, p. 6.
28. Armes, *op. cit.*, pp. 250, 258. Honorably discharged in 1870, Armes reëntered the army in 1878 as a captain, Tenth Cavalry, and served until 1883. Francis B. Heitman, HISTORICAL REGISTER AND DICTIONARY OF THE UNITED STATES ARMY, FROM ITS ORGANIZATION, SEPTEMBER 29, 1789, TO MARCH 2, 1903 (two vols., Washington, D. C., 1903), Vol. I, p. 169.
29. Two Beaver Creeks were shown on some contemporary maps, one tributary to the Solomon River in Kansas, the other to the Republican River in Nebraska. What actually was the North Fork of the Solomon was designated on these maps as the Beaver Creek tributary of the Solomon. And the Bow Creek tributary of the Solomon (the Middle Branch of the Solomon on some maps) was shown as the North Fork. It seems clear enough, however, that Armes and Jenness believed they were on the Beaver Creek tributary of the Solomon. Armes gave his location in his diary on August 22, 1867, as "Beaver Creek, Kan." Armes, *op. cit.*, p. 244. And Jenness notices in his account the close proximity of the Solomon and mistakenly placed the fighting on August 22 on that stream. Jenness, "The Battle on Beaver Creek," *Kansas State Historical Society Transactions*, Vol. IX, pp. 443-445, 449. Armes' and Jenness' location of the fight is supported by the statement of a Fort Hays newspaper correspondent that Armes was attacked on the Beaver after crossing the Saline and Solomon Valleys. Communication of Marshall, August 21, 1867, *Weekly Union*, September 21, 1867.

Armes' failure in his official report to indicate which Beaver Creek he meant together with his strong intimation that he believed before he was attacked that he would find the Indians on the Republican may have caused some of his contemporaries to assume that he meant the Beaver Creek tributary of the Republican. Presumably, on the basis of the Armes report, Hancock told General Sherman and Governor Crawford that the fight occurred "on the Republican." And Colonel Corbin commented in transmitting the Armes report to higher headquarters that it was fought "near the Republican." Armes to Corbin, August 24, 1867, in Armes, *op. cit.*, pp. 245, 247; Hancock to Sherman, August 24, 1867; *House Executive Document* No. 240, 41st Congress, Second Session, pp. 145-146; Hancock to Crawford, August 24, 1867, *Kansas Daily Tribune*, August 27, 1867; Corbin to McKeever, August, 1867, Fort Hays, LS, DM, RWD, NA.

30. Farley (ed.), "Reminiscences of Allison J. Pliley," *Trail Guide*, Vol. II, p. 3; Hadley, *Farm and Home Sentinel*, January 1, 1906, "Indian Depredations and Battles," Vol. I, p. 78, Library, Kansas State Historical Society; Stahl to Spaulding, November 7, 1932, Library, Kansas State Historical Society; Blackburn, "The Eighteenth Kansas Cavalry," *Trail Guide*, Vol. IX, pp. 11-12.

31. See Armes to Corbin, August 24, 1867, in Armes, *op. cit.*, p. 245; Jenness, "The Battle on Beaver Creek," *Kansas State Historical Society Transactions*, Vol. IX, p. 444; Moore to Crawford, August 31, 1867, Correspondence of Governors — Crawford, Archives, Kansas State Historical Society; communication of Marshall, August 31, 1867, *Weekly Union*, September 21, 1867.

32. If Armes covered some twenty miles on each of his three marches after leaving his camp on the Saline forty-five miles northwest of Fort Hays on August 19, as one presumes from his diary and official report that he did, then he was by his own accounts on the Prairie Dog on the twenty-first. He states that he camped after the first march on the Saline, but he evidently means the South Fork of the Solomon, since he was moving northward and he had traveled approximately the same distance as that between the Saline and the South Fork. His second march, he says, took him to the Solomon River. What later maps show as Bow Creek was shown on some early maps as the North Fork of the Solomon though it was designated simply as the Solomon. It is less than ten miles from Bow Creek (the North Fork) to the North Fork (the Beaver Creek tributary). But Armes tells us that he moved "ten or fifteen miles" during the night of his third march, made camp and then resumed the march at 2:00 a. m.; he did not stop again until 9:00 a. m., next morning. The first one-half of his third march would have taken him north of what was apparently on Armes' map the Beaver Creek tributary of the Solomon. Thus Armes' own accounts of his movements indicate the stream immediately north of Beaver Creek as the correct site of the fight. That stream was Prairie Dog Creek. Diary entries, Aug. 18, 19, 20, 21, 22, 1867, Armes to Corbin, August 24, 1867, in Armes, *op. cit.*, pp. 243-245.

33. Sherman to Hancock, August 7, 1867, Fort Hays, LS, DM, RWD, NA; *Daily Conservative*, August 9, September 1, 1867; *Kansas Daily Tribune*, August 9, 1867; Hadley, *Farm and Home Sentinel*, January 1, 1906, "Indian Depredations and Battles," Vol. I, p. 79, Library, Kansas State Historical Society; Berthrong, *op. cit.*, pp. 289-290; Leckie, *op. cit.*, pp. 57-59. One wonders if Moore and Elliott's march to the Prairie Dog upon Armes' return on August 24 was not in violation of Sherman's orders. Perhaps a subsequent engagement would have been excused on the grounds that it was merely a continuation of the battle of the Prairie Dog.

THE BATTLE OF BEECHER ISLAND

IN 1867 federal commissioners concluded a general peace treaty with the Southern Plains Indians under which they were to accept reservations in Indian Territory and receive annually from the government food, clothing and other items necessary for their sustenance. In the spring of 1868, however, the Cheyennes and Arapahoes, most of whom were congregated on the Pawnee Fork and Walnut Creek tributaries of the Arkansas River, west of Fort Larned, Kansas, became restive. They were unhappy not only with their new reservation, but also because their annuities, which included arms and ammunition, had not arrived. Early in June a large war party consisting mainly of Cheyennes made an attack against the Kaws on their reservation near Council Grove, Kansas, in retaliation for a defeat suffered at their hands a few months earlier. During the expedition the raiders plundered farm houses, stole livestock, and caused considerable alarm among the settlers.

The Kaw raid caused the Indian Office to hold up on the delivery of arms and ammunition until it could be determined whether the Indians intended to keep the treaty of 1867 or go on the warpath. When it appeared to observers that they intended no outbreak, the arms and ammunition were issued early in August. Less than a week later, a large party of Cheyennes, seemingly without provocation, swept through the Saline and Solomon Valleys in Kansas, killing, wounding, raping, and stealing. Some thirty frontiersmen were killed and wounded, seven women ravished, and one woman and two little girls captured. The damage might have been even greater had it not been for the appearance of cavalry from Fort Harker.[1]

The Saline and Solomon raids were followed by attacks on the Santa Fe and Smoky Hill roads in both Kansas and Colorado. In an assault on a Mexican wagon train near Fort Dodge on August 28, a party of Cheyennes and Arapahoes killed and scalped sixteen Mexicans and burned their bodies together with the wagons. In another incident, the Indians attacked Scouts William Comstock and Abner S. (Sharp) Grover as they were leaving a Cheyenne camp on the Solomon, killing Comstock and wounding Grover.[2]

In response to the appeals of Governor Samuel J. Crawford of Kansas and Acting Governor Frank Hall of Colorado Territory for federal help, Lieutenant General William T. Sherman, commander of the Division of the Missouri, urged Major General Philip H. Sheridan, commander of the Department of the Missouri, to exert himself to the limit in meeting the danger. Although Sheridan had only 2,600 men in his

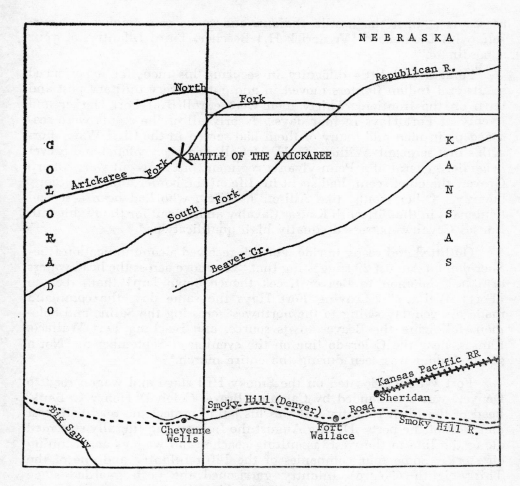

FORT WALLACE, THE DENVER ROAD, AND THE ARICKAREE FORK

This sketch map by the author shows parts of Western Kansas and Eastern Colorado where the march to and from Beecher Island took place.

entire command with which to "catch" the elusive hostiles, he nevertheless began preparations for a major campaign. To expedite his operations, he established his headquarters at Fort Hays.[3]

Short-handed as he was, Sheridan could not send cavalry to each scene of attack. He could ask the State of Kansas to provide a regiment of cavalry, which he eventually did, but raising such a force would take some time. Consequently, Sheridan decided to establish a mobile force of scouts for immediate service on the frontier. On August 24, he directed one of his staff officers, Major (Brevet Colonel) George A. Forsyth to employ "without delay" fifty "first class hardy frontiersmen to be used

69

as scouts against the hostile Indians, and to be commanded by your-self, with Lieutenant [Frederick H.] Beecher, Third Infantry, as your subordinate."[4]

Forsyth had little difficulty in securing his men, for experienced scouts and Indian fighters moved in and out of every military post and town on the frontier. Thirty men were enrolled at Fort Harker and twenty at Fort Hays in four days. Nearly all of the scouts were sea-soned plainsmen and many of them had served in the Civil War. For-syth's first sergeant, William H. H. McCall, had been colonel and brevet brigadier general of a Pennsylvania regiment in the recent war. Sharp Grover, the chief scout, had spent his life on the border and spoke Sioux fluently. Other scouts, like Allison J. Pliley, who had been a second lieutenant in the Fifteenth Kansas Cavalry and a scout for the Eighteenth Kansas Cavalry, possessed equally high qualifications.[5]

Outfitted and ready to ride, Forsyth received a communication from Sheridan on August 29 suggesting that "you move across the head waters of [the] Solomon to Beaver Creek thence down [up] that creek to [Fort] Wallace." Leaving Fort Hays the same day, the command made a seven-day swing to the northwest, crossing the Saline and Solo-mon, following the Beaver to its source, and reaching Fort Wallace, Kansas, near the Colorado line on the evening of September 5. Not a single Indian was seen during the entire march.[6]

Fort Wallace, located on the Smoky Hill stage and wagon road to Denver, was commanded by Captain (Brevet Colonel) Henry C. Bank-head of the Fifth Infantry. It was his job to protect the road both east and west of the post. During August the Indians had literally swarmed along the line to the west, assaulting coaches and wagons and running off stock. Some four companies of the Fifth Infantry and one of the Thirty-eighth (Negro) Infantry garrisoned the post, guarded stage stations, and escorted the coaches. Bankhead's need for cavalry with which to pursue Indian raiding parties and patrol the frontier undoubt-edly explains why Forsyth's scouts and two companies of Tenth (Negro) Cavalry were sent to Fort Wallace in late August and early September.[7]

On September 7, twenty-five Indians killed and scalped two men near Sheridan, the western terminus of the Kansas Pacific Railroad thirteen miles to the east, and drove off seventy or eighty mules be-longing to a wagon train camped on Turkey Creek. One Indian, identi-fied as an Arapaho, was killed and a teamster slightly wounded in the raid on the train. Learning of the attacks, Bankhead sent Captain George W. Graham's troop of Tenth Cavalry in pursuit, but it was unable to overtake the fleeing Indians.[8]

Returning to the post, Graham was ordered to proceed west and clear the Denver road of Indians. On September 15 he was attacked on the Big Sandy, thirty miles south of Deering Wells, by about one

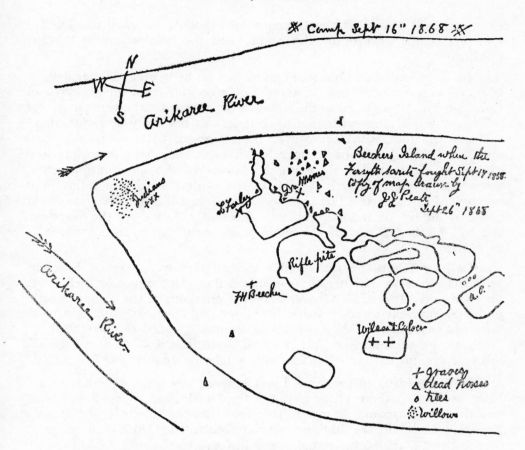

MAP OF THE BATTLESITE AT BEECHER ISLAND

J. J. Peate, a member of the rescue column that came from Fort Wallace, made this map of the battleground. The map appeared in the BEECHER ISLAND ANNUAL, Vol. IV (1908). It is reproduced through the courtesy of the State Historical Society of Colorado, Denver.

hundred warriors. Graham's troopers repulsed the attack, killing eleven Indians and several ponies, but the loss of twenty-eight horses and mules killed or captured forced them to return to Fort Wallace.[9]

While Graham was on the Big Sandy, Captain (Brevet Lieutenant Colonel) Louis H. Carpenter's company of Tenth Cavalry was trailing about two hundred Indians who had run off some 1,200 horses, mules, and cattle from a point near Pond City four miles west of Fort Wallace. Although Carpenter succeeded in recovering the stolen stock, he was unable to overtake the raiders. Because Graham's company, which came in on September 19, was not in condition to return immediately to the field, Bankhead ordered Carpenter to take up on the Denver road where Graham had left off. Carpenter marched out on September 21 riding toward Kiowa station whence he expected to leave the Denver road and scout toward the Big Sandy and the headwaters of the Republican.[10]

In the meantime, Colonel Forsyth had on September 10 decided, in response to a communication brought by a courier from the governor of Colorado Territory, to go to the Bijou Basin where a large war party was raiding the outlying settlements. But just as his command was about to leave the fort, word came over the telegraph that the Indians had attacked a freighter's train near Sheridan, killing two teamsters and capturing some stock. Reaching the scene of the depredation about seven hours later, Forsyth picked up the raiders' trail and followed it northward until dark. The next morning it took him toward the Beaver Creek tributary of the Republican. Presently, however, the warriors, one by one, began leaving the main party, causing the trail eventually to vanish.[11]

Calling a halt, Forsyth held a consultation with Grover, Beecher, and McCall as to whether the command should continue or turn back. Beecher said little while Grover and McCall thought the raiders would probably proceed directly to their villages and return with reinforcements before they could be overtaken. Forsyth ended the conversation, however, by announcing that he was "determined to find and attack the Indians, no matter what the odds might be against us."[12]

Thus deciding to press on, Forsyth spent the next three days carefully examining the country between the North Fork of the Republican and the main stream. It was in this area that the governor of Colorado Territory had said the Indians were concentrated. On the morning of September 14, the scouts struck a small, fresh trail which took them up the Arickaree Fork (known also as the Dry Fork) of the Republican. Presently, the trail "led into a large and well beaten track and there was no doubt but that we had discovered the road to the encampment of some of the hostile tribes."[13]

As the trail widened on the next day, some of the men, according to Scout John Hurst, questioned

> . . . the wisdom of following such a large party of Indians with such a small force of men. It was evident they [the warriors] had their families with them and could not travel as fast as a war party alone, and we realized that we would soon overtake them. We made known our anxiety to Colonel Forsyth, and he asked us if we "did not enlist with him to fight Indians?" That ended the discussion, but, all the same, it did not convince us of the wisdom of the course.[14]

Another matter of concern to the men was their dwindling supply of provisions. But "as we had a small supply of salt I [Forsyth] concluded to push on trusting that we might find game enough to subsist upon and find and fight the Indians, before returning to Fort Wallace."[15]

On the afternoon of September 16 the little command camped on the north bank of the Arickaree Fork in a small, "well-grassed" valley. In the middle of the stream, some ninety feet from either side, lay a small island about two hundred feet long and forty feet wide. It was "in reality merely a land heap," sparsely covered by a few cottonwood and willow trees with a thin stream of water a few inches in depth running along each side.[16]

Unknown to the scouts two large villages of Brulé Sioux and one of Cheyenne Dog Soldiers and a few Northern Arapahoes lay along the river about twelve miles away.[17]   Among the chiefs were Pawnee Killer of the Sioux and Tall Bull, Bull Bear, and White Horse of the Cheyennes.   Another important personage in the Dog Soldier camp was Roman Nose, who though not a tribal chief was one of the Cheyennes' most outstanding war leaders.[18]   Late that same day a small hunting party came in with the news that "soldiers" were camped nearby.   Thus the main body of Indians learned of Forsyth's presence in the vicinity.[19]

At daybreak on September 17, eight Indians attempted to stampede Forsyth's stock by dashing through the herd whooping and yelling and waving robes and blankets.   Seven animals broke their lariats and were captured.   Almost in a moment, the camp was alive with the sound of rifle fire and the cry of "Indians! Turn out! Indians!" Realizing that he was in an "untenable" position, Forsyth ordered the men to saddle up.   The order had no sooner been obeyed than warriors in large numbers swarmed on all sides.   If we may believe Forsyth,

> The ground seemed to grow them. They appeared to start out of the very earth. On foot and on horseback, from over the hills, out of the thickets, from the bed of the stream, from the north, south, and west, along the opposite bank, and out of the long grass on every side of us, with wild cries of exultation they pressed towards us. A few sharp volleys from the command, who stood coolly to horse, each man having his bridle thrown over his left arm, staggered them for a moment, and then they hastily fell back out of range.[20]

Surrounded and badly outnumbered, Forsyth decided to make a stand "on the adjacent island."[21]   Leading their horses, the scouts moved almost in a solid front to the west end of the tract.[22]   The movement was covered by several of the "best shots" under Beecher, Grover, and McCall who kept up a rapid fire with their seven-shot Spencer carbines from the flanks.   Three scouts remained in the tall grass under the river bank to cover the east end of the island.   Reaching their destination, Forsyth had his men tie the animals securely to trees and bushes and to lie down in a rough circle and dig pits in the sand with their hands and carbines for protection.

While the scouts were retreating, a large portion of the warriors took up positions in the tall grass and weeds along the river banks. Others remained on their ponies just outside range of the scouts' guns watching the fight. The action was also witnessed by the Indian women and children from the distant hills.

Well-armed, according to Forsyth, mainly with the latest type breech-loading rifles,[23] the warriors poured in a deadly fire upon the island. By 9:00 a.m. all of the horses and mules had been shot down and several men were killed or wounded. Most of the losses occurred before the scouts completed the digging of the rifle pits. One of the casualties was the command's doctor, Acting Assistant Surgeon John H. Mooers, who was shot in the head. Although wounded in the right thigh and the left leg and grazed on the head, Colonel Forsyth continued to direct the defense of the island. At 9:30 a.m. about three hundred mounted warriors collected in a gorge upstream[24] and charged forward en masse.[25] But all, save one who rode on undaunted and unharmed, broke away in the face of the scouts' devastating fire and passed on either side of the island. With the exception of three men, who were paralyzed with fear,[26] the scouts fought desperately.

Hard fighting continued throughout the remainder of the day with the warriors firing from cover and occasionally charging on horseback. At 2:30 p.m. and again at 5:00 p.m. the Indians charged the island in force, but both assaults were repulsed. Several braves were shot off their ponies so close to the pits that their comrades were unable to retrieve their bodies. One of the Indian casualties during the day was Roman Nose, who was killed while leading one of the charges.[27]

At sundown, the fighting ceased, and for the first time Forsyth could take stock of the command's predicament. Nearly one-half the men, including Lieutenant Beecher, were dead or wounded; their rations had been used up before the battle; their medical supplies had been captured in the early-morning dash upon the animals; and the only person who was competent to attend the wounded was dying. It was eighty-five miles to Fort Wallace, the nearest army post, and even if runners succeeded in getting through it would be many hours before they returned with troops. Nevertheless, getting word to Fort Wallace seemed to be the little band's only hope. Two men, Jack Stilwell and Pierre Trudeau, volunteered to undertake the dangerous mission, and shortly after midnight they left the island, crawling toward the Indian encirclement.

The command's situation was, however, not entirely bad, since it was in an excellent position for defense and possessed an abundance of ammunition. During the night, the men connected and strengthened the rifle pits, dug out a secure place for the injured and covered them with saddle blankets, deepened a small well which one of the scouts had dug during the day, secured the ammunition which they had in the saddle bags, and cut off strips of flesh from the dead animals for food. A light rain which began falling in the evening apparently did not affect their activities one way or another.[28]

Fighting was resumed the next morning with a "slight charge" at dawn but it was easily repulsed, and thereafter the Indians contented themselves to snipe at the scouts from the nearby banks, hills, and ravines. Forsyth believed the warriors intended to try "to starve us out," but it would appear in retrospect that they had become discouraged by the scouts' determined stand of the day before and their strong defensive position on the island. During the day the Indians signaled their desire for a parley by raising a white flag. Some "controversy" occurred among the scouts as to whether it should be recognized, but fearing a trick, Forsyth decided to reject the overture, and had Grover shout his decision to the warriors in their own language. Evidently they misunderstood what Grover said because a delegation started immediately toward the island. A half-dozen shots from the scouts' carbines, however, corrected the misunderstanding and sent the messengers scampering for cover.[29] In the evening Forsyth sent two more scouts out with instructions to bring help from Fort Wallace. But the messengers, Allison J. Pliley and Chauncey B. Whitney, soon returned, having been unable to slip through the Indian encirclement.

Intermittent firing continued throughout the next day. At about noon, Grover observed that the women and children were withdrawing.[30] Evidently the Indians were planning to abandon the field. But even if they left, the command's condition was such that it must soon have relief and Forsyth had no way of knowing whether Stilwell and Trudeau had made it through the Indian lines. Consequently, Forsyth penciled a message on some small note paper to Colonel Bankhead and that evening gave it to Pliley and John Donovan to take to Fort Wallace. The message reveals the desperate plight of Forsyth's command.

> I sent you two messengers on the night of 17th inst., informing you of my critical situation. I tried to send two more last night but they did not succeed in passing the Indian pickets and returned. If the others have not arrived, then hasten at once to my assistance. I have eight badly wounded & 10 slightly wounded men to take in & every animal I had was killed save seven which the Indians stampeded. Lt. Beecher is dead & Acting Asst. Surgeon Moore [Mooers] probably cannot live the night out. He was hit in the head on Thursday & has spoken but one rational word since. I am wounded in two places, in my right thigh & my left leg broken below the knee. The Cheyennes numbered four hundred and fifty (450) alone or more. Mr. Grover says they never fought so before. They are splendidly armed with Spencer and Henry rifles. We killed at least thirty-five of them & wounded many more, besides killing & wounding a quantity of their stock. They carried off most of their killed during the night but three of their men fell into our hands. I am on a little island & have still plenty of ammunition left. We are living on mule & horse meat & are entirely out of rations. If it was not for so many wounded I would come in & take the chances of whipping them if attacked. They are evidently sick of their bargain. I had two of the members of my company killed on the 17th, viz Wm. Wilson and George W. Culver.

You had better start with not less than 75 men & bring all the wagons & ambulances you can spare. Bring a 6 pdr. howitzer with you. I can hold out here for 6 days longer if *absolutely necessary*, but please loose no time.

Very respy,
Your obt Svt
Geo. A. Forsyth,
Bvt Col. USA,
Comdg Co Scouts

P.S. My Surgeon having been mortally wounded, none of my wounded have had their wounds dressed yet. So please bring out a Surgeon with you.[31]

The story of the fighting on the fourth day was about the same as that of the day before, but on the fifth day, September 21, the main body of Indians withdrew, leaving only a few warriors behind, presumably to watch the command's movements. They, too, disappeared two days later. With the Indians' departure the scouts' main concern was to find food enough for subsistence until the arrival of relief. Apparently any animal that ventured near was considered game, for Scout Sigmund Schlesinger wrote in his diary on the 22nd, "Killt a Coyote & eat him all up."[32] Some prickly pears were also found, but mainly the men dined on putrid horse meat. At one point Forsyth suggested that since the messengers might not have succeeded in penetrating the Indian lines the uninjured should strike out for Fort Wallace in an attempt to save themselves. They refused to do so, however, preferring instead to remain with the wounded in case the Indians should return.[33]

But rescue was in the offing, for Trudeau and Stilwell had got through to Fort Wallace. After leaving the island, the two men had found themselves at dawn on September 19 on the South Fork of the Republican and virtually in the midst of a large Indian camp. They escaped detection, however, by hiding all day in a nearby swamp. Continuing their journey during the night, they observed early the next morning a party of Cheyennes riding directly toward them. Quickly crawling into a nearby buffalo carcass surrounded by weeds, the scouts watched as a lone Indian approached within a few yards and turned away. As he left a rattlesnake hissed as it coiled to strike. Stilwell, however, rose to the emergency and thwarted the reptile's attack with a well-directed spray of tobacco juice. Finally, reaching the Denver road, the messengers turned east and followed it to Fort Wallace, arriving there at about 7:00 p.m., September 22.[34]

Colonel Bankhead had been concerned for several days because he had received no word from Forsyth and his command had carried only a week's supply of rations.[35] After hearing the two scouts' report, Bankhead wired General Sheridan telling him what they had said:

Two scouts from Col. Forsyth's camp just in on foot. They left four night[s] and a half ago the camp on the dry fork [Arickaree] of the

— *Courtesy Kansas State Historical Society*

COLONEL GEORGE A. FORSYTH

—*Courtesy the Kansas State Historical Society, Topek*

COLONEL L. H. CARPENTER

A PLEA FOR IMMEDIATE ASSISTANCE

*This five-page message from Colonel Forsyth was carried to Fort Wallace
by two volunteer scouts.*

78

Republican and report as follows: About 7 or 8 days after we left here [Fort Wallace] early in the morning just at daybreak about 10 Indians attempted to run off stock. Just between daylight and sunrise about 3 or 400 Indians appeared on a Bluff about 1½ or 2 miles off coming fast towards us. We went across to a little island & they commenced firing upon us. They kept up the fight steady until about 11 o'clock [a.m.] & then there was scattering shots until about 8 o'clock [p.m.], then the firing began sharper than ever & the Indians came on thicker. Colonel Forsyth estimated them at 700. They fought us until sundown. At sundown they made one desperate charge & they still continued firing odd shots until 11 o'clock at night. [The messengers' story of the fighting on September 17 differs slightly with those of Forsyth and others, though no two accounts agree precisely on the details.] I [presumably Stilwell][36] received orders from Col. Forsyth to take a man & try to go to Fort Wallace for assistance. I started and crawled about one [and] ½ or two miles on my hands & knees through the Indians. At day light we heard firing back at camp about 5 miles from us & the sounds of firing continued until about 11 o'clock & along in the evening we heard more shots. Col. Forsyth's left leg is broken by a ball & he is shot through the right thigh. Lieut. Beecher is shot in several places & supposed to be dying. His back is broken and he begged the men to kill him. Dr. Moore [Mooers] was shot in the head while dressing the Col.'s wounds. He was crazy when we left camp. Two men are killed and about 18 or 20 wounded. Col. Forsyth wants wagons, ambulances, ammunition & provisions sent to him & a strong party of men. The men were living on horseflesh when I left. I had but 1½ pound[s] of horseflesh to come to this post. All Col. Forsyth's stock was killed, he wants some artillery. Quite a number of Indians were killed. Col. Forsyth has but very little ammunition. [This statement does not comport with Forsyth's message, quoted above, his official report, or the fact that each man went into the fight with 250 rounds of ammunition.][37] The names of the scouts are F. [S.] E. Stilwell and Peter Trudell [Trudeau]. The last man I [Bankhead] know and think his story is reliable. I will have at least 100 men including cavalry ready to start at once with 1 or 2 mountain howitzers. As soon as I can get more reliable information as to the exact position of the camp will telegraph.[38]

Sheridan promptly replied that Bankhead should use every resource at his disposal in succoring Forsyth's group. He should inform Carpenter, who was on the Denver road, and Lieutenant Colonel (Brevet Brigadier General) Luther P. Bradley, who had been ordered from Fort Sedgwick, Colorado, to the forks of the Republican with six companies of Twenty-seventh Infantry and two companies of the Second Cavalry, of Forsyth's plight. Neither money nor horseflesh were to be spared in going to the rescue.[39]

Bankhead immediately dispatched a courier to find Carpenter and deliver a message directing him "to proceed at once" to Forsyth's relief.[40] Next, after some difficulty in obtaining the services of scouts, presumably owing to the Indian danger, Bankhead sent a body of messengers under one of Forsyth's scouts to find Bradley. Because the wagons for the transportation of the troops were away at Sheridan and did not arrive back until after midnight, Bankhead himself was unable to start his own column until 4:00 a.m., September 23. The force numbered one hundred and six men and consisted of one company of Thirty-eighth Infantry, a detachment of Fifth Infantry, one company of Tenth Cavalry, a party of scouts, and Assistant Surgeon Theophilus H. Turner. Among the guides was one of the messengers from Forsyth's command. The expedition was joined on the Beaver by the couriers Bankhead had sent to find Bradley. They had been driven back by Indians.

Noticing that the country between the South and Arickaree Forks was marked on his map as impassable even for cavalry, and since he was not sure of Forsyth's exact location, the colonel decided to proceed to the main Republican and follow it until he struck the Arickaree Fork whence he would march upstream. While on the headwaters of Thickwood Creek, he was attacked by a party of Indians who charged his rear guard. Corralling the train, Bankhead fired one of the howitzers at some twenty-five or thirty warriors on a bluff, and the Indians disappeared.

The next day, September 25, the expedition moved down the Thickwood to the Republican and crossed the South Fork going upstream. Late in the afternoon a squad of cavalry from General Bradley's command rode in. Bradley had crossed Bankhead's trail downstream and sent cavalry to investigate it. Learning that General Sheridan wished him to assist in the rescue, Bradley directed Major James S. Brisbin to take his cavalry and join Colonel Bankhead. The next morning the combined forces struck Forsyth's trail on the Arickaree and were met shortly thereafter by couriers who informed them that Forsyth had been relieved the day before by Colonel Carpenter. Leaving the rest of the command to follow, Bankhead took Dr. Turner and the company of Tenth Cavalry and galloped on to the island, arriving there just before noon.[41]

Carpenter's command of seventy men, including a party of scouts under J. J. Peate and an assistant surgeon, Dr. Jenkins A Fitzgerald, had been overtaken by the courier from Fort Wallace at about 10:00 a.m., September 23, a few miles west of Cheyenne Wells. Bankhead's message (it was actually written for him by Lieutenant Hugh Johnson) stated that Forsyth was on the Dry Fork of the Republican, but Carpenter did not know and his map did not indicate which of the three forks of the Republican was known by that name. He estimated, however, from Bankhead's directions that Forsyth was almost directly north of where he was on the stage road. Crossing some dry streams in the afternoon, he had them thoroughly scouted before moving on. Reaching the South Fork on the afternoon of September 24, he discovered "a large, fresh trail over which at least 2,000 head of ponies had recently been ridden or driven . . ." Fearing that he had been spotted by the Indians and that they might be preparing to attack him, he corralled his wagons. But the Indians did not come, and he, with several men, rode to a nearby hill from whence to scan the countryside. At the top of the hill the little party found a number of recently constructed scaffolds containing the bodies of several warriors who had been shot to death. The trail undoubtedly belonged to those Indians who had fought Forsyth! Across the river and up a small ravine, Carpenter found "a small tepee of clean, white robes, and on a frame inside lay the body of a warrior wrapped in buffalo robes. He was evidently some one of consequence . . ." The body was, Carpenter tells us, subsequently identified as Roman Nose's.[42] Since the Indians had apparently been coming from the fight with Forsyth, Carpenter decided to follow their back trail.[43]

Early the next morning, Carpenter's company was joined by five scouts from Fort Wallace, one of whom was Donovan. After leaving the island on the third night, Donovan and Pliley had headed south toward the stage road. The daylight hours of September 20 they spent concealed in a buffalo wallow. A most anxious moment occurred when a small war party rode near their hiding place. Some three nights later the exhausted scouts reached Cheyenne Wells where they ate, slept, drank "a little whiskey," and boarded the first stage for Fort Wallace. On September 24, Donovan and four other scouts started out with dispatches for Colonel Bankhead.[44] But they became lost and by sheer luck happened onto Carpenter on the South Fork.

Learning of the critical condition of Forsyth's command from Donovan, Carpenter took Dr. Fitzgerald, the scouts, a portion of his troops, and an ambulance and rode on ahead, leaving the wagons and the rest of the men to follow at a more leisurely pace. Presently, the back trail left the river and turned northward. Twenty miles across the prairie brought Carpenter to a dry sand river, which he soon discovered was the Dry Fork he had been looking for. From a tall hill, he observed "what appeared to be an island" and "some figures" moving around nearby. A short ride later he was on the island. Forsyth was found "lying in a place scooped out in the sand" and "too weak, shattered and nervous to be able to talk much . . ."[45] He pretended to be reading a book that one of the men had found in his saddle pocket; actually, however, "I [Forsyth] had all I could do to keep from breaking down, as I was sore and feverish and tired and hungry, and I had been under a heavy strain . . ."[46] The rescue from the point of view of the scouts is perhaps told best by Scout Whitney:

> 25th of September, 1868. — A day long to be remembered by our little band of heroes. Arose at daylight to feel all the horrors of starvation slowly but surely approaching. Got a light breakfast on rotten meat. Some of the boys wandered away to find something to satisfy and appease their hunger. About ten o'clock the cry of Indians rang through the works. Some of the men being out, eight or ten of us took our guns to rescue them if possible. The word was given that it was *friends*. In a few moments, sure enough, our friends did come. Oh, the unspeakable joy! Shouts of joy and tears were freely commingled. Such a shaking of hands is seldom witnessed. Soon our hands were filled with something

81

for the inner man, both in the shape of victuals and stimulants. The day passed off in joy and gladness among friends who condoled with us over our hardships and shouted for joy at our success against the enemy.[47]

Carpenter's men distributed bacon and hard bread among the survivors and moved the wounded to tents which they pitched about a quarter of a mile from the island, out of range of the terrible scent emanating from the dead men and animals. Dr. Fitzgerald found many of the scouts' wounds "in a festering and fevered condition." Blood poisoning had developed in Forsyth's case, but it had not reached a point beyond medical control. The worst instance was that of Scout Louis Farley, who had been wounded in the thigh. Dr. Fitzgerald tried to save his life by amputating his leg, but the ordeal was too much for him, and he died shortly after the operation.[48]

Soon after his arrival on September 26, Colonel Bankhead dispatched a courier to Fort Wallace with a message for General Sheridan at Fort Hays telling him some of the details of the fight and the rescue. There were "few cases on record" the colonel observed, "of more desperate fighting and continued endurance, without food, except horse-flesh, surrounded by the dead and dying." Sharp Grover estimated the number of Indians in the fight at six hundred. Of this number "at least" seventy-five "must have been" killed or wounded. Of the fifty-two men in the command Forsyth had lost five killed and fifteen wounded. Carpenter had "struck the trail and place where they [the Indians] had encamped probably for two or three days after leaving here, and the trails show they were going southeast toward the Beaver." The bodies of the dead scouts were too decomposed to permit their immediate removal. The doctors had given their consent to the removal of the wounded to Fort Wallace the next day.[49]

Leaving the battleground at 10:30 a.m., September 27, Bankhead's force, including Carpenter's and Forsyth's commands,[50] camped for the night on the South Fork of the Republican. During the march, several of the scouts who were riding ahead of the column encountered four Indians, one of whom they killed. But as the scouts were mounted on "brokendown mules" they were unable to overtake the others. Many Indian graves were found in the evening near Bankhead's camp and on the following day, "Some of them undoubtedly Indians killed in Col. Forsyth's engagement."[51]

Arriving at Fort Wallace on September 29, the wounded were placed in the post hospital. The rest were early in October sent by wagons to Sheridan and thence by train to Fort Hays where they were reörganized under the direction of a new commanding officer, Lieutenant Silas Pepoon, Tenth Cavalry. Colonel Forsyth remained at Fort Wallace and eventually recovered despite his refusal to permit the amputation of one of his legs. General Sheridan visited him there in October.[52]

Soon after Forsyth's recovery, he wrote his official report of the fight. In it he stated that Grover had set the number of warriors engaged "at between eight and nine hundred." Forsyth himself had earlier estimated the Indians' strength at four hundred and fifty, "but information since obtained leads [me] to the belief that Grover's estimate was the correct one." (Apparently Grover's estimate had risen after leaving the island, since he is reported on September 26, as noticed above, to have given the number as six hundred.) None of the men, the colonel asserted, believed they had fought fewer than seven hundred and fifty warriors. Thirty-two Indians were killed and about three times that many wounded.[53] The scouts fired an average of sixty rounds each "and as most of the men were good marksmen firing coolly at short ranges, the enemy suffered severely." Many of the casualties had been inflicted while the Indians were attempting to remove their dead and wounded from the battlefield. Twenty warriors had been found, after the rescue, buried in two spots near the island, and two more noticed in some bushes. Forsyth gave his own losses as four killed and seventeen wounded though two of the injured had subsequently died, one (Louis Farley) before leaving the battlefield.[54]

In December, two companies of the Fifth Infantry commanded by Captain Edmond Butler and guided by Sharp Grover returned to the island for the purpose of recovering the remains of the dead scouts. It was a most difficult journey owing to the extreme cold and recent snow. Near the Arickaree on the morning of December 23, Butler's scouts discovered a small party of Indians, of whom one, an Ogallalah Sioux chief named Black Bull indicated in sign language that it was friendly. In a talk with Captain Butler, Black Bull stated that there were three hundred lodges in the vicinity. Butler told the chief the purpose of the expedition and bluntly warned him that his men "would shoot every Indian that came in range" of their guns. Black Bull had no sooner left than Butler "closed up his wagons in two lines" and "deployed" his men in case the Indians should make an attack. But none came and the expedition marched on to the island and went into camp nearby.

Grover pointed out the location of the graves of Forsyth's men to Dr. Turner, whose task it was to exhume and secure their remains. Only two bodies — those of George W. Culver and Farley — were found; Dr. Mooers', William Wilson's and Lieutenant Beecher's had been removed by the Indians. Wilson and Culver had been buried in the same grave, but the Indians had not suspected the presence of a body beneath Wilson's and, consequently, Culver's remains had not been disturbed. Farley's grave had not been molested presumably because the Indians had not found it. Also missing from the site was a Spencer carbine, a pistol, and part of a blanket left by Forsyth's rescuers. Strewn over the area were many pieces of clothing and relics of the fight.

While Dr. Turner was working among the graves, about fifty war-

83

riors appeared on a bluff about eight hundred yards away. As he wished to question them about the removal of the bodies, Butler sent Grover to bring the chiefs in. But the chiefs, one a Sioux the other a Cheyenne, knew nothing about the disinterrment of the remains. As they rode away three of the scouts "raised their carbines at them" whereupon Butler shouted "stop that." Butler's words were misunderstood by the troops guarding Dr. Turner as an order to fire, and they delivered a volley at the warriors on the bluff. The result was a desultory exchange of shots at long range for nearly an hour, apparently with no casualties to either side. Fearing that the Indians might summon help for a major assault, Butler moved the command to a flat, open prairie about three miles to the southeast. But the Indians did not attack, and the expedition marched out the next morning for Fort Wallace.[55]

The stand on the Arickaree Fork was one of several successive battles which eventually brought peace to the Central Plains frontier. Because of its sensational nature, it soon became one of the best known Indian fights of the time. For his performance in the fight, Forsyth was breveted a brigadier general and recommended for the Congressional Medal of Honor. Partly in recognition of their roles in Forsyth's relief, Colonel Bankhead was breveted a brigadier general and Colonel Carpenter was awarded the Congressional Medal of Honor. The island where the stand was made was subsequently named Beecher Island in honor of Lieutenant Beecher who died on it. In 1905 the States of Colorado and Kansas commemorated the battle by placing a monument on the site with the names of the members of Forsyth's command inscribed thereon.[56] It was washed away in a great flood which swept over eastern Colorado in 1935, but a new monument stands today as a reminder of one of the truly spectacular episodes in the struggle between red men and white for possession of the American West.

NOTES

1. Lonnie J. White, "The Cheyenne Barrier on the Kansas Frontier, 1868-1869," *Arizona and the West*, Vol. IV (Spring, 1962), pp. 51-54; Donald J. Berthrong, THE SOUTHERN CHEYENNES (Norman, 1963), pp. 289-306; Carl Coke Rister, BORDER COMMAND: *General Phil Sheridan in the West* (Norman, 1944), p. 65; Topeka, *Kansas State Record*, June 10, 17, July 1, August 26, September 2, 1868; *Junction City* (Kansas) *Weekly Union*, June 6, August 22, September 12, 22, 1868; *Leavenworth* (Kansas) *Daily Conservative*, August 16, 19, September 6, 1868; Lawrence, *Kansas Daily Tribune*, August 16, 1868; Wynkoop to Murphy, August 10, 1868, *House Executive Document* No. 1, Fortieth Congress, Third Session., p. 530. The little girls were subsequently left on the prairie by their captors and found by the military.
2. Douglass to Keough, September 3, 1868, Fort Dodge, Letters Sent. Department of the Missouri, Records of the War Department, National Archives; *Weekly Union*, September 12, 1868; *Daily Conservative*, September 10, 1868; Philip H. Sheridan, PERSONAL MEMOIRS (2 vols., New York, 1888), Vol. II, pp. 292-294.
3. *Kansas State Record*, August 26, 1868; Samuel J. Crawford, KANSAS IN THE SIXTIES (Chicago, 1911), p. 291; Rister, *Border Command*, p. 66; White, "Cheyenne Barrier on the Kansas Frontier," *Arizona and the West*, Vol. IV, pp. 56-57.
4. Forsyth's report, March 31, 1869, Phillips Collection, Division of Manuscripts, University of Oklahoma Library (hereafter cited Forsyth's report); Rister, *Border Command*, p. 80.

5. G. A. Forsyth, "A Frontier Fight," *Harper's New Monthly Magazine* (hereafter designated *HNMM*), Vol. XCI (June, 1895), pp. 43-44; Alan W. Farley (ed.), "Reminiscences of Allison J. Pliley, Indian fighter," *Trail Guide*, Vol. II (Kansas City, Missouri, June, 1957), pp. 1-2. There is some evidence to indicate that Grover joined the command at Fort Wallace.

6. Forsyth's report.

7. Bankhead of Belger, August 24, 27, 29, 31, September 1, 3, 1868, Fort Wallace, Telegrams Sent, Department of the Missouri, Records of the War Department, National Archives (hereafter cited For Wallace, TS, DM, RWD, NA); *Kansas Daily Tribune*, September 17, 1868. A force of Tenth Cavalry had been camped near Pond Creek in August, but it had departed about the middle of the month, leaving only a few men behind at Fort Wallace to look after certain regimental property.

8. Bankhead to Crosby, September 8, 1868, Fort Wallace, TS, DM, RWD, NA; Bankhead to Graham, September 7, 1868, Fort Wallace, Letters sent, Department of the Missouri, Records of the War Department, National Archives (hereafter cited as Fort Wallace, LS, DM, RWD, NA); *Kansas Daily Tribune*, September 10, 1868.

9. Bankhead to Crosby, September 8, 14, 19, 1868, Fort Wallace, TS, DM, RWD, NA; Bankhead to Graham, September 7, 1868, Bankhead to Forsyth, September 14, 1868, Fort Wallace, LS, DM, RWD, NA. Graham was subsequently breveted major for his performance in this battle. Francis B. Heitman, HISTORICAL REGISTER AND DICTIONARY OF THE UNITED STATES ARMY, FROM ITS ORGANIZATION, SEPTEMBER 29, 1789, TO MARCH 2, 1903 (2 Vols., Washington, 1903), Vol. I, p. 467.

10. Bankhead to Crosby, September 19, 22, 1868, Fort Wallace, TS, DM, RWD, NA; Bankhead to Graham, September 18, 1868, Fort Wallace, LS, DM, RWD, NA; *Kansas Daily Tribune*, September 17, 1868.

11. Forsyth's report.

12. Forsyth, "A Frontier Fight," *HNMM*, Vol. XCI, pp. 44-45.

13. Forsyth's report.

14. Scout John Hurst, "The Beecher Island Fight," *Kansas State Historical Society Collections*, Vol. XV (1919-1922), p. 531. (Kansas State Historical Society hereafter designated KSHS.) See also Forsyth, "A Frontier Fight," *HNMM*, Vol. XCI, p. 45.

15. Forsyth's report; Scout Tom Murphy, "The Battle of the Arickaree [*sic*] on Beecher Island, September 16 [*sic*], 1868," MS article, Arickaree File, Manuscript Division, KSHS.

16. Forsyth's report; Forsyth, "A Frontier Fight," *HNMM*, Vol. XCI, p. 46.

17. George B. Grinnell, *The Fighting Cheyennes* (Norman, 1958), p. 281, states that the Indians were camped down river from the scouts. Forsyth, however, indicates in his report that his command was moving upstream, presumably toward the river's source. If so, the Indians must have been camped upstream; otherwise, he would already have encountered them.

18. *Ibid.* George Bent says that the Sioux were under Spotted Tail. Bent to George Hyde, February 23, 1904, George Bent Letters, Coe Collection, Yale University Library, microfilm copies, Manuscript Division, KSHS. Both Bent and Grinnell were friends of the Indians and spent much time with them. Donald Berthrong, *The Southern Cheyennes*, p. 311, apparently accepts Grinnell's statement that Pawnee Killer was the leader. Both Pawnee Killer and Spotted Tail were Brulé Sioux chiefs.

19. Bent to Hyde, June 10, 1904, George Bent Letters, Manuscript Division, State Historical Society of Colorado. Grinnell's account of the Indians' discovery of the scouts varies somewhat from Bent's. According to Grinnell, some young Sioux who had left a war party to return to their villages discovered the scouts moving in the same direction as they were. Riding on to their camps, they spread the word of the "soldiers'" approach. On the morning of the September 16, a large war party rode out "in the direction where they supposed the troops to be" for the purpose of ambushing them. But the scouts, unaware of the location of the villages, had taken a direction away from the camps. And it was not until the following morning that the Indians found Forsyth's command. Grinnell, *Fighting Cheyennes*, pp. 281-282. Both Grinnell's and Bent's accounts are based on Indian sources.

20. Forsyth, "A Frontier Fight," *HNMM*, Vol. XCI, pp. 46-47. See also Forsyth's report.

21. Scout Hurst would have us believe that Forsyth ordered the retreat to the island at the suggestion of Scout Jack Stilwell. Hurst, "The Beecher Island Fight," *KSHS Collections*, Vol. XV, p. 532. See also William E. Connelley (ed.), "Life and Adventures of George W. Brown," *ibid.*, Vol. XVII (1926-1928), pp. 102-103.

22. Forsyth intimates that they moved to the south end of the island, but according to a map of the battlesite prepared in 1868 by an army scout named J. J. Peate, the river where the fight occurred ran east and west instead of north and south. Map by Peate, in *Beecher Island Annual*, Vol. IV (August, 1908), p. 22. Forsyth is reported to have acknowledged during a visit to the island in 1905 that he was turned around at the time of the fight. *Beecher Island Annual* (Beecher Island, Colorado, Ninety-third Anniver-

sary edition, Beecher Island Battle Memorial Association, [1961]), p. 30. Mrs. Hendricks, who has examined the area, informs me that the river runs "nearly straight east and west" at the point in question. Letter of Mrs. Hendricks to author, August 3, 1965.

23. Forsyth's report. Grinnell states, however, that the Indians possessed, besides their traditional weapons, only a few old muzzle-loaders. Grinnell, *Fighting Cheyennes*, p. 282. Each scout possessed a Spencer carbine, a Colt revolver, and 250 rounds of ammunition.

24. Forsyth says the Indians amassed downstream, but he evidently meant upstream. See maps in Harry H. Anderson (ed.), "Stand at the Arikaree," *Colorado Magazine*, Vol. XLI (Fall, 1964), p. 338; James S. Hutchins, "The Fight at Beecher Island," in GREAT WESTERN INDIAN FIGHTS (Garden City, New York, 1960), p. 168. According to Forsyth, the Indians were formed for the charge by the "peal" of an artillery bugle. Forsyth, "A Frontier Fight," *HNMM*, Vol. XCI, pp. 50-51.

25. The Indians' version of the early fighting differs considerably from that of the whites. The Indians told Grinnell and Hyde that no shots were fired by the scouts during the dash on the animals at daylight and that the main body of Indians did not come up until some time after the scouts had entrenched themselves on the island. They stated also that the first charge was made immediately upon the arrival of the main body at the scene of action. Grinnell, *Fighting Cheyennes*, pp. 283-284; Bent to Hyde, June 10, 1904, George Bent Letters, Manuscript Division, State Historical Society of Colorado. Jack Stilwell and Pete Trudeau's story, however, quoted elsewhere in this article, in part supports that of the Indians.

26. Hurst, "The Beecher Island Fight," *KSHS Collections*, Vol. XV, p. 533. Forsyth, however, states that only one man "failed" him. Forsyth, "A Frontier Fight," *HNMM*, Vol. XCI, p. 49.

27. Forsyth asserts that Roman Nose was recognized by Grover early in the fight and that he was killed while leading the first charge. Forsyth, "A Frontier Fight," *HNMM*, Vol. XCI, pp. 49-53. Grinnell maintains, however, that Roman Nose did not participate in the early fighting and that he was not killed until later in the day. The "medicine" of Roman Nose's war bonnet, which had always protected him in battle, had been broken prior to the fight as the result of his eating with an iron instrument. Because he had not had time to go through a purification ceremony, he had expected to be killed in the fight. He was, Grinnell tells us, shot in the back by the scouts concealed in the grass on the mainland as he rode past them leading the charge upon the island. Grinnell, *Fighting Cheyennes*, pp. 286-287. See also Bent to Hyde, May 24, 1906, George Bent. Letters, Coe Collection, Yale University Library, microfilm copies, Manuscript Division, KSHS.

Grinnell does not believe, contrary to the later statements of Forsyth and others, that the scouts recognized Roman Nose because, he avers, no one in the command, including Grover, knew Roman Nose. Grinnell's allegations are seemingly supported by the fact that none of the official correspondence at the time, including Forsyth's own official report, mentions Roman Nose. But one finds it difficult to believe that he was not recognized, since it is known that several men in the command had scouted for the army and Roman Nose was no stranger to the Southern Plains frontier. One of the scouts, Allison J. Pliley, had been with the Armes expedition in 1867 when it had been defeated on Prairie Dog Creek, Kansas, by a large body of Indians under Roman Nose and others. Forrest R. Blackburn, "The 18th Kansas Cavalry and the Indian War," *Trail Guide*, Vol. IX (March, 1964), pp. 1-15. And Pliley himself reports having seen Roman Nose at Medicine Lodge Creek in 1867. Farley (ed.), "Reminiscences of Allison J. Pliley," *Trail Guide*, Vol. II, p. 6.

28. Forsyth's report: Forsyth, "A Frontier Fight," *HNMM*, Vol. XCI, pp. 47-58; Hurst, "The Beecher Island Fight," *KSHS Collections*, Vol. XV, pp. 532-534; Scout Sigmund Schlesinger, "The Beecher Island Fight," *ibid.*, pp. 541-544; "Diary of Chauncey B. Whitney," *ibid.*, Vol XII, pp. 297-298; Merrill J. Mattes, "The Beecher Island Battlefield Diary of Sigmund Schlesinger," *Colorado Magazine*, Vol. XXIX (July, 1952), p. 169; Anderson (ed.), "Stand at the Arikaree," *ibid.*, Vol. XLI, pp. 337-342. Other accounts by participants are in the several *Beecher Island Annuals*, copies of which may be found in the library of the KSHS. One of the articles is a reprint of Forsyth's story of the fight from his book, THRILLING DAYS IN ARMY LIFE (New York, 1902), The details of the fight given by participants vary slightly.

29. Forsyth's report: Forsyth, "A Frontier Fight," *HNMM*, Vol. XCI, pp. 58-61; Hurst, "The Beecher Island Fight," *KSHS Collections*, Vol. XV, p. 535; Mattes, "The Beecher Island Battlefield Diary of Sigmund Schlesinger." *Colorado Magazine*, Vol. XXIX, p. 169. Forsyth says in his report that the white flag incident occurred on the third day and in his article on the fourth, but Scout Schlesinger recorded it in his diary on the second day.

30. The Indians told Grinnell that the women and children did not come out, as Forsyth and others said they did, to watch the fight. The only women who appeared near the battlefield "were those who came with travois to carry away the dead." Grinnell, *Fighting Cheyennes*, p. 292.
31. Forsyth to Bankhead, September 19, 1868, Arickaree File, Manuscript Division, KSHS. The Arickaree apparently was also known as Delaware Fork, since Forsyth gave that name in the heading of his message. Other names were the Dry Fork and the Bobtail Deer Creek.
32. Mattes, "The Beecher Island Battlefield Diary of Sigmund Schlesinger," *Colorado Magazine*, Vol. XXIX, p. 169.
33. Forsyth, "A Frontier Fight," *HNMM*, Vol. XCI, pp. 60-61.
34. Winfield Freeman, "The Battle of the Arickaree," *KSHS Transactions*, Vol. VI (1900), pp. 354-356; William H. Leckie, THE MILITARY CONQUEST OF THE SOUTHERN PLAINS (Norman, 1963), pp. 78-79; MS article by Mrs. Della Hendricks, owned by the author. Mrs. Hendricks knew several of Forsyth's scouts personally.
35. Bankhead to Crosby, September 14, 22, 1868, Fort Wallace, TS, DM, RWD, NA; Bankhead to Graham, September 15, 1868, Bankhead to Carpenter, September 22, 1868, Fort Wallace, LS, DM, RWD, NA.
36. Stilwell was in charge of the two-man party. See Forsyth, "A Frontier Fight," *HNMM*, Vol. XCI, pp. 56-57.
37. *Ibid.*, 42-43; Forsyth's report.
38. Bankhead to Crosby, September 22, 1868, Fort Wallace, TS, DM, RWD, NA. See also *Junction City Weekly Union*, September 26, 1868.
39. Bankhead to McKeever, October 5, 1868, Fort Wallace, TS, DM, RWD, NA; Johnson to Carpenter, September 22, 1868, Fort Wallace, LS, DM, RWD, NA; Anderson (ed.) "Stand at the Arikaree" *Colorado Magazine*, Vol. XLI, p. 341.
40. Johnson to Carpenter, September 22, 1868, Fort Wallace, LS, DM, RWD, NA.
41. Bankhead to McKeever, October 5, 1868, Fort Wallace, LS, DM, RWD, NA. Bankhead arrived on the island some twenty-six hours after Carpenter.
42. Grinnell states, however, that Roman Nose was buried on a scaffold and that the body in the tepee belonged to a Dog Soldier Cheyenne named "Killed by a Bull." Medicine Woman "helped the wife of Roman Nose to bring up her lodgepoles to raise the scaffold for his burial." Grinnell, *Fighting Cheyennes*, p. 291. As a further complication, Mrs. Hendricks doubts that Roman Nose was interred on a scaffold because, she says, it was not his people's custom to bury the dead in this manner. She tells us that Jack Stilwell, who some years after the fight traversed the route taken by the Indians from the island, was convinced he was buried on "the high bluffs of the Republican River, one-half mile west of the crossing directly north of Bethune, Colorado. On the highest part of the terrain was found a circular wall of stones similar to wagon wheel shaped markings used by the Cheyennes to mark the tombs of chieftains." MS article by Mrs. Hendricks; Letter of Mrs. Hendricks to Lorrin and Carroll Morrison, August 24, 1965.
43. Carpenter to Martin, April 22, 1912, Arickaree File, Manuscript Division, KSHS (also printed in *KSHS Collections*, Vol. XII, pp. 299-302); Carpenter to Lewis, October 2, 1868, in *Beecher Island Annual* (Beecher Island, [1961]), pp. 94-95.
44. Order signed by post adjutant, September 24, 1868, Fort Wallace, LS, DM, RWD, NA; Farley (ed.), "Reminiscenses of Allison J. Pliley, Indian Fighter," *Trail Guide*, Vol, II, pp. 8-9. Pliley claims that after he and Donovan reached Fort Wallace he rode to General Bradley's camp near the mouth of Frenchman's Fork on the Republican to tell him of Forsyth's plight and that Bradley promptly dispatched a force to Forsyth's assistance. Pliley's account of the rescue, written many years after the fight, does not entirely comport with contemporary evidence.
45. Carpenter to Martin, April 22, 1912, Arickaree File, Manuscript Division, KSHS; Carpenter to Lewis, October 2, 1868, in *Beecher Island Annual* (Beecher Island, [1961]), pp. 94-95.
46. Forsyth, "A Frontier Fight," *HNMM*, Vol. XCI, p. 61.
47. "Diary of Chauncey B. Whitney," *KSHS Collections*, Vol. XII, p. 298.
48. E. A. Brininstool, "The Rescue of Forsyth's Scouts," *KSHS Collections*, Vol. XVII 1926-1928), pp. 850-851; Anderson (ed.), "Stand at the Arikaree," *Colorado Magazine*, Vol. XLI, pp. 337-342; Carpenter to Martin, April 22, 1912, Arickaree File, Manuscript Division, KSHS.
49. Bankhead to Crosby, September 26, 1868, in Sheridan to Sherman, September 28, 1868, Phillips Collection, University of Oklahoma Library. A slightly condensed copy of the letter is also in *Junction City Weekly Union*, October 3, 1868. Bankhead, perhaps deliberately, gave the impression in his message that he had arrived at the battlefield on September 25. It is clear enough, however, that he did not actually arrive until a day later.
50. Brisbin's detachment presumably rejoined Bradley's command on the Republican.

51. Bankhead to McKeever, October 5, 1868, Fort Wallace, TS, DM, RWD, NA; J. J. Peate's account of the relief, *Beecher Island Annual* (Beecher Island, [1961]), pp. 62-63.
52. Bankhead to Crosby, September 30, October 2, 1868, Fort Wallace, TS, DM, RWD, NA; Lewis to Lauffer, October 4, 1868, Fort Wallace, LS, DM, RWD, NA; *Leavenworth Times and Conservative*, October 8, 22, 1868; Carpenter to Martin, April 22, 1912, Arickaree File, Manuscript Division, KSHS. Sheridan issued a general field order on October 1 expressing his thanks and "high appreciation of the gallantry, energy and bravery displayed" by Forsyth's command. *Times and Conservative*, October 13, 1868.
53. A quarter of a century later, Forsyth claimed that an Indian chief subsequently told him that about 970 Indians participated in the fight and their loses were 75 killed and " 'heaps' wounded." Forsyth, "A Frontier Fight," *HNMM*, Vol. XCI, p. 62.
54. Forsyth's report. Forsyth's list of the killed in his article is inaccurate. For example, he used Scout Chalmers Smith's first name as a surname to make two casualties out of Smith and he does not mention Scout G. W. Culver as one of the killed. Bankhead, who, as noticed above, reported Forsyth's losses as five killed and fifteen wounded, does not list Smith as a casualty. According to Ray G. Sparks, Scout Thomas O'Donnell later died at Fort Wallace, making six deaths in all. Sparks to author, March 2, 1967.

   Grinnell's and Bent's figures as to numbers and losses differ considerably from those of Forsyth. Grinnell says that "probably six hundred" warriors participated in the fight, Bent about "300 or 350." Both Grinnell and Bent gave the number of Indians killed as nine. Grinnell, *Fighting Cheyennes*, p. 291; Bent to Hyde, February 23, 1904, Bent Letters. Coe Collection, Yale University Library, microfilm copies, Manuscript Division, KSHS.

   Although Forsyth may indeed have exaggerated the number of Indian casualties, one finds it difficult to accept the low figure given by Grinnell and Bent, since the warriors were exposed at short ranges during their charges and in their attempts to remove the dead and wounded. One might question why, if their losses were as slight as Bent and Grinnell suggest, the Indians became discouraged after the first day and eventually abandoned the field.
55. Turner to Butler, December 23, 1868, Butler to Lewis, December 28, 1868, copies, Arickaree File, Manuscript Division, KSHS; Bankhead to McKeever, December 27, 1868, Fort Wallace, TS, DM, RWD, NA. Captain Butler subsequently won the Congressional Medal of Honor for his performance in the action at Wolf Mountain, Montana, in 1877. Heitman, *Historical Register and Dictionary* . . ., Vol. I, pp. 268-269. Grover was later shot to death in a saloon. Reuben Waller's narrative, *Beecher Island Annual* (Beecher Island [1961]), p. 88; Mrs. Frank C. Montgomery, "Fort Wallace and Its Relation to the [1961]), p. 88; Mrs. Frank C. Montgomery, "Fort Wallace and Its Relation to the Frontier," *KSHS Collections*, Vol. XVIII, pp. 226-227.
56. Heitman, *Historical Register and Dictionary* . . ., Vol. I, pp. 189, 284, 430; Berthrong, *Southern Cheyennes*, pp. 314-317; "Beecher Island Monument," *KSHS Transactions*, Vol. IX (1905-1906), p. 453; Letter of AAG to AG, March 23, 1894, Phillips Collection, Division of Manuscripts, University of Oklahoma Library; MS Article by Mrs. Hendricks. Washed away by a flood in 1935, the monument was subsequently restored and placed on higher ground. A little settlement now stands at the site. The exact location is in Yuma County, Colorado, fifteen miles from Wray on the Burlington Railroad. Owing to shifting sands closing the south channel, the island itself no longer exists. E. A. Brininstool, FIGHTING INDIAN WARRIORS (Harrisburg, 1953), pp. 123-124; *Beecher Island Annual* (Beecher Island, [1961]), pp. 117-118; Letter of Mrs. Hendricks to author, August 10, 1965.

WINTER CAMPAIGNING WITH
SHERIDAN AND CUSTER:

The Expedition of the Nineteenth Kansas
Volunteer Cavalry

AT MEDICINE LODGE CREEK in 1867 federal commissioners concluded a treaty with the Southern Plains Indians under which they were to accept reservations in Indian Territory and receive annuities from the government. The United States Senate was, however, slow in ratifying the treaty, and when spring came in 1868 the Indians were still roaming at will and waiting impatiently for their annuities, which included arms and ammunition.

In June, 1868, a large war party, composed mainly of Cheyennes, engaged their enemies, the Kaws, in combat near Council Grove, Kansas. This incident caused the Indian Office, when the annuities were finally made available in July, to withhold the arms and ammunition from the Cheyennes until their intentions could be determined. When it appeared that they did not plan an outbreak, the delivery was made. A few days later, in August, more than two hundred braves, principally Cheyennes, swept through the Saline and Solomon River Valleys of Kansas, killing, raping, stealing, and destroying. They were soon joined on the warpath by other warriors, who stuck the Santa Fe and Smoky Hill stage and freight roads.

Major General Philip H. Sheridan, commander of the Department of the Missouri, had at the time only twenty-six hundred men with which to meet the uprising. In need of additional troops, Sheridan authorized his aide, Major (Brevet Colonel) George A. Forsyth, to recruit fifty experienced plainsmen as scouts for patrol duty on the frontier. Sent to Fort Wallace, Kansas, Forsyth's command was on September 17, 1868, attacked on the Arickaree Fork of the Republican River in Colorado Territory and badly shot up by several hundred Cheyennes and Sioux.[1]

To the south, an expedition of Seventh Cavalry and Third Infantry under Lieutenant Lolonel (Brevet Brigadier General) Alfred Sully, commandant of the District of the Upper Arkansas, marched from Fort Dodge, Kansas, into Indian Territory and engaged some eight hundred hostiles in the sand hills adjoining the North Canadian River. After some brisk, indecisive skirmishing, Sully retreated, eventually returning to Fort Dodge on September 18.

Late in September, Sheridan's department was reinforced by seven companies of Fifth Cavalry. From Fort Harker, Kansas, the troopers marched northward to Prairie Dog Creek where Major (Brevet Colonel) William B. Royall divided them into three portions. On October 14, Cheyenne Dog Soldiers under Tall Bull assaulted the weakest force, killing two men and running off twenty-six horses. Meanwhile, Major (Brevet Major General) Eugene A. Carr, who had been assigned to command the regiment, arrived at Fort Wallace and started northward with two companies of Tenth (Negro) Cavalry to look for his command. Attacked by Tall Bull's warriors on Beaver Creek, the Negro troopers corralled their wagons and fought off their assailants. Carr returned thence to Fort Wallace and finally joined his command at Buffalo Tank on the Kansas Pacific Railroad on October 22. Marching his men northward, Carr encountered a large body of Cheyennes and Sioux south of Beaver Creek and engaged them in a running fight until the wily warriors seemingly vanished from the plains.

In the meantime, Sheridan and his superior, Lieutenant General William T. Sherman, commander of the Division of the Missouri, had decided on a more aggressive policy. They would no longer fight mainly on the defensive; instead they would seek out the hostiles for the purpose of punishing them and would force all the Southern Plains tribes — the Cheyennes, the Arapahoes, the Kiowas, the Comanches, and the Kiowa-Apaches — to go on their reservations.[2] Despite the advice of experienced plainsmen, among them Jim Bridger, that winter campaigning on the Plains was sheer folly, they planned to move against the hostiles while they were in their winter haunts on the Red, Canadian, and other streams in Indian Territory and their ponies were weak from a shortage of grass. Because the Interior Department insisted that some means be devised for the protection of innocent Indians, provision was made for the concentration of "friendlies" at Fort Cobb, Indian Territory, where they would be under the supervision of Colonel (Brevet Major General) William B. Hazen and safe from attack by the military. To expedite his operations, Sheridan, who was in immediate charge of the campaign, moved his headquarters from St. Louis to Fort Hays, Kansas.

Sheridan's plans were for three columns to converge on the Indian Territory from three directions. The main movement would be made from Fort Dodge by an expedition under General Sully. Supporting Sully would be forces under General Carr from Fort Lyon, Colorado, and Major (Brevet Lieutenant Colonel) Andrew W. Evans from Fort Bascom, New Mexico. In about mid-November, 1868, Sully with eleven troops of Seventh Cavalry and five companies of infantry marched from Fort Dodge into Indian Territory and established a supply depot —

named Camp Supply — at the point where Wolf and Beaver Creeks joined to form the North Canadian River.[3]

Apparently Sherman and Sheridan had expected their main trouble to be with the Cheyennes and Arapahoes. Actually, only a part of the Cheyennes and a few of the Arapahoes had participated in the depredations. Sherman, however, considered them all "at war" because the peaceful tribesmen had "not restrained" their warring comrades "nor have they on demand given up the criminals as they agreed to do" in the treaty of 1867.[4] Although the Kiowas and Comanches had raided on the Texas frontier during the summer, they had not joined in the outbreak in Kansas. In a council at Fort Larned, Kansas, in September, arrangements were made for General Hazen to conduct these Indians from their camps on the Arkansas River to Fort Cobb. But after the conference, they left on a buffalo hunt and never returned, causing Sheridan to conclude that they, too, had gone on the warpath.[5]

Sheridan now informed Sherman that he did not have troops enough to deal effectively with so many hostile tribes. Consequently, Sherman sought and received authority from the Secretary of War for Sheridan to call on the governor of Kansas for a regiment of volunteer cavalry. On October 9, Sheridan telegraphed Governor Samuel J. Crawford that

> . . . I am authorized to call on you for one regiment of mounted volunteers to serve for a period of six months[,] unless sooner discharged[,] against hostile Indians on the Plains. I therefore request that you furnish said regiment as speedily as possible to be rendezvoused and mustered into the service of the United States at Topeka[,] Kansas. The regiment [is] to consist of one colonel, one lieutenant colonel, 3 majors[,] twelve captains[,] twelve first lieutenants, twelve second-lieutenants[,] twelve companies of one hundred men each including the requisite number of non-commissioned officers specified in the United States Army Regulations (1863) [,] the pay[,] allowances and emoluments of officers and men to be the same as that of United States troops. The men will be rationed from the time of their arrival at the rendezvous[,] and will be furnished with arms, equipments, horses and clothing from the date of muster into the service of the United States.

The next day, October 10, the governor issued a proclamation calling for the organization of a regiment of volunteers at the "earliest possible moment." His swift action undoubtedly was not unexpected since he had told the President on August 22, shortly after the Saline and Solomon raids, that if volunteers were needed, he would "furnish . . . all that may be necessary . . ." Acting in accordance with Crawford's proclamation, the state adjutant general appointed recruiting officers in about a dozen counties.[6]

By October 26 most of the companies had been recruited and a training camp — named Camp Crawford in honor of the governor — was established on the Kansas River adjacent to Topeka, the capital city.

Presumably with some exceptions the company officers were elected by the men and the regimental officers appointed by the governor. By prearrangement with his successor, Governor Crawford, whose gubernatorial term was nearing an end, resigned his executive position to accept appointment as the regiment's colonel. Horace L. Moore of Lawrence was appointed lieutenant colonel and William C. Jones, Charles Dimon and Richard Jenkins, majors. Colonel Crawford did not join the regiment until shortly after it left Topeka, and consequently it was organized and the men armed, mounted, equipped, and trained under the supervision of Major Jones and Colonel Moore, commanders of Camp Crawford, respectively.[7]

Most of the enlisted volunteers were young men in service for the first time. Among them, however, were a few "old soldiers"; these were "judiciously distributed" throughout the regiment so as to give the greenhorns the benefit of their "example." Although the volunteers evidently made considerable progress in "drill and general discipline" during their brief training period at Camp Crawford and during their later service, one surmises from reading the contemporary sources that their competence in these areas left much to be desired.

The officers were, in contrast to the enlisted men, "principally experienced men." Presumably a considerable number of them had served in the Civil War; at least two, Colonels Crawford and Moore, had been field officers in that war. And several had served on the plains. Colonel Moore, Captain George B. Jenness, and Captain David L. Payne had been officers in the Eighteenth Kansas Cavalry during the Indian campaign of 1867. Captain Allison J. Pliley had accompanied the Eighteenth Kansas as scout, and he had been with Forsyth on the Arickaree. Captain Jenness was at the time of his appointment a major in the state frontier militia battalion which had been formed in the summer of 1868 to protect the Kansas frontier.[8]

Apparently though the volunteers worked hard in anticipation of service in the field, they had time enough to play. Some who were unable to obtain passes slipped out of camp into town, through the courtesy of friendly guards. Several men from Leavenworth allegedly amused themselves in Topeka by beating up Negroes. A number of those who did not go to town gambled. On Sunday, November 1, the volunteers were visited by preachers and others, including a number of young ladies accompanied by their mothers. The men were "on their good behavior" during the day, but that night, according to Private David L. Spotts of Company L, "Some donned their citizen clothes and went out with the visitors and now there is whiskey in camp, and the noise is the effect of it. Several are now in the guard house, others ought to be."[9]

Early in November the regiment, numbering slightly over twelve hundred officers and men, was ordered by General Sheridan to move out. Companies D and G were to proceed by rail to Fort Hays and escort a supply train thence to the mouth of Beaver Creek where Sully was to establish the supply depot (Camp Supply) noticed above. The remaining ten companies were to march directly to that point from Camp Crawford.

Breaking camp on November 5, the main command paraded ostentatiously through the crowd-lined streets of Topeka and headed toward Camp Beecher (also know as Wichita) on the Arkansas River some one hundred fifty miles to the southwest. The Kansans' route led them either through or near the villages of Burlingame, Emporia, and El Dorado. As they had received only a five-day supply of rations, they were compelled to buy food from settlers with their own money. In one instance, three volunteers helped themselves to some feathered "fruit" which they found roosting in a tree near a farm house.

Near Emporia, the regiment encountered a "severe rainstorm which drenched us freely all day and the following night." On the heels of the rain fell "a covering of snow, which was received with cheers, curses, jokes, and all the different emotions and passions found in a full [*sic*] regiment of soldiers." The skies soon cleared, but not before a number of men apparently decided that campaigning on scant rations in bad weather was not to their liking and deserted.[10]

Coming to the Arkansas River on November 12, the soldiers bivouacked near Camp Beecher, a collection of crude adobe and wooden buildings. Here was stationed a company of regular infantry and one of state militia. Sheridan had promised to have ten days' rations and forage on hand for the regiment at this point. But much to the dismay of Colonel Crawford, half the rations had been consumed by the regulars and only a small supply of damaged forage had arrived. Moreover, the regular army captain in charge seemed contemptuous of the volunteer officers, and until Crawford threatened him with summary measures, he stubbornly refused to release the supplies.[11]

Notwithstanding the critical shortage of provisions, Crawford decided to press on, presumably hoping to live off the country as much as possible. His decision to do so was not an easy one since the winter season was approaching, it was some one hundred forty miles to his destination, the country to be traveled was mainly an uninhabited wilderness, and both his men and horses were relatively untrained and untried.

Guiding the command as it left the Arkansas on the fourteenth were Scouts William (Apache Bill) Seamans and Jack Stilwell. Apache Bill, the leader of the pair, had scouted out of Fort Dodge and Stilwell had been with Forsyth's scouts on the Arickaree. They had been sent to Crawford by General Sheridan, who considered both of them "com-

petent." Of the two, however, apparently only Apache Bill was supposed to know the country beyond Camp Beecher. That he was not the
most savory character on the frontier is suggested by the fact that he
had been accused earlier in the year by the commandant of Fort Dodge
of "introducing liquor into the Indian country" and allegedly found
guilty. He would later be acquitted of a charge of stealing government
horses and mules.[12] The Kansans would soon have cause to question
Apache Bill's knowledge of the Indian Territory.

The weather turned bad again on November 15. In the evening,
the rain-drenched "and shivering command" went into camp in a grove
of cottonwood trees on the sandy banks of the Ninnescah River. During
the night the wind began "blowing a blizzard from the north" and the
rain changed to "heavy sleet." To make matters worse, the strong wind
blew down nearly all the tents. Neither large fires nor exercise was
enough to keep the men even partially comfortable. As soon as the
storm subsided, a number of the volunteers deserted, and if we may believe Private Spotts, "no one seems to care or blame them."[13]

Three more days of marching brought the soldiers to Medicine
Lodge Creek. By this time they had "passed beyond the timber" and
had come onto the prairie proper. Their meager rations had been amply
supplemented after leaving Camp Beecher with buffalo meat, but the
buffalo herds had by now virtually disappeared. Of more immediate
concern at the moment, however, were the horses and mules; the forage
having played out, their only food was dry buffalo grass. Consequently,
as the troopers halted at the various company campsites on the creek,
they immediately led their mounts out to graze.

One trooper, however, was more interested in having wood — a
relatively scarce item on the prairie — for his campfire than in tending
to his horse. Halting, he dismounted, threw his saddle on the ground,
tied his lariat to the saddle, and rushed away to secure "a piece of wood"
lying nearby. He had no sooner left than the horse caused the saddle
to move by pulling on the lariat. Frightened by the unexpected jerk
of the saddle, the animal bolted away with the saddle bouncing behind
him. The excitement was too much for the horses nearby to stand steady,
and soon the mounts of several companies were stampeding through
the camp and in the direction from whence they had come. Details under Captains Pliley and Charles H. Finch, commanding officers of Companies A and L, respectively, searched for the runaways throughout the
night and following day. According to Captain Jenness, three hundred
horses were stamped, and of these about one-third were recovered.
Besides the loss in valuable horses, the regiment lost a day's march in
looking for them.[14]

Bad weather set in again on the night of the twenty-first, and the
volunteers floundered forward throughout the next day in a hard, driv-

—*Courtesy, Kansas State Historical Society*

GEN. PHILIP H. SHERIDAN

—*Courtesy, Kansas State Historical Society*

GEN. GEORGE A. CUSTER

—*Courtesy, Kansas State Historical Society*

GOV. SAMUEL J. CRAWFORD

—*Courtesy, Kansas State Historical Society*

COL. HORACE L. MOORE

95

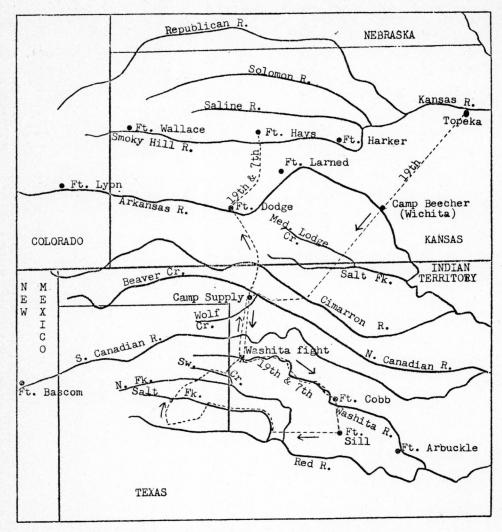

ROUTE MAP OF THE WINTER CAMPAIGN

Sketch map, drawn by the author, showing the approximate route of the Nineteenth
Kansas Volunteer Cavalry and Seventh U. S. Cavalry, from
November, 1868, to April, 1869

ing snow. As a further discomfort, they were forced — owing to the wretched condition of the animals — to walk most of the time. Late in the afternoon, they pitched their tents on the snow-covered banks of Sand Creek, evidently south of the Kansas-Indian Territory line, within sight of "the mountainous hills of the Cimarron."

The worst news of the day, however, was that Apache Bill, because either he did not know the country or he could not get his directions in the snowstorm, had become lost.[15] In a meeting of the officers, Crawford sought their advice as to whether they should push on blindly in the hope of eventually finding the supply camp or return to the Arkansas River. "A diversity of opinion ensued," but if we may believe Captain Jenness, "upon one of the company commanders facetiously remarking 'that there was no danger of starvation so long as a horse or mule remained,' the colonel decided in favor of adhering to the original plan, and pressing forward." Presumably it was also decided at this council to send a party on ahead to find the supply depot and bring back relief. This task was assigned to Captain Pliley, undoubtedly one of the most competent officers in the command. Pliley with fifty picked men and horses left the camp at 10:00 o'clock p. m., on the same evening as the conference.[16]

The storm was still raging the next morning, whereupon Colonel Crawford ordered the command to remain put. Having seen no buffalo in several days and having completely exhausted their provisions, the troopers were becoming desperately hungry. Several hunting parties sent out during the day returned empty-handed. Most of the volunteers' time, however, was spent trying to secure grass enough "to sustain" their starving animals. This "could only be done by each man's kicking away the deep snow in spots of a rod or so square, and allowing the ravenous animals to crop short the stunted buffalo grass . . ." Many of the animals "died at the picket lines from hunger and cold."[17]

When the snow ceased to fall on the twenty-fourth, the Kansans struck camp and resumed the march. But progress was so slow, owing to the deep snow, the poor condition of the animals, and the broken terrain, that they made only a few miles before nightfall. They pitched their tents that evening "in a snowfield surrounded by high hills and deep ravines," about three miles from the Cimarron River. On the hillsides they found hackberry trees, "and, though the fruit was all seed, at best, and now dried on the tree, it was sweet and agreeable, and was eaten, seeds and all . . ." But more satisfying was a small supply of buffalo meat brought in during the day by a hunting party.[18]

It was discovered on the morning of the twenty-fifth, presumably by Apache Bill, that he had brought the regiment too far south; it should have struck the Cimarron some thirty miles above where it was. This news was received with considerable displeasure by the tired and harassed troopers, who, according to Captain Jenness, expressed an

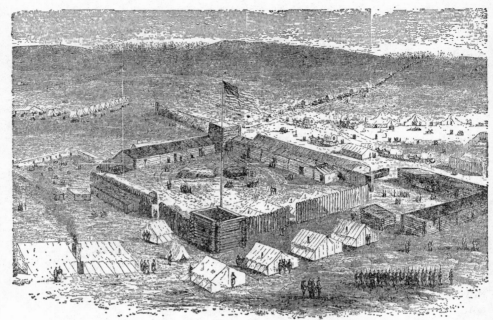

CAMP SUPPLY

This artist's sketch of Camp Supply appeared in Harper's Weekly *on February 27, 1869*

"itching desire" to hang their chief scout. Aware of their attitude. "His royal scoutship hung close to the colonel's quarters," thus giving the unhappy soldiers no chance to carry out their "threats."[19]

Since the previous day's march had been so slow and game had become almost non-existent, Crawford decided to push on with part of the column on the best horses, leaving the rest to remain in camp until the arrival of a relief party.[20] Leaving Major Jenkins with the wagon train and three hundred sixty men,[21] Crawford started the remainder of the command forward at 11:00 o'clock a. m. After some difficulty in finding a place to cross the Cimarron River, the volunteers marched for forty-five miles across gulches "so deep, narrow and steep, that only one man could pass at a time, and lead his horse." Leaving the breaks of the Cimarron, they came onto "the uplands," whence they turned and proceeded nearly due west.

On the evening of the twenty-seventh they camped on the North Canadian River. Since there were no trails going down-river, the scouts concluded that the supply camp was located up-stream. Trudging up the river the next day, November 28,[22] the Kansans met a party of scouts, who informed them that Camp Supply was about five miles ahead. Not-

MARCHING TO THE WASHITA

*The Seventh U. S. Cavalry, under command of General George Armstrong Custer,
on its way to attack the Cheyenne Indian village on the Washita River. This
work of a contemporary artist appeared in* Harper's Weekly
on December 19, 1868.

withstanding their weak condition, the tired and hungry men gave forth a loud cheer "and kept it up for a long time." At Camp Supply, they found tents already pitched, bedding, and rations waiting for them.

Captain Pliley's party had come in on the twenty-fifth, and Pliley had gone back to the Cimarron with several supply wagons and an escort. The wagons and men under Major Jenkins were found where they had been left. Their main diet had been hackberries. Although the men had at first named their encampment "Camp Hackberry Point," they had subsequently changed it to "Camp Starvation." They and the relief party reported at Camp Supply on December 1. Despite its many tribulations, the regiment came through from Camp Beecher without a casualty though several men suffered from pneumonia and frostbite.[23]

The two companies sent from Topeka to Fort Hays for escort duty to Camp Supply had arrived on November 21. With them had come General Sheridan, who wished "to give the campaign my personal attention" and "prove that operations could be successfully conducted in spite of winter"; the Forsyth scouts, now commanded by Lieutenant Silas Pepoon; and a troop of Tenth Cavalry.[24]

Sheridan's first problem was to settle a dispute between Lieutenant Colonels Sully and George A. Custer as to which was the commander of the expedition. Sully with the Seventh Cavalry, five companies of infantry, and a four hundred fifty-wagon supply train, had come from Fort Dodge and established Camp Supply on November 18. Presumably since the Nineteenth Kansas was assigned to this command and the

Articles of War stated that brevet rank was effective when volunteer and regular officers acted together, Brevet Major General Custer attempted at Camp Supply to assume command from Brevet Brigadier General Sully. Evidently because Custer was within his rights and he was one of Sheridan's favorites, Sheridan resolved the matter in favor of Custer and sent Sully back to Fort Dodge.[25]

During their marches to Camp Supply, both Sully and Sheridan had crossed a fresh Indian trail leading northeast. Without waiting for the Nineteenth Kansas, which he expected to arrive on the twenty-fourth,[26] Sheridan ordered Custer to take the Seventh Cavalry and follow the back trail to the Indians' village. Although the heavy snow on the twenty-second obliterated the trail, Custer presently struck another "near where the Texas boundary crosses the [South] Canadian River" and followed it to the Indians' village on the Washita River.

Dividing his command into four detachments, Custer surprise-attacked the village at daylight on the morning of November 27. The Indians — Cheyennes under Black Kettle — soon recovered from the initial shock of the assault, and for several hours a severe battle raged with both sides fighting desperately. Presently, large numbers of Cheyenne, Araphao, Kiowa, Comanche, and Kiowa-Apache warriors from villages down-stream, which Custer had not seen, began appearing on nearby hills. A few of them joined the fray. Realizing that he was in an untenable position, in case the newcomers should attack in force, Custer marched his men out under cover of darkness and did not halt until they were a safe distance from the battlefield. Much to the unhappiness of some of his officers, Custer left the scene without taking time to learn the fate of a detachment of sixteen men under Major Joel H. Elliott, which had last been seen pursuing some Indians downstream.

The next day Custer sent a message ahead to Camp Supply telling Sheridan about the fight. In it, Custer reported killing one hundred three warriors, including Black Kettle, killing and wounding "some" squaws and "a few" children, capturing fifty-three women and children, destroying eight hundred seventy-five ponies and mules, burning fifty-one lodges, seizing a large amount of stores and equipment, and recovering two white children captives. His own losses, including the Elliott detachment which he evidently presumed had been wiped out, numbered thirty-five men killed and wounded. The impression conveyed in his report was that he had won a great victory. Arriving at Camp Supply on December 2, Custer's cavalry passed triumphantly in review before Sheridan, the regulars, and the Kansas volunteers.[27]

Sheridan would have liked to follow up Custer's "stroke" immediately, but he could not do so owing to the poor condition of the men and animals of the Nineteenth Kansas. Moreover, many of the volunteers were without mounts. Sheridan subsequently stated that seven hundred horses had been lost during the Nineteenth's march from Camp Beecher, but a more accurate estimate was given by Captain Jenness, who set the number at about two hundred forty.[28]

Presumably because he did not wish the progress of the expedition impeded by slow-moving foot soldiers, Sheridan assigned the men without horses to a special detachment under Major Dimon. Also detached to this outfit were Companies G and M, both of which were at least partially mounted. During the remainder of the Nineteenth's service, this detachment did garrison duty at Camp Supply and escorted supply trains mainly to and from posts in Kansas.[29]

After giving the Kansans nearly a week to recuperate, Sheridan ordered them and the Seventh Cavalry to move out. Counting Custer's Osage trailers, Pepoon's scouts, and a number of white guides, the foremost of whom was Ben Clark and California Joe, the expedition numbered some seventeen or eighteen hundred men. Three Indian women captives were taken along for the purpose of "giving information respecting the country." The eleven companies of regulars "occupied" the front of "the line of march," the ten companies of volunteers the rear. Between them moved over three hundred six-mule wagons carrying supplies for a thirty-day march. Although Sheridan accompanied the column, he left the exercitation of command to Custer. Sheridan's plans called for the expedition to march southwardly to the Washita and thence down that stream toward Fort Cobb. He hoped to find the hostiles on the Washita and bring them "to terms."

As if marching through deep snow in sub-freezing weather was not bad enough, a blizzard blew in on about the eighth. Coming to the South Canadian River, the column was forced to halt while work details with axes cleared a path through the ice. The temperature was reported as about eighteen degrees below zero. On the evening of the tenth, the expedition camped on the snow-covered banks of the Washita, just below Custer's battlefield.[30]

The next day Sheridan, Custer, Crawford, and other officers with a one-hundred-man escort of Seventh Cavalry visited the battleground in the hope of learning the fate of the Elliott detachment. Signs of a terrific struggle were everywhere evident. Most of the Indian dead had been either "concealed or removed," but a few bodies had evidently been left in plain sight. Besides the Indian remains, the party found those of a young white woman and child, identified by the Kansans as Mrs. Clara Blinn and her two-year-old son. They had been with the Indians since their capture "below Fort Lyon" on the Arkansas River in October. They had obviously been killed by the Indians during the fight.[31] Some distance down-stream, the officers found the frozen and mutilated remains of Elliott and his men lying in a circle in a hollow

101

where they had been surrounded and made their last stand. The ground, Captain Jenness noticed, "was covered with cartridge shells, showing that they had made a desperate fight, and [had] been overcome only when they had used up their ammunition."[32]

That Black Kettle's warriors had been guilty of hostilities on the Kansas frontier was plainly apparent. Among the belongings found in the charred ruins of their lodges were photographs, clothing, bedding, and other items taken from farm houses on the Saline and Solomon Rivers. A large book of illustrations told the officers that the Cheyennes had been "especially" active on the Smoky Hill stage and freight road in the vicinity of Fort Wallace. And several pieces of mail were identified as those taken from two expressmen who had been killed by Indians en route from Bluff Creek, Kansas, to Fort Dodge, on about November 20.[33]

Resuming the march on the twelfth, the soldiers moved downstream through falling snow. The Indian villages, they learned, had extended for several miles beyond the one destroyed by Custer. The Indians had left considerable property behind in their haste to leave the vicinity of the fight. Much of it the troops burned. Presumably among the material they did not destroy were "a carefully wrapped package" containing nearly four hundred dollars in greenbacks and "a buckskin bag" filled with one hundred eighty-two dollars in gold coins.[34]

On December 17 the Osage trailers came in to report a large Indian camp to the front. With them was a courier with a message from General Hazen saying, in effect, that he had given the Indians — Kiowas, Comanches, and Kiowa-Apaches — camped between the expedition and Fort Cobb his guarantee of protection. Presently, a party of chiefs from the Kiowa village immediately ahead rode out and asked for a parley. In conference with Satanta and Lone Wolf, Custer told the chiefs that Hazen's note would be honored if they would promise to remove their people to Fort Cobb and remain there. This the chiefs agreed to do.

During the talk Custer noticed large numbers of well-armed and highly painted warriors "in the neighboring ravines and upon the surrounding hill-tops." The general believed they would have attacked the column had its strength not been "far greater than they had imagined." The presence of the Nineteenth Kansas, without which the expedition would have appeared much less formidable, may have prevented a pitched battle.

Sheridan's decision not to attack the Kiowa village was, Captain Jenness relates, most "disagreeable to the officers and men of the Nineteenth, many among whom had suffered from Indian depredations on the frontier, and a few had suffered the loss of relatives at their bloody hands." Actually Sheridan favored punishment for the Kiowas, but he did not believe that he could ignore Hazen's message, since Hazen was General Sherman's personal appointee.[35]

Satanta and Lone Wolf proposed that they and a large body of warriors should accompany the expedition on to Fort Cobb as evidence of their good faith while the rest of their people moved their lodges to that point "by easy stages, . . . claiming this to be necessary from the poor condition of the ponies." Sheridan agreed to this proposition. Soon after the resumption of the march, however, Sheridan noticed that the warriors were "slipping away one by one." Suspecting, correctly as it turned out, that somehow he had been deceived, Sheridan ordered Satanta and Lone Wolf arrested.

Arriving at Fort Cobb on the eighteenth, Sheridan found that most of the Comanches and Kiowa-Apaches were either there or coming in. The Cheyennes and Arapahoes had gone south to the North Fork of the Red River after the Washita fight and were still there. The only Kiowas at the post were those he had brought with him — Satanta and Lone Wolf — though their people were supposed to be coming up. But the Kiowas did not appear, whereupon Sheridan notified the captive chiefs that unless their people came in within forty-eight hours, he would have them hanged. Indian runners immediately carried word of Sheridan's threat to the Kiowas, who had fled southward from their camps on the Washita. By the time set for the execution, nearly all members of the tribe had arrived at Fort Cobb.[36]

The volunteers' first encampment at Fort Cobb was on the Pond Creek tributary of the Washita not far from the post buildings, which consisted of nothing more than "a large warehouse and quarters for probably one or two companies."[37] They lived comfortably in dugouts, with fireplaces, constructed by digging holes several feet deep in the ground and stretching shelter tents over them, until late in December when heavy rains flooded their quarters and forced them to remove to higher ground. Although the Indians were camped some distance away evidently along both the creek and the river, they sometimes kept the soldiers awake "by dancing and yelling" far into the night. The troopers were often visited during the day by squaws who came "to barter pelts, moccasins, and Indian trinkets" for coffee and sugar. Occasionally, the Kansans visited the Indian villages to satisfy their "curiosity" as to the Indian "mode of life."

Evidently Christmas day was the loneliest time of the expedition. The volunteers' thoughts naturally turned to home, and "a gloomier set of men could hardly be found anywhere." Each mess prepared a special dinner of wild turkey or venison and General Hazen treated the officers to eggnog at his quarters. Jenness subsequently recalled doing "Full justice . . . to the General's hospitality" and returning "to camp considerably enlivened by our visit."

103

While at Fort Cobb, the Nineteenth was called out by Brevet Brigadier General Forsyth (presumably J. W. Forsyth), one of Sheridan's staff,
for a thorough inspection. Insofar as arms, equipment, and condition of
the men were concerned, the unit "passed a very creditable examination," but it was a different story in regard to the animals. According
to Colonel Moore, one hundred forty-eight horses had died en route
from Camp Supply to Fort Cobb and apparently many others were in
bad shape. Jenness intimates that Forsyth blamed the Kansans for this
situation and attributes Forsyth's attitude to prejudice on his part as a
regular officer against volunteers. Forsyth's report, Jenness later declared, indicated

> . . . plainly the hostile feeling entertained by regular officers for volun-
> teers, and which had been very plainly indicated on several occasions
> during our association with Custar [Custer] and his officers. The 19th
> Kansas, as a body of fighting men, could have whipped two Regiments
> like the 7th Cav. and had we ever encountered the Indians, there is no
> question in my mind but what the 19th would have been the bulwark of
> the command. The reflections on the Regt. were sweetened a little by
> a special complimentary mention of Capts. [John Q. A.] Norton and
> Pliley, but there was [were] many companies in the command as good
> or better than either of these. It was not the fault of the men that our
> horses died [en route from Camp Supply to Fort Cobb]. It was the
> direct result of the unfortunate and unavoidable march and exposure
> [from Camp Beecher] to Camp Supply.

According to Jenness, the horseless men were "sent back to Camp
Supply with instructions to report to Major Dimon."[38]

In the meantime, Sheridan had decided to abandon Fort Cobb in
favor of a new post to be built about thirty miles to the south on the
site of an old Wichita Indian village at the eastern base of the Wichita
Mountains, where Medicine Bluff Creek emptied into Cache Creek.
From this new site on the Kiowa and Comanche reservation, the army
would better protect the Texas frontier and watch the movements of
the Kiowas and Comanches.[39]

Early in January, 1869, the expedition struck camp and headed
toward Medicine Bluff Creek. The going was extremely slow owing to
the jaded condition of the animals and the large number of muddy
spots on the trail. Finding the grazing good, the command halted often
in a futile effort "to recuperate" the animals.

Nearly every volunteer who left an account of the expedition commented on the splendid countenance of the country below Fort Cobb.
Soon after the column's arrival at its destination, one of the volunteers,
probably Captain Milton Stewart of Company K, wrote a letter to the
Junction City Weekly Union:

> The country lying between here and Cobb is one of the finest I have
> ever passed through. It is watered by never failing springs, gushing
> from the rocks of the Washita [Wichita] mountains; differing in every
> essential from the miserable sloughs of the plains. The soil is rich,

and judging from the rank growth of the grass, must be highly productive. The margin of all the streams is thickly fringed with timber, principally oak. Mt. Scott is apparently the loftiest peak of the range of mountains. It is just before me as I write — "grand, gloomy and peculiar." From its summit you can see . . . the Red River 40 miles distant — a mere thread to the naked eye — winding its meandering course through as lovely a stretch of timbered country as ever the eye rested upon.[40]

Thus the volunteers observed the fine farming lands in Indian Territory and made known their findings to the people at home. It is not surprising that Kansans were subsequently among the most avid of those who "boomed" the opening of lands south of the Kansas line to homesteaders. Among the volunteers was Captain David L. Payne, future leader of the Oklahoma Boomer Movement.[41]

A new post was soon constructed by Negro troopers of the Tenth Cavalry. The officers of the Seventh Cavalry wanted to call it Fort Elliott after Major Elliott who had died in the Washita fight, and it was known for a time as Camp Wichita, but Sheridan subsequently named it Fort Sill in memory of a West Point classmate, Brigadier General Joshua W. Sill, who had been killed in the Civil War.[42]

Much of the volunteers' time at this station seems to have been spent in hunting, playing baseball, killing rattlesnakes, and racing horses. One of the fastest horses in camp was the privately-owned mount of Captain Pliley. His and Captain Finch's horses were stolen on one occasion by deserters, but the two officers with Custer's Osage trailers tracked the thieves down, finding them one morning at about daybreak. Instead of returning the men to camp, the officers sent them toward the "rising sun" on foot.[43]

While the expedition remained at Fort Sill, Sheridan decided, since so few of the surviving horses were serviceable, and it was difficult to procure forage, to dismount all the volunteers except the officers. The good mounts were turned over to the Seventh Cavalry while the others together with the condemned animals of the Seventh were taken to Fort Arbuckle, some seventy miles to the southeast. Of the ten companies of Kansans, Captain Pliley's allegedly was the only one to turn in "all the horses" that it had started out with. After the volunteers lost their horses, they were drilled "as infantry."[44]

In the meantime, events had been taking place which would soon cause the expedition to take up the line of march once again. Operating on the Canadian and Red Rivers to the west were the supporting columns of General Carr and Colonel Evans. On Christmas day, 1868, Evans struck a hostile Comanche camp on the North Fork of the Red River, killing twenty-five Indians and destroying the village. Most of the Comanches escaped, but they wanted no more trouble with the bluecoats and gave themselves up at Forts Bascom and Cobb.[45]

Although Carr's and Evans' columns saw relatively little action, their operations were important, for they caused the Cheyennes and Arapahoes untold hardship during the winter by keeping them constantly on the move. Late in December, while Sheridan and Custer were still at Fort Cobb, Little Robe of the Cheyennes and Yellow Bear of the Arapahoes with other leaders came in and asked for peace. Sheridan immediately accepted their friendly overtures and sent them back to their villages to bring in their people. A newspaper correspondent with the Seventh Cavalry described the several chiefs as "a lot of poor, half-starved creatures" whose people had not had time, owing to the movements of the military, either "to graze their ponies" or "to kill meat for themselves."[46]

Shortly after Sheridan and Custer's arrival at Medicine Bluff Creek, Little Robe and Yellow Bear returned from their villages. They had urged their people to come in but they were not sure their advice would be heeded. With Sheridan's permission, Custer took the two chiefs and a small detachment of men out to find the Indians and bring them in. With this force rode a young Kansan named D. A. Brewster who had joined the expedition at Camp Supply as a "substitute teamster." His sister, Mrs. Anna Belle Morgan, had been captured and her husband wounded in an October raid on the Solomon. During the march westward from Fort Sill, Brewster learned from Little Robe that the Cheyennes were holding two young Kansas women prisoners. One of them answered the description of his sister.

Finding the Arapahoes on Mulberry Creek, a tributary of the Red River, in the Texas Panhandle, Custer received assurances from their principal chief, Little Raven, that they would go immediately to Fort Sill. Custer then set out to find the Cheyennes, but as they were moving west and he was low on supplies, he soon returned to Fort Sill, arriving there on February 7, 1869. The Arapahoes came in a few days later and made camp near the Kiowas, Comanches, and Kiowa-Apaches, who had been forced to accompany Sheridan and Custer from Fort Cobb to Medicine Bluff Creek.[47]

The Cheyennes and about eighty lodges of Arapahoes were the only Indians now remaining at large. With major campaigning seemingly near an end, Sheridan warned the chiefs of the tribes gathered about Fort Sill against future hostilities and freed Satanta and Lone Wolf. And as "state affairs" now seemed more important than Indian campaigning, Colonel Crawford resigned his commission and returned to Topeka. Forthwith, Lieutenant Colonel Moore was promoted to colonel, Major Jones to lieutenant colonel, and Captain Stewart became a major.[48]

Sheridan decided to send Custer with the Seventh Cavalry and the Nineteenth Kansas to find the remaining hostiles and demand their

106

surrender. To facilitate Custer's operations, Sheridan proposed to establish a temporary supply depot to the west. Escorted by Pepoon's scouts, Sheridan journeyed to Camp Supply late in February to make arrangements for supplying the depot directly from that point. While there he received orders to proceed to Washington immediately. En route he learned that he had been promoted to lieutenant general, and in Washington he was reässigned as commander of the Division of the Missouri.[49]

After some delay in procuring "ten days short rations," Custer's command, now numbering some fifteen hundred men, left Fort Sill on March 2. For a few days Custer marched the expedition at a moderate gait in order that the dismounted volunteers might become accustomed to walking. Nevertheless, the steady pace was too much for many of the Kansans and presumably some of the Seventh's horses and, on the North Fork of the Red River, Custer sent nearly three hundred volunteers and one hundred fifty regulars together with part of the supply train under Captain (Brevet Lieutenant Colonel) Edward Myers to the command's supply depot near the old Custer battlefield on the Washita. The "cripples" reported at the camp on March 9, one day after the arrival of Captain (Brevet Major) Henry Inman with provisions and a part of Major Dimon's detachment from Camp Supply as escort.[50]

From the North Fork Custer's command, with the Seventh in the lead, traveled westward to the Salt Fork. Finding a small, fresh Indian trail, Custer followed it up-stream into the Texas Panhandle. On the afternoon of March 8 the Osage trailers spotted eight Cheyenne warriors and a squaw busily erecting lodges during a rainshower. Surrounding the camp, the regulars charged "at a gallop" only to find the Indians gone. They had undoubtedly been warned of the soldiers' approach by the barking of two staghounds, owned by none other than the general himself. There is evidence to indicate that the regulars considered themselves a cut above their volunteer cohorts, and this instance gave the Kansans an opportunity to take them down a notch. "We are," wrote Private Spotts in his diary that evening, "having a joke on the Seventh for letting the Indians escape."[51]

As the expedition's supplies were dwindling rapidly and it no longer had a trail to follow, Custer held a meeting of the officers in the evening to decide whether or not to continue the search. The decision was to go on for several days more in the hope of either finding the Cheyennes' camp or a trail leading to it. During the next three days the command marched westward, southward, and southwestward, in that order. Crossing Mulberry Creek and coming almost to the Red River, the scouts found a small, cold Indian trail going northwest. By this time, the men were subsisting mainly on mule meat, the animals on "the buds and bark" of cottonwood trees and the scant, dry grass. The death of some of the draft animals owing to starvation forced Custer to abandon a number of the wagons.

Nevertheless, he decided to follow the trail as rapidly as possible. It led him in a northeasterly direction across the Salt Fork. Presently, it became larger and warmer. So as not to attract the Indians' attention, Custer prohibited night fires and unnecessary noise. In the interest of expediting the pursuit, he ordered all surplus equipage burned.

Soon after crossing the North Fork of the Red River on March 15, Hard Rope, the head Osage guide, reported a large pony-herd grazing about a mile ahead. Sighting the troopers, the Indian herders immediately ran their ponies toward Sweetwater Creek several miles away. Custer, who was riding with a "few men" some distance in front of the column, sent word back for it to "close up."

Riding on ahead with his orderly, he signaled to some warriors, who were watching him from their ponies on a nearby sandhill, asking for a parley. From them, the general learned that the Cheyennes were camped in two villages, numbering altogether two hundred sixty lodges, in the valley of Sweetwater Creek just ahead. The village of the principal chief, Medicine Arrows, was directly to the front; the other, under Little Robe, who had left Custer's earlier expedition out of Fort Sill to return to his people, was some ten miles down-stream near the Texas-Indian Territory line.

A "few moments" later, the group was joined by Medicine Arrows and other chiefs. Medicine Arrows urged Custer to accompany him to his village for a council. The general's presence would satisfy his people that no attack would be made upon them. Sending back orders to the approaching soldiers not to attack, Custer with Lieutenant (Brevet Lieutenant Colonel) William W. Cooke, who had come up during the discussion, rode amidst the party of warriors to the village. Custer said later that he chose to talk because he feared that the Indians might be holding the two white women and that they would be killed by their captors in case of a fight. En route to the camp, Custer learned that the women, Mrs. Morgan and Miss Sarah C. White, were indeed captives in the village. Miss White had been captured in August, 1868, near Lake Sibley, just east of the Republican River.[52]

Custer's orders not to attack were, to say the least, not appreciated by the volunteers, who wanted revenge for the destructive raids the Cheyennes had committed on the Kansas frontier during the previous year. Their reaction is perhaps described best by First Sergeant James A. Hadley of Company A:

> As the men gripped their repeating carbines and saw that each had a cartridge in the barrel and seven others in the magazine, an officer came from Custer with the order to Colonel Moore: "Don't fire on those Indians." The men, stupid with wonder, hardly realized what it meant, before another aide brought Moore the orders for his position. The Nineteenth was marched into the valley at the upper end of the village and halted in a column of troops to "rest in place." The men of the Nine-

teenth, not knowing the reason for this, and fearing their general had been tricked, as had so often been the case, were angry. Neither Custer nor Moore ever knew what a critical time it was for about ten minutes. It looked, at one time, like they could not be restrained. The line officers urged, begged and cursed. The accidental discharge of a carbine, or the shout of a reckless soldier, would have precipitated a killing that could not have been stopped, and would have entailed consequences impossible to estimate. Nothing was known along the line of [the] captive white women . . .

Some of the men who had lost relatives and friends in Indian raids branded Custer a "coward" and a "traitor." Colonel Moore called the order "a wet blanket, saturated with ice-water."[53]

While the column was moving into position about the village, the Nineteenth at the upper end and the Seventh at the lower, Custer was in council with the chiefs. He was sorely handicapped during the proceedings by the absence of his interpreter, a Mexican named Romero, who had fallen behind during the day's march and had not yet come up. Perhaps partly for this reason little came of the conference. The general's main success seems to have been in smoking the ceremonial pipe without becoming sick. When the pipe-smoking ritual was finished, Medicine Arrows poured the ashes over the toes of Custer's boots which, unknown to Custer, was intended to bring the officer bad luck.

After the council, Medicine Arrows showed his guest to a campsite just out of view of the village, and there the command pitched its tents. During the afternoon, Custer's "lookouts" reported that the Indians were preparing to leave. To cover their movements, a delegation of chiefs and warriors brought a group of "musicians" to the general's tent ostensibly for the purpose of entertaining him. While watching their performance, Custer "quietly passed the word" to the officers sitting with him around the campfire to leave "one by one" and instruct "their most reliable men" to gather about gradually, interspersing themselves among the Indian onlookers. The performers had no sooner concluded their show and left than Custer arose amidst the assembly of Indians and soldiers and gave the order to "Take these Indians prisoners!" For a few tense moments, it appeared that the Indians, all of whom were armed, would fight; instead, however, they made a dash for safety. Custer avoided a bloody incident by shouting to his men not to fire. Four warriors — three of whom were the notable Dog Soldier chiefs Big Head, Dull Knife, and Fat Bear — failed to get away, and Custer had what he wanted, hostages.

Custer immediately sent out one of the Indians with a message to the Cheyennes saying that he would not destroy the lodges of the deserted camp if the owners would encamp near the village down-stream and demanding that the tribe surrender the two white women and proceed to Fort Sill.[54] That night several braves visited the soldiers' bivouac

109

to ascertain whether the remaining three hostages were still alive. The next afternoon, March 16, Little Robe with a group of head men rode in for a talk. The chiefs apparently expressed themselves "heartily sick of war" and in favor of removing to Fort Sill, but the conference hit a snag on the matter of the white captives. Little Robe stated that the owners of the young women would not give them up without payment of a ransom. Custer demanded that they be released "unconditionally." Since Medicine Arrows' people had camped near Little Robe's, the general gave them permission, as he had promised he would, to come back and get their lodges. Colonel Moore subsequently recalled that the Indians "pulled down" the entire camp in "a surprisingly short time" and hauled it pony-back down-stream.

The following day, March 17, Custer declined a proposition brought to him by a chief that the Cheyennes would "consider" freeing their captives if he would first release him. In order that messages might be exchanged more quickly, Custer on the eighteenth moved his camp closer to the Indian camp. Another visit by an Indian emissary failed to secure the women's liberty. Finally, after the general "had almost exhausted the patience of the troops, particularly of the Kansas regiment," Custer called the chiefs together in his tent and told them that "if by sunset the following day," March 19, the women prisoners had not been "delivered up" he would "hang to a tree," which was then designated, "the three captive chiefs, after which he would "follow and attack" their village. One of the Kansans, Private William D. Street of Company I, stated later that he doubted whether Custer could have carried out the latter threat because he "did not have fifty horses in his command that would stand a forced march of fifteen miles . . ."

When the Indians did not appear with the captives the next morning, Custer ordered ropes prepared and a limb selected for the hanging. In the afternoon, both officers and men of the command began assembling "near headquarters, and upon the small eminences nearby, eagerly watching the horizon in the direction of the village . . ." At about 3:00 o'clock a small party of warriors approached and halted on a distant knoll. One of them then rode forward and offered to exchange the women for two of the chiefs. Custer refused to do so. The warrior no sooner rejoined the group on the knoll than "two figures" descended from a single pony and started toward the camp. Custer, who was watching these proceedings through his "field glass," soon identified them as the young women.

Since "the Kansas volunteers had left their homes and various occupations to accomplish, among other results, the release of the two girls . . . I [Custer] deemed it appropriate that that regiment should be the first to welcome the two released captives to friends and freedom." Accordingly, the general detailed the three ranking officers of the Nineteenth "to go out and receive them." As the reception committee advanced, Mrs. Morgan's brother, Brewster, whom Custer had detained near his side for fear he might in anger at the Indians provoke an incident, broke away and bounded past the three officers to clasp his sister in his arms. As the little aggregation returned to camp, it passed between two lines formed by the volunteers. Both women were pale-looking and shabbily dressed. They had been treated quite cruelly by the "jealous" squaws who had not only forced them to bear a heavy work load, but also had often whipped them. They had, however, suffered their greatest indignities at the hands of the several warriors with whom they had been forced to live. Both women were allegedly pregnant at the time of their recovery; Mrs. Morgan, however, was hopeful that her pregnancy pre-dated her capture.[55]

Late in the afternoon, a delegation of chiefs visited Custer to "urge the release of the three chiefs." The general told them that he would give them up when the Cheyennes reported at Fort Sill. The chiefs promised that they would do so, though at the moment their ponies were in no condition to travel. Custer avers in his report to Sheridan, dated March 21, 1869, that he would have attacked the village after the recovery of the women had not his supplies been exhausted. Custer's report also contained a statement highly complimentary of the Kansas volunteers:

> Serving on foot they have marched in a manner and at a rate that would put some of the regular regiments of infantry to the blush. Instead of crying out for empty wagons to transport them, each morning every man marched with his troop, and, . . . company officers marched regularly on foot at the head of their respective companies . . .

Evidently unknown to Custer, some of the Kansans had been riding in the empty wagons at every opportunity.[56]

Having thus brought the Cheyennes to terms, Custer on March 21 moved his tired, hungry, and worn command northeastward toward Inman's supply camp on the Washita. Both animals and men suffered severely on the march. Coming to within a short distance of the depot, Custer halted the exhausted troopers and sent word to Inman for him to bring out a relief train with supplies and some empty wagons to carry the men who could walk no further. Apparently the horses of the Seventh Cavalry were in such bad shape by this time that the regiment was nearly dismounted. Despite the desperate condition of the foot-sore, the starving, and the weary, several companies of the Nineteenth chose to press on rather than to wait for relief. Arriving at the supply camp, some of the ravenous troopers stuffed themselves so much that they became sick. As the men's clothing "was black and brown and hanging in rags and tatters" and their general appearance "hard," many of their former comrades did not recognize them.[57]

After a short rest of two days, the expedition, together with the

111

men at the supply station, on March 26, left for Camp Supply. Arriving at that point on the twenty-eighth, the entire Kansas regiment was reunited and completely dismounted. Since the Indian campaign had been brought to a successful conclusion and the Nineteenth's period of service was nearly up, Custer moved the column out again two days later, destination Fort Hays via Fort Dodge. Though weary in body, the homeward-bound Kansans were high in spirit. Private Spotts commented en route to Fort Dodge that the "boys" never seemed to tire of "cheering for they break out every once in a while."

The expedition camped just northeast of Fort Dodge on April 2. It had no sooner done so than many of the volunteers went into "town," a collection of houses, saloons and, presumably, other buildings along the river near the stockade, to celebrate their homecoming. Although Custer evidently had intended to lay over a few days at this point, he decided on the afternoon of the third — since both officers and men were drinking heavily and threatening to make trouble — to push on to Fort Hays.

The journey to Fort Hays, over a good wagon road, was hampered only by a light snow. Pitching camp near the post on April 7, the volunteers began taking inventory of their losses in property and turning in their arms and equipment. Since leaving Topeka they had marched about twelve hundred miles. During that time ninety men had deserted, four had died of illness, and two had been killed accidentally.[58]

Thanks to the efforts of Colonel Crawford and General Sheridan, the volunteers were paid for their service shortly before they were mustered out. Concerned because they had received no pay, Crawford had, after returning from Fort Sill to Topeka, gone to Washington and taken the matter up with the Secretary of War. Informed that Congress had recently adjourned without making provision for the compensation of the Nineteenth, Crawford had enlisted the aid of General Sheridan, who had just come from the frontier, and they together had persuaded the Secretary to order the payment out of his contingent fund.[59]

While the volunteers waited at Fort Hays to be discharged and notwithstanding the fact that they had little money for several days after their arrival, many of them managed to have a good time drinking and fighting in nearby Hays City. Private Spotts declared in his diary that he had "never seen so many drunken men at one time before," and that

> It is a fight nearly every night—citizens vs. soldiers. Sometimes the citizens get together and clean out the soldiers by small squads, and keep them from uniting. Perhaps the next night the soldiers will get in a body and run every man in citizen's clothes out of town or disarm them and shut them up.

According to Private Alfred A. Runyon of Company M, "Shots were

112

fired at every minute of the night" and several men killed as the result of "serious affrays" with Hays City "roughs." Presumably the good people of the town breathed a sigh of relief when the volunteers were finally mustered out on April 18 and they departed for their homes on the next east-bound train.[60]

The former soldiers left behind them a relatively peaceful frontier. By early April nearly all the Southern Plains Indians either had come in or were coming in to Fort Sill. Subsequently, all the Cheyenne captives taken by Custer in the Battle of the Washita and on the Sweetwater, with the exception of two of the hostages captured on the latter stream, who were killed while trying to escape from the stockade at Fort Hays, were restored to their people.[61]

Although the volunteers may have been disappointed at not having engaged the Indians in combat, they themselves were probably the reason there had been no battles. The additional strength they gave to Custer's expedition undoubtedly caused the hostiles to abandon any thoughts of resistance which they may have entertained. The Kiowas and Comanches would soon be raiding in Texas again; but, with the exception of a few weeks in the summer of 1869 when a renegade band of Cheyenne Dog Soldiers under Tall Bull depredated in northwestern Kansas, there would be little Indian hostility on the Kansas frontier until 1874.[62] Partly responsible for this partially peaceful situation was the Nineteenth Kansas Volunteer Cavalry.

NOTES

1. For a more thorough treatment of Forsyth's fight, see the preceeding chapter.
2. Military campaigns on the Plains were often opposed by the Indian Office; but inasmuch as the Indian outbreak of 1868 was seemingly unprovoked, most of the Indian officials concerned supported Sherman and Sheridan's policy. Murphy to Mix, September 19, 1868, Mix to Otto, September 25, 1868, Otto to Secretary of War, October 1, 1868, Wynkoop to Mix, October 7, 1868, Report of Commissioner of Indian Affairs for 1868, *House Executive Document*, No. 1, 40 Cong., 3 Sess., pp. 535-542.
3. P. H. Sheridan, Personal Memoirs (two volumes, New York: 1888), Vol II, pp. 281-309; Sheridan to Sherman, November 16, 1868, Emporia (Kansas) *News*, December 11, 1868; Leavenworth (Kansas) *Times and Conservative*, September 24, 1868; Carl Coke Rister, Border Command: *General Phil Sheridan in the West* (Norman: 1944), pp. 45-94; William H. Leckie, The Military Conquest of the Southern Plains (Norman: 1963), pp. 63-90; Donald J. Berthrong, The Southern Cheyennes (Norman: 1963), pp. 289-317; Marvin H. Garfield, "Defense of the Kansas Frontier, 1868-1869," *Kansas Historical Quarterly*, Vol. I (November, 1932), pp. 451-464; Lonnie J. White, "The Cheyenne Barrier on the Kansas Frontier, 1868-1869," *Arizona and the West*, Vol. IV (Spring, 1962), pp. 51-60.
4. Sherman to Secretary of War, September 17, 26, 1868, Report of Commissioner of Indian Affairs for 1868, *House Executive Document*, No. 1, 40 Cong., 3 Sess., pp. 536, 539. Sherman stated that since the Cheyennes and Arapahoes wanted war "I propose to give them enough of it to satisfy them to their hearts' content . . ."
5. Sheridan to Crawford, October 8, 1868, Governors' Correspondence, Crawford's Telegrams, Archives, Kansas State Historical Society (hereafter cited KSHS); Samuel J. Crawford, Kansas in the Sixties (Chicago: 1911), p. 318; Sheridan to Sherman, November 11, 1868, Emporia *News*, December 11, 1868; Leckie, *Military Conquest*, pp. 90-91. Actually they had gone to the vicinity of Fort Cobb on their own. Notably absent, how-

ever, were the renown Kiowa chiefs Satanta, who was away on a raid in Texas, and Kicking Bird, who was leading an expedition against the Utes. Three bands of Comanches also remained out; one on the Canadian River, two on the Washita River.

6. Sheridan to Crawford, October 9, 1868, Governors' Correspondence, Crawford's Telegrams, Archives, KSHS; Crawford, KANSAS IN THE SIXTIES, pp. 319-320; Proclamation, October 10, 1868, Junction City, Kansas, *Weekly Union*, October 17, 1868; Crawford to President Andrew Johnson, August 22, 1868, *Kansas State Record*, Topeka, August 26, 1868; *Times and Conservative*, October 13, 1868. Sheridan susequently telegraphed Crawford that the twelve companies should each contain ninety-nine men instead of one hundred. Sheridan to Crawford, October 12, 1868, Governors' Correspondence, Crawford's Telegrams, Archives, KSHS.

7. George B. Jenness, "History of the 19th Kansas Cavalry," unpublished manuscript, Manuscript Division, KSHS (hereafter cited Jenness MS); David L. Spotts, CAMPAIGNING WITH CUSTER AND THE NINETEENTH KANSAS VOLUNTEER CAVALRY ON THE WASHITA CAMPAIGN, 1868-1869 (Los Angeles: 1928), pp. 15, 40; James A. Hadley, "The Nineteenth Kansas Cavalry, and the Conquest of the Plains Indians," Kansas State Historical Society *Transactions* (hereafter cited as *KSHS Transactions*), Vol. X (1907-1908), pp. 41-433. For the names of the officers and men in each company, *see* Spotts, *Campaigning With Custer*, pp. 15-27. Although Dimon was mustered in as a captain, he was promoted to major on October 30, 1868. The roster in *ibid*. evidently erroneously dates his promotion as March 23, 1869.

8. Lonnie J. White, "Warpaths on the Southern Plains: The Battles of the Saline River and Prairie Dog Creek," JOURNAL *of the* WEST, Vol. IV, No. 4 (October, 1965), pp. 485-503; Jenness MS; Alan W. Farley (ed.), "Reminiscences of Allison J. Pliley, Indian Fighter," *Trail Guide*, Vol. II (Kansas City, Missouri, June, 1957), pp. 1-11; Forrest R. Blackburn, "The 18th Kansas Cavalry and the Indian War," *ibid.*, Vol. IX (March, 1964), pp. 1-15; Edward C. Manning, "A Kansas Soldier," *KSHS Transactions*, Vol. X, pp. 427-428; Hadley, "The Nineteenth Kansas Cavalry," *ibid.*, Vol. X, p. 433. Pliley and Jenness were appointed to their places by the governor. These appointments were presumably in line with Sheridan's wish that the governor appoint officers rather than permit their selection by the men. Sheridan believed that if the governor did so he would "get better officers." Sheridan to Crawford, October 12, 1868, Governors' Correspondence, Crawford's Telegrams, Archives, *KSHS*. One suspects, however, from the scant evidence on the matter that most of the officers were elected by the men. See Spotts, *Campaigning with Custer*, p. 40.

9. Spotts, *Campaigning with Custer*, pp. 41-43; Hadley, "The Nineteenth Kansas Cavalry," *KSHS Transactions*, Vol. X, p. 432.

10. Communication of Sergeant M. A. Victor, December 15, 1868, Emporia *News*, January 8, 1869; "A. L. Runyon's Letters from the Nineteenth Kansas Regiment," *Kansas Historical Quarterly*, Vol. IX (February, 1940), pp. 62-64; Spotts, *Campaigning with Custer*, pp. 45-49; Horace L. Moore, "The Nineteenth Kansas Cavalry," *KSHS Transactions*, Vol. VI (1897-1900), p. 38.

11. Jenness MS; Letter of Dr. Russell, November 14, 1868, Emporia *News*, November 27, 1868; "Copy of Diary of Luther A. Thrasher," *KSHS Transactions*, Vol. X, p. 661; Hortense B. Campbell, "Camp Beecher," *Kansas Historical Quarterly*, Vol. III (May, 1934), pp. 172-185; Crawford, KANSAS IN THE SIXTIES, pp. 322-324. Crawford said later that the officer in command, Captain Samuel L. Barr, Fifth Infantry, was subsequently reprimanded "for consuming" the supplies, which had been sent there from Fort Riley, intended for the Nineteenth Kansas. Presumably the regulars had partaken of the provisions because they had none of their own. The regimental Quartermaster, Luther A. Thrasher, noted in his diary that he had "some hard words and late hours" with Captain Barr.

12. Douglass to McKeever, June 18, 1867, March 24, 1868, Douglass to Townsend, July 30, 1868, Fort Dodge, Letters Sent, Department of the Missouri, Records of the War Department, National Archives; Topeka *Kansas Daily Commonwealth*, May 21, 1869; Hadley, "The Nineteenth Kansas Cavalry," *KSHS Transactions*, Vol. X, p. 435; Sheridan, *Memoirs*, Vol. II, p. 310. Apache Bill was subsequently killed by a Texas cowboy.

13. Jenness MS; Spotts, *Campaigning with Custer*, pp. 54-56.

14. Crawford to Martin, July 13, 1908, Nineteenth Kansas File, Manuscript Division, *KSHS*; Jenness MS; Hadley, "The Nineteenth Kansas Cavalry," *KSHS Transactions*, Vol. X, p. 436; Moore, "The Nineteenth Kansas Cavalry," *ibid.*, Vol. VI, p. 33; "Runyon's Letters," *Kansas Historical Quarterly*, Vol. IX, p. 65; Letter of E. R. [P.?] Russell, December 1, 1868, Lawrence, *Kansas Daily Tribune*, December 22, 1868; Spotts, *Campaigning with Custer*, pp. 56-57. Jenness' account of the cause of the stampede differs somewhat from those of Spotts' and Hadley's. Jenness says that the regiment was going into camp with the wagons "swinging into their places in the rear of their respective companies" when a "six mule team, left for a moment by its driver," became frightened and dashed through the camp "at full speed," frightening the horses and causing them to stampede. I have, however, chosen to accept Spotts' and Hadley's ac-

counts (given in text above) because they are nearly identical. Hadley sets the number of horses stampeded as over five hundred, Runyon one hundred fifty or two hundred, Crawford about three hundred. Crawford estimates the number of horses lost as "about nine or ten," Runyon about seventy-five, Moore about eighty, Spotts nearly one hundred. The exact number has not been ascertained.

15. Jenness MS; Spotts, *Campaigning with Custer*, p. 59; Letter of Russell, December 1, 1868, *Kansas Daily Tribune*, December 22, 1868. Jenness asserts that Apache Bill got the command lost because he did not know the country while Assistant Surgeon Russell states that it was "so dark" during the snowstorm that he "could not get the direction." This matter will be considered further in a subsequent note.

16. Jenness MS; Hadley, "The Nineteenth Kansas Cavalry," *KSHS Transactions*, Vol. X, pp. 438-439. Private William D. Street of I Company avers the Pliley party did not leave until the next morning, November 23. Street to Martin, November 5, 1908, Nineteenth Kansas File, Manuscript Division, *KSHS*.

17. Jenness MS. Two Sand Creeks are shown on contemporary maps, one tributary to the the Cimarron River, the other to the Nestuganta River; but neither would seem to be the stream on which the command was camped on the twenty-second and twenty-third. The Sand Creek tributary of the Cimarron is much too far to the west of the route described by contemporaries while the Sand Creek tributary of the Nestuganta is a little too far north of the Cimarron. It is possible that they were either on another small creek named Sand Creek or that they were mistaken as to the name of the stream. According to J. R. Mead, an Indian trader who was not with the expedition, the volunteers camped on Medicine Lodge Creek "several miles above its mouth" and moved thence southward when "Their proper route was by the junction of Medicine and Salt Fork . . . thence southwest . . ." Mead to Martin, July 11, 1908, *KSHS Transactoins*, Vol. X, p. 664.

18. The hunters reported "that the buffalo were suffering even worse than ourselves or horses. This unexpected blizzard had caught them upon the unsheltered prairies, and there they would seek some deep ravine, or hollow and chilled through and completely covered by the storm, they would stand and allow the men to approach within ten feet of them, and shoot them down, without any effort on their part to escape." Jenness MS.

19. "John McBee's Account of the Expedition of the Nineteenth Kansas," *KSHS Collections*, Vol. XVII (1926-1928), p. 362; Communication of M. S. (probably Captain Milton Stewart), December 20, 1868, *Weekly Union*, February 6, 1869; Crawford, KANSAS IN THE SIXTIES, p. 324; Sheridan, *Memoirs*, Vol. II, p. 321; "Runyon's letters," *Kansas Historical Quarterly*, Vol. IX, pp. 64-68; Mead to Martin, July 12, 1906, Street to Martin, November 5, 1908, Nineteenth Kansas File, Manuscript Division, *KSHS*; William E. Connelley (ed.), "Life and Adventures of George W. Brown," *KSHS Collections*, Vol. XVII (1926-1928), p. 106. Most of the volunteers who left accounts of the expedition are hard on Apache Bill for getting the command lost. One Kansan who defended him, William D. Street, points out that no one in the expedition knew exactly where Camp Supply was located since it had not been established when the volunteers left Topeka. And he intimates that the scouts might not have gotten lost had not the snow storms obscured the landmarks. Another volunteer, A. L. Runyon, speaks of Apache Bill as "one of the best guides," but mistakedly thought that "he brought us straight through." Private John McBee reports a rumor that Apache Bill deliberately led the command astray because he did not want his Cheyenne wife hurt as the result of a military attack on her people's village. George W. Brown, one of Pepoon's scouts, who accompanied Captain Pliley with the relief train from Camp Supply to Camp Starvation (discussed below in the text), defends Apache Bill, saying that he was a good scout, but the volunteers thought he should "know to a gnat's heel the location of every stream and little old blind spring in the country . . ." General Sheridan declares that the regiment got lost because it did not follow "the advice of the guide sent to conduct it to Camp Supply." Crawford, however, asserts that Sheridan apologized to him at Camp Supply for sending him guides "who knew nothing about the country through which we passed." J. R. Mead, who claims that he knew the Cimarron country well, maintains that "there was no reason or sense in getting into the 'Bad lands' and cañons of the Cimmarrone" when there were "two ways around them."

 That Apache Bill was responsible for getting the command lost, there seems little doubt; but whether he did so because he was unfamiliar with the country or because he could not read the landmarks in the snow, it is impossible to ascertain from the evidence.

20. Hadley, "Nineteenth Kansas Cavalry," *KSHS Transactions*, Vol. X, p. 439; Jenness MS; Crawford, KANSAS IN THE SIXTIES, p. 323. Hadley states that Crawford remained at the camp, but Jenness and the colonel himself tell us that he led the force that pushed on.

21. This is the figure given by Crawford. Hadley sets the number as over six hundred, Jenness as about one-half the regiment.

22. This is the date given by Moore, Hadley, and Spotts. Although other accounts give different dates, it seems certain enough that the twenty-eighth is the correct one.

23. D. B. Randolph Keim, SHERIDAN'S TROOPERS ON THE BORDERS: *A Winter Campaign on the Plains* (Philadelphia: 1885), pp. 106-107; Moore, "The Nineteenth Kansas Cavalry," *KSHS Transactions,* Vol. VI, p. 39; Jenness MS; Communication of Victor, December 15, 1868, Emporia *News,* January 8, 1869; Communication of Russell, December 1, 1868, *Kansas Daily Tribune,* December 22, 1868; Mahlon Bailey, "Medical History," Nineteenth Kansas File, Manuscript Division, *KSHS* (printed in *Kansas Historical Quarterly,* Vol. VI).

24. Sheridan left Fort Hays on November 15 escorted by Pepoon's scouts and a company of Tenth Cavalry. Evidently the two troops of volunteers had already gone on with a supply train to Fort Dodge. At Fort Dodge they joined Sully's command, accompanying it as far as Bluff Creek, Kansas, where they were left behind to await Sheridan and escort him thence to Camp Supply. Keim, *Sheridan's Troopers,* pp. 88-93.

25. George A. Custer, MY LIFE ON THE PLAINS (Norman: 1962), pp. xii-xvii; Marguerite Merington (ed.), THE CUSTER STORY (New York: 1950), p. 216; Sheridan, *Memoirs,* Vol. II, pp. 307-312; *Harper's Weekly,* Vol. XIII (February 27, 1869), p. 140; Rister, BORDER COMMAND, pp. 96-100; Leckie, *Military Conquest,* p. 97. Until the decision to launch a winter campaign against the hostiles, Custer had been on inactive duty as the result of a court martial in 1867. At Sheridan's request, Custer was in 1868 recalled to active duty. The infantry battalion at Camp Supply was commanded by Major John H. Page, Third Infantry. It consisted of three companies of Third Infantry, one of the Fifth, and one of the Thirty-eighth (Negro).

26. Sheridan to Sherman, November 24, 1868, *Times and Conservative,* December 5, 1868.

27. Custer to Sheridan, November 28, 1868, *House Executive Document* No. 240, 41 Cong., 2 Sess., pp. 162-165; Custer, MY LIFE ON THE PLAINS, pp. 213-270; Communication of corresopndent, November 28, 1868, *Times and Conservative,* December 2, 1868; Rister, BORDER COMMAND, pp. 101-112; Berthrong, *Southern Cheyennes,* pp. 325-327. One of Custer's troopers, Delos G. Sanbertson, was allegedly scalped alive, Emporia *News,* July 2, 1869. Custer may not have punished the Indians as much as he thought. Professor Berthrong cites "Three reliable sources" placing the number of warriors killed at between nine and twenty, the number of women and children at between eighteen and forty.

28. Jenness states that "an average of not more than eighty men in each company" had horses at Camp Supply. Jenness MS. Hadley, however, would have us believe that all but seventy-five mounts survived the march. Hadley, "The Nineteenth Kansas Cavalry," *KSHS Transactions,* Vol. X, p. 443. Sheridan states falsely that the volunteers were entirely dismounted as the result of the march to Camp Supply and served the rest of the campaign as "foot-troops." Sheridan, *Memoirs,* Vol. II, pp. 321-322.

29. Jenness MS; "Runyon's Letters," *Kansas Historical Quarterly,* Vol. IX, pp. 68-72; Moore, "The Nineteenth Kansas Cavalry," *KSHS Transactions,* Vol. VI, p. 40; Post adjutant to post trader and post sutler, March 27, 1869, Fort Dodge, Letters Sent, Department of the Missouri, Records of the War Department, National Archives. The men of this command evidently found their main excitement in hunting and drinking. As the result of a complaint from Major Dimon that whiskey was being "indiscriminately sold in large quantities" to the volunteers at Fort Dodge, the post adjutant ordered the post sutler and post trader not to let them have liquor "save by the glass, and not then unless the applicant is provided with a written order signed by Major Dimon in person."

30. Sheridan, *Memoirs,* Vol. II, pp. 323-327; Keim, *Sheridan's Troopers,* p. 128; Hadley, "The Nineteenth Kansas Cavalry," *KSHS Transactions,* Vol. X, pp. 443-445; Moore, "The Nineteenth Kansas Cavalry," *ibid.,* Vol. VI, p. 41; Jenness MS.

31. Custer to Crosby, December 23, 1868, *House Executive Document* No. 240, 41 Cong., 2 Sess., pp. 155-157; Carl Coke Rister, BORDER CAPTIVES (Norman: 1940), pp. 156-157; Communication of M. S., December 20, 1868, *Weekly Union,* February 6, 1869; Communication of Mrs. Blinn, November 17, 1868, *Times and Conservative,* December 23, 1868. Custer says in his report of December 23 that they were found in the Kiowa camp. Mrs. Blinn wrote in a note to an Indian trader in November that they were with the Cheyennes. General Hazen asserted that they were held by the Arapahoes and killed by them. The truth has not been ascertained.

32. Jenness MS; Keim, *Sheridan's Troopers,* pp. 144-147; George B. Grinnell, THE FIGHTING CHEYENNES (Norman: 1956), pp. 300-301, 304-305. One of Elliott's men was found some distance from the others. The remains of Elliott and Mrs. Blinn and her child were taken to Fort Arbuckle for interment. Elliott's men were buried in a trench on "the crest of a beautiful knoll, overlooking the valley of the Washita." Custer states in his report of the fight that a ten-year old white boy was also killed by the Indians during the attack.

33. Jenness MS; Sheridan to Nichols, December 19, 1868, January 1, 1869, Custer to Crosby, December 23, 1868. *House Executive Document* No. 240, 41 Cong., 2 Sess., pp. 151-156; Sheridan, *Memoirs,* Vol. II, pp. 328-330; Communication of Hustin, December 1, 1868,

116

Times and Conservative, December 6, 1868; Extract from Sheridan's annual report for 1869, *ibid.,* December 12, 1869. Sheridan subsequently used this evidence of the Cheyennes' hostility in an effort to silence critics in the service of the Indian Office who maintained that Black Kettle's had been a friendly camp and that the Washita fight was another Sand Creek affair. (At Sand Creek in 1864 a regiment of Colorado volunteers had fallen on Black Kettle's village and massacred a portion of its inhabitants while it was under the protection of the commanding officer at Fort Lyon, Colorado.) Although it was true that Black Kettle had on November 20 sought protection from General Hazen at Fort Cobb, Hazen had declined to make peace with him on the grounds that he had no authority to do so, since Sheridan had begun active campaigning. Probably a more important reason — since Hazen subsequently gave protection to Indians of other tribes (see discussion below in text) — Hazen believed that unless the Cheyennes were punished there would be no permanent peace.

Neither Sheridan nor his superior, Sherman, was deterred by the Indian sympathizers. As Sheridan saw it, Custer had "wiped out old Black Kettle and his murderers and rapers of helpless women." Sheridan had through Chief Little Raven of the Arapahoes invited Black Kettle to come in before the campaign started, but he had not done so. Sherman, also, expressed himself "well satisfied with Custer's attack" and declared that he "would not have wept if he [Custer] could have served Satanta's and Bull Bear's bands in the same style." He told Sheridan "to go ahead, kill and punish the hostile" tribes. "I hope this winter's work will bring peace on the plains, so that we will not again be harassed by the endless murders and depredations that made this Indian war indispensable." Sherman to Sheridan, Hazen, and Grierson, December 23, 1868, Wynkoop to Taylor, January 26, 1869, *House Executive Document* No. 240, 41 Cong., 2 Sess., pp. 10-11, 177-178; Sheridan to Sherman, November 1, 1869, *House Executive Document* No. 1, 41 Cong., 2 Sess., pp. 2, 47-48; Berthrong, *Southern Cheyennes,* pp. 323-324, 331-332. There is evidence to indicate that while Black Kettle himself was friendly enough he could not control his young men who favored war.

34. See Hadley, "The Nineteenth Kansas Cavalry," *KSHS Transactions,* Vol. X, p. 445.
35. Jenness MS; Custer to Crosby, December 22, 1868, *House Executive Document* No. 240, 41 Cong., 2 Sess., pp. 157-158; Sheridan, *Memoirs,* Vol. II, pp. 333-334; Custer, *My Life on the Plains,* pp. 290-294.
36. Sheridan to Nichols, December 19, 1868, Alford to Hazen, December 7, 1868, *House Executive Document* No. 240, 41 Cong., 2 Sess., pp. 151-155; Sheridan to Nichols, December 24, 1868, Sheridan Papers, Library of Congress; Keim, *Sheridan's Troopers,* pp. 152-160, 163; Communication of M. S., December 20, 1868, *Weekly Union,* February 6, 1869. About half the Kiowas, including Satanta's band, had also gone south after the Washita fight, but evidently they had by mid-December rejoined the rest of the tribe on the Washita.
37. Fort Cobb, "situated on Pond Creek, about a mile from its junction with the Washita river," was garrisoned by three companies of Tenth Cavalry and one of Sixth Infantry. Keim, *Sheridan's Troopers,* pp. 161-163.
38. Jenness MS; Spotts, *Campaigning with Custer,* pp. 80-94; Moore, "The Nineteenth Kansas Cavalry," *KSHS Transactions,* Vol. VI, pp. 42-43; Keim, *Sheridan's Troopers,* p. 171. The drink Jenness called eggnog was presumably that described by Keim as "Milk punch, concocted of the condensed material, sugar, and Texas 'spirits' . . ."
39. Sheridan to Nichols, January 8, 1869, Sheridan Papers, Library of Congress; Keim, *Sheridan's Troopers,* pp. 231-251; Sheridan, *Memoirs,* Vol. II, pp. 338-339.
40. Communication of M. S., January 11, 1869, *Weekly Union,* February 27, 1869. See also communication of M. S., February 2, 1869, *ibid.,* March 13, 1869.
41. Carl Coke Rister, LAND HUNGER: *David L. Payne and the Oklahoma Boomers* (Norman: 1942), pp. 21-22.
42. Leckie, *Military Conquest,* p. 112; Spotts, *Campaigning With Custer,* p. 111; W. S. Nye, CARBINE AND LANCE: *The Story of Old Fort Sill* (Norman: 1962), pp. 75-77, 84-86.
43. Spotts, *Campaigning with Custer,* pp. 120, 122, 127. Another volunteer states that the deserters refused the officers' demand that they surrender and, consequently, "they were dealt with in accordance with their deserts." Communication of M. S., February 22, 1869, *Weekly Union,* March 13, 1869.
44. Jenness MS; Sheridan to Nichols, February 9, 1869, Sheridan Papers, Library of Congress; Spotts, *Campaigning with Custer,* pp. 99-136; "Runyon's Letters," *Kansas Historical Quarterly,* Vol. IX, p. 73.
45. *Kansas Daily Tribune,* January 28, 1869; RECORD OF ENGAGEMENTS WITH HOSTILE INDIANS WITHIN THE MILITARY DIVISION OF THE MISSOURI FROM 1868-1882 (Washington: 1882), p. 17; Leckie, *Military Conquest,* pp. 114-118.
46. Interview of Sheridan with Little Robe and Yellow Bear, January 1, 1869, Sheridan to Nichols, January 1, 1869, Sheridan Papers, Library of Congress; Communication of correspondent, January 4, 1869, *Times and Conservative,* February 7, 1869. Sheridan had late in December sent a Kiowa-Apache chief named Iron Shirt and one of the captive

Indian women, Mah-wis-sa (Black Kettle's sister), to the Cheyenne and Arapaho camps to try and persuade the hostiles to come in. Presumably the visit of the delegation headed by Little Robe and Yellow Bear was in response to this effort.

47 Custer, MY LIFE ON THE PLAINS, pp. 317-343; Sheridan to Nichols, February 9, 1869, Sheridan Papers, Library of Congress; *Weekly Union*, December 26, 1868. Custer states in his book that he marched as far as Mulberry Creek while Sheridan reports that he proceeded to a point on the North Fork of the Red River. The truth has not been ascertained.

48. Jenness MS; Rister, *Border Command*, p. 143; Leckie, *Military Conquest*, pp. 112-113. Crawford seems to have been well-liked by the volunteers and there is no evidence that they resented his leaving the command.

49. Sheridan, *Memoirs*, Vol. II, pp. 344-347.

50. Custer to Sheridan, March 21, 1869, Sheridan Papers, Library of Congress (hereafter cited Custer's report); Hadley, "The Nineteenth Kansas Cavalry," *KSHS Transactions*, Vol. X, pp. 441-447; "Runyon's Letters," *Kansas Historical Quarterly*, Vol. IX, p. 73; Jenness MS; Custer, MY LIFE ON THE PLAINS, pp. 343-344; Communication of M. S., March 21, 1869, *Weekly Union*, April 10, 1869. Custer states in his report that eight hundred men remained with him, but other figures indicate a number somewhat higher than that.

51. Custer's report; Custer, MY LIFE ON THE PLAINS, pp. 346-349; Spotts, *Campaigning with Custer*, pp. 137-143.

52. The Indians had taken Miss White, eighteen years old, on August 13 from her parents' home near Lake Sibley. Her mother avoided capture by hiding in some bushes nearby. Her father, who was working in a field four miles away, was killed. Several children at the house and in the field were not taken. Topeka *Kansas State Record*, September 2, 1868; *Kansas Daily Tribune*, September 13, 1868.

53. Hadley, "The Nineteenth Kansas Cavalry," *KSHS Transactions*, Vol. X, pp. 447-451; Moore, "The Nineteenth Kansas Cavalry," *ibid.*, Vol. VI, pp. 44-45; Spotts, *Campaigning with Custer*, pp. 137-152; Custer, MY LIFE ON THE PLAINS, pp. 349-358; Custer's report.

54. Both Custer and Sheridan state in their books that Custer called on the Cheyennes to proceed to Camp Supply. This is probably an error. One receives the impression from contemporary sources that Fort Sill was the collection point. And one notices that although the Cheyennes eventually made their way to Camp Supply that they first went to Fort Sill.

George Bent subsequently identified the three prisoners retained by Custer as Curly Hair, Lean Face, and Fat Bear. Lean Face, according to him, was the Cheyenne called Dull Knife by the whites. George E. Hyde, LIFE OF GEORGE BENT: *Written from His Letters* (Norman, 1968), p. 326.

55. See the *Kansas Daily Tribune*, April 11, 1869; "Runyon's Letters," *Kansas Historical Quarterly*, Vol. IX, p. 74, note 29.

56. Custer's report; Custer, MY LIFE ON THE PLAINS, pp. 358-375; Moore, "The Nineteenth Kansas Cavalry," *KSHS Transactions*, Vol. VI, pp. 45-46; Hadley, "The Nineteenth Kansas Cavalry," *ibid.*, Vol. X, pp. 451-454; Spotts, *Campaigning with Custer*, pp. 154-161; Street to Martin, July 19, 1909, Nineteenth Kansas File, Manuscript Division, KSHS; Bent to Hyde, September [?], 1905, George Bent Letters, Library, State Historical Society of Colorado. Custer states in his book that those volunteer officers who had condemned him for his order not to attack the Cheyenne village on March 15 subsequently admitted to him afterwards that his had been the correct course. Most of the accounts left by members of the Nineteenth are generally friendly to Custer.

57. Street to Martin, July 19, 1909, Nineteenth Kansas File, Manuscript Division, KSHS; "Runyon's Letters," *Kansas Historical Quarterly*, Vol. IX, p. 74. According to Runyon, Custer was lavish in his praise of the volunteers, saying that they first wore the Seventh's horses out "and then the men."

58. Spotts, *Campaigning with Custer*, pp. 169-189; Bailey, "Medical History," 19th Kansas File, Manuscript Div., KSHS. Mrs. Morgan was met by her husband at Fort Dodge and Miss White was returned to her family from Fort Hays.

59. Crawford, *Kansas in the Sixties*, p. 330; Hadley, "The Nineteenth Kansas Cavalry," *KSHS Transactions*, Vol. X, p. 446, note 14; [Samuel J. Crawford], "The Nineteenth Kansas Volunteers," *ibid.*, Vol. X, pp. 657-659. The money used to pay the volunteers was replaced by an appropriation voted at the next session of Congress.

60. Spotts, *Campaigning with Custer*, pp. 182-189; "Runyon's Letters," *Kansas Historical Quarterly*, Vol. IX, p. 75.

61. Berthrong, *Southern Cheyennes*, pp. 338-339.

62. Leckie, *Military Conquest*, pp. 127-207; White, "The Cheyenne Barrier," *Arizona and the West*, Vol. IV, pp. 61-64; G. Derek West, Lowell H. Harrison, Lonnie J. White, and Ernest R. Archambeau, THE BATTLES OF ADOBE WALLS AND LYMAN'S WAGON TRAIN, 1874 (Panhandle-Plains Historical Society, Canyon, Texas: 1964).

INDIAN BATTLES IN THE TEXAS PANHANDLE, 1874

IN THE YEARS IMMEDIATELY FOLLOWING Sheridan's punitive winter campaign of 1868-1869, the Southern Cheyennes, the Southern Arapahoes, and the Kiowa-Apaches had remained relatively peaceful on their reservations in western Indian Territory. The Kiowas and Comanches, however, had continued raiding across the southern border of their reserve into Texas. Since President Grant's peace policy was in effect, the raiders encountered only a minimum of military resistance, causing them to believe that "the United States did not intend to fight them."[1]

By 1874 the Indian situation on the Southern Plains was deteriorating rapidly. Young warriors yearned to revenge the loss of relatives in raids on the Texas frontier. The Indians were annoyed by Kansas and Texas horse thieves who constantly raided their pony herds. Unhappy, among other things, with reservation life, many of them sought solace in the white man's liquor which they obtained from illegal whiskey peddlers. Their minds numbed by poisonous alcohol, they did little hunting, and consequently they and their families were forced to subsist on the scanty rations provided by the government. Warriors who hunted found to their great distress that the buffalo herds were being destroyed by white hunters who killed the mangy critters solely for their hides. The slaughter had started in 1871 after eastern tanners had discovered a means of turning buffalo hides into serviceable leather.

Not without reason, then, small parties of Kiowas, Comanches, and Cheyennes in May and June, 1874, took to the warpath to begin what would be the last major Indian uprising on the Southern Plains. The ensuing Indian war — known as the Red River Indian War — would produce some of the most sensational fights in western history. The most notable of the battles fought in the Texas Panhandle, the major battleground of the war, are described below.[2]

THE BATTLE OF ADOBE WALLS

During the spring of 1874, as the Kiowas, Comanches, and Southern Cheyennes were becoming increasingly unhappy with the white man's road and they were beginning to raid in both Texas and Kansas, a messiah, a young medicine man of the Kwahadi Comanches named Ishatai, emerged to give direction to their efforts. An astronomer,

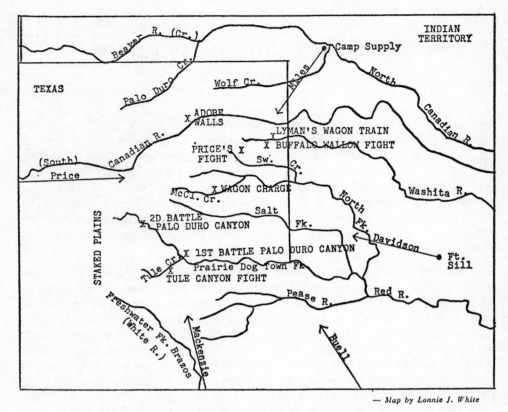

— *Map by Lonnie J. White*

APPROXIMATE SITES OF INDIAN BATTLES
IN THE TEXAS PANHANDLE, 1874

weather prophet, and magician, Ishatai's extraordinary powers had been
the subject of considerable talk among the Comanches for some time.

At his call, the Comanches late in May, 1874, assembled for a sun
dance, the first in their history, on the North Fork of the Red River.
Mexican whiskey flowed freely throughout the proceedings. A general
war council which met at the conclusion of the ceremonies was attended
by representatives of all the Southern Plains tribes. Presiding over the
council's deliberations was Quanah, a young Comanche war chief and
son of Cynthia Ann Parker, a white captive.[3] At his right sat Ishatai,
who called for war against the whites. Ishatai told his listeners that
he had been informed by the Great Spirit that if they would drive the
white man out of their country the buffalo would come back in great
herds and the Indians would be powerful and prosperous again. Ishatai
had been given the power to make a special paint, one that would repel
bullets. To prove that he had the blessings of the Great Spirit, he
pulled three arrows, one by one, seemingly out of the air.

Impressed by his performance, the Indian leaders, or at least some of them, accepted Ishatai as a medicine man endowed with special powers. All that had to be decided now was where to strike the first blow of their projected all-out war. The answer was provided by Quanah who suggested they attack the buffalo hunters at Adobe Walls on the main (or South) Canadian River in the Texas Panhandle.[4]

By 1874 most of the buffalo in western Kansas had been slaughtered, causing the hide hunters to seek new hunting grounds in the Texas Panhandle. As the hunters began drifting southward in the spring, some Dodge City merchants and hunters decided to establish a supply center near the ruins of an old trading post named Adobe Walls on the north bank of the Canadian River.[5] The new Adobe Walls consisted in late June, 1874, of A. C. Myers and Fred Leonard's store and corral, a well, a mess house, Thomas O'Keefe's blacksmith shop, James Hanrahan's saloon, and Charles Rath and Robert M. Wright's store. The buildings were of sod or sod-timber construction and were arranged in a rough north-south line.[6] Although many hunters collected at the post to await the arrival of the buffalo herds from the south, they did not undertake to fortify the buildings, preferring instead to play cards or swill whiskey in Hanrahan's saloon.

Presently, the herds appeared and the hunters, armed with their Sharps "Big 50"[7] buffalo guns, left Adobe Walls to begin the hunt. But they no sooner did so than parties of Indians began attacking isolated hunting camps, killing several men and mutilating their bodies and causing many of the hunters to return to the relative safety of Adobe Walls. When after a few days, however, no more raids were reported, the hunters began going out again.

At Adobe Walls on the evening of June 26, 1874, there were about twenty-eight men and one woman. Among the hunters, businessmen, and employees were: William (Billy) Dixon, William B. (Bat) Masterson, Billy Tyler, James W. McKinley, Ike and Shorty Shadler, Hanrahan, Leonard, Andrew Johnson, William (Old Man) Keeler, Billy Ogg, and Mr. and Mrs. William Olds, who operated a restaurant in the back of Rath and Wright's store. Word of the impending Indian attack had reached Camp Supply, Indian Territory, and it had by this time been conveyed to the merchants at Adobe Walls by a government scout named Amos Chapman. But this information had not been made known to the hunters and employees because the merchants were afraid that if they knew what was coming they would leave, and the post with all its valuable supplies would be left unprotected. Consequently, most of the men at Adobe Walls were unaware of any extraordinary danger as they bedded down for the night, several of them outside the buildings.

At about 2:00 o'clock in the morning of June 27, the men sleeping in the saloon were suddenly awakened by a loud, sharp noise that sounded like a gunshot. Believing that the ridgepole was breaking, several of the hunters threw some of the dirt off the roof and braced the pole with a prop. Hanrahan, the owner of the saloon, suggested that since they were up they might as well stay up. Any thought of dissent undoubtedly vanished when Hanrahan offered free drinks at the bar. There is evidence to indicate that the cracking noise was actually that of a gunshot fired by one of the merchants, perhaps Hanrahan, who wished to keep the hunters awake and ready for the Indian attack that he knew was coming.

Billy Dixon, a partner of Hanrahan's in the hide business, who had planned to leave for the buffalo herds in the morning anyway, decided that since he was up he might as well make an early start. While he rolled up his bedding and placed it in his wagon Billy Ogg, one of Hanrahan's employees, went out to drive in the horses from where they were grazing near East Adobe Walls Creek. Looking up, Dixon observed through the dim light of the "dusky dawn" the shadowly forms of riders coming towards the buildings. Then he saw them "suddenly spread out like a fan," give a war whoop, and dash forward. It was Indians, "hundreds" of them! Quickly tethering his saddle horse to the wagon, Dixon threw a shot in the direction of the charging Indians and scrambled into the saloon, closely followed by Ogg.

The defenders of Adobe Walls made their stand from the saloon and the two stores. Hastily barricading the doors and windows, the men knocked holes in the chinking between the logs and opened fire with their rifles. The Indians had expected to catch the inhabitants of Adobe Walls asleep and carry the place in one fell swoop, but thanks to the ridgepole incident the men were awake and the Indians' charge was repulsed.

After breaking off the charge, the Indians rode wildly around the buildings, pouring bullets and arrows into the walls and through the windows. Some of them beat on the doors with rifle butts, or caused their horses to kick on the doors, as others looted the wagons and drove off stock. Several times during the early fighting the Indians withdrew, rallied, and charged. Their movements were, however, directed by bugle calls, and in each instance the defenders knew what the Indians were going to do before they did it. After a while the warriors dismounted and took up positions behind corral pickets, overturned wagons, and hide-piles, whence they poured in a galling fire upon the whites.

The inhabitants of Adobe Walls suffered three casualties during the morning's fighting. The Shadler brothers had been caught in their wagons and killed in the initial assault. Later, Billy Tyler had been mortally wounded while he and Fred Leonard were outside seeking to protect the horses in Myers and Leonard's corral. Bat Masterson, who was in the saloon, braved death to come to his dying friend's side in

Myers and Leonard's store. And Old Man Keeler risked his life to fetch Tyler a drink of water from the well.

Mounted on a white horse and naked except for a coat of "bullet-proof" paint and a sage-stem cap, Ishatai watched the fight from a distant hill. It soon became apparent to him and his comrades that his "medicine" was not working. Three warriors were killed in the initial charge and Quanah, the Indians' leader, lost his horse in one of charges. The chief himself was temporarily incapacitated by a spent bullet or ricochet which numbed an arm and shoulder. In another instance the Indians' bugler, probably a Negro deserter from the Tenth Cavalry at Fort Sill, was killed while looting one of the wagons. And, as if these incidents were not enough to discredit Ishatai's medicine in the eyes of his companions, a stray bullet whizzed over the crest of a ridge where the Indian leaders were holding a council and killed the medicine man's horse whose body was covered with bullet-proof paint. The disgraced messiah himself allegedly advised his comrades to give up the fight, saying "No use fighting when heap gun shoot today and kill tomorrow."[8] Discouraged by the failure of Ishatai's medicine and the strong resistance by the whites, the warriors finally broke off the attack at about 4:00 o'clock in the afternoon.

On the ground around the buildings lay the bodies of eleven or more braves. The exact number of Indian losses is not known since the Indians removed many of their dead and wounded from the field. Nor is it known precisely how many warriors participated in the fight. The whites estimated the number as between two hundred and seven hundred or more. Although warriors from all five Southern Plains tribes participated in the battle, they were principally Cheyennes and Comanches. Among the Kiowas at Adobe Walls were the noted chiefs Satanta and Lone Wolf.[9]

For several days parties of Indians hung around the post at some distance, but none seemed interested in making another attack. On June 29, Billy Dixon, a crack shot, knocked an Indian off his pony while he and several comrades were casually watching the buildings at a reported 1,538 yards away. On July 1, William Olds, while on duty in a newly-built, sod-timber lookout tower, was killed by the accidental discharge of his rifle as he scrambled down the ladder to report a party of Indians nearby.

Borrowing a horse from some hunters who came in on the twenty-eighth, a volunteer named Henry Lease rode out to bring help from Dodge City.[10] During the next few days, as word of the engagement spread, numerous hunters drifted in to the safety of Adobe Walls. These men helped the survivors of the battle to dispose of the dead men and animals and to build fortifications. Before burying the slain Indians, the hunters severed their heads from their bodies and stuck them on the gateposts of the corral.

When relief did not come immediately and since they had no way of knowing whether Lease had got through the Indian lines, about twenty-five men took off for Dodge City. There they learned that Lease had arrived safely, but the merchants had been delayed in dispatching help by their decision to send wagons for the purpose of salvaging as much of their property as possible. It was not until the end of July that the relief expedition arrived at the post.

The fight at Adobe Walls was clearly a victory for the defenders. Armed with long-range buffalo guns and fighting from behind good cover, the whites were, as one Comanche participant declared, "too much for us."[11] The Indians' only success was in causing a temporary cessation of extensive buffalo hunting in 1874. Although the Indians had committed a number of hostile acts before the attack, the Battle of Adobe Walls was the first major action of the year, and as such, it, more than any other event, marks the beginning of the Red River Indian War of 1874-1875.[12]

The First Battle of the Palo Duro Canyon[13]

Despite the failure of their first great effort against the whites, the Indians remained on the warpath. By the end of July, large numbers of Cheyennes, Comanches, and Kiowas were raiding across the Texas, New Mexico, Kansas, and Colorado frontiers.[14] In one instance, on July 12, a large party of Kiowas under Lone Wolf attacked twenty-seven Texas Rangers in Lost Valley, Texas, near Jacksboro. The Kiowas kept the Rangers pinned down in a ravine for about one-half a day before they (the Indians) finally withdrew. The Rangers lost one man killed and three wounded, one mortally. The Indian casualties were estimated as three killed and three wounded.[15]

Clearly faced with a serious outbreak, the Army began preparations for the most extensive and comprehensive campaign ever undertaken on the Southern Plains. The architects of the operation were Lieutenant General Philip H. Sheridan, commander of the Division of the Missouri, and his ranking subordinates on the Southern Plains frontier, Brigadier General (Brevet Major General) John Pope, commander of the Department of the Missouri, and Brigadier General (Brevet Major General) Christopher C. Augur, commander of the Department of Texas. Their plans were for five columns to converge on the hostiles from all sides and force them to surrender. Colonel (Brevet Major General) Nelson A. Miles was to move from Fort Dodge, Kansas, to Camp Supply, Indian Territory, and thence southwest; Major (Brevet Colonel) William R. Price was to march eastward from Fort Union, New Mexico Territory; Colonel Ranald S. Mackenzie, a former brigadier general and brevet major general of volunteers, was to proceed north from Fort Concho, Texas; Lieutenant Colonel (Brevet Major General) John W.

(Black Jack) Davidson was to operate west from Fort Sill; and Lieutenant Colonel (Brevet Brigadier General) George P. Buell was to move northwest from Fort Griffin, Texas, and penetrate the region between Davidson and Mackenzie. Although the northern boundary of Indian Territory and the western line of Texas divided the Departments of the Missouri and Texas, departmental borders were not to be respected by commanders in the field during the campaign.

The Indians were given fair warning of the Army's intentions to move against them. Those professing to be friendly were directed to enroll at their agencies and answer roll call. If they did not do so, they would be treated as hostiles. Some of the Indians accepted the sanctuary of their agencies, but a large number of them chose to remain on the warpath. Apparently only a few, if any, of the Arapahoes and Kiowa-Apaches participated in the ensuing war.[16]

Of the five commands sent against the hostile Cheyennes, Comanches, and Kiowas, General Miles' saw the greatest amount of action. Organized at Fort Dodge early in August, it numbered seven hundred forty-four men and consisted of eight troops of the Sixth Cavalry divided into two battalions, four companies of the Fifth Infantry, a small artillery detachment, and a large body of Delaware and white scouts. En route to Camp Supply in about mid-August, Miles sent First Lieutenant Frank D. Baldwin, Fifth Infantry, with forty-nine soldiers and scouts to reconnoiter "along the line" of the Palo Duro tributary of the Beaver River southward to Adobe Walls.

Baldwin's force went into camp near Adobe Walls on the eighteenth. Twenty-two hunters were still living inside the buildings. As Baldwin and several men were riding toward the post on the morning of August 19 they heard Indian yells and looked up to see a large party of warriors pursuing five hunters, two on horses and three in a wagon, toward the buildings. One of the hunters was cut off, killed, and scalped. Riding to the rescue, Baldwin drove the Indians off. Returning to his camp for reinforcements, Baldwin learned that Second Lieutenant Austin Henely, Sixth Cavalry, with sixteen men had taken up the chase and followed the braves into the sand hills south of the Canadian. Baldwin and a number of Delaware scouts overtook Henely and together they pursued the Indians for twelve miles.

Though Baldwin thought it safe enough for the hunters, who were well-armed, to remain, they discreetly decided to accompany the lieutenant's party back to the main command. While moving down the Canadian on the twentieth, Baldwin's scouts killed one Indian and wounded another. Since the signs showed that many Indians had recently been in the vicinity, Baldwin in the evening sent two scouts, of whom one was Bat Masterson, on ahead with a message for Miles telling him what he had found.[17]

In the meantime, Miles had left Camp Supply on August 20, marching westward into the Texas Panhandle along Wolf Creek. Upon receiving Baldwin's message on August 23, Miles moved southward to the Canadian River where he was joined on the twenty-fourth by Lieutenant Baldwin's scouting party. Believing the Indians to be concentrated further south, Miles continued on to the Washita. In an effort either to halt or to slow his advance, the Indians burned off large portions of the prairie in his front.

Picking up an Indian trail below the Washita, Miles followed it to the Sweetwater Creek tributary of the North Fork of the Red River. There Miles discovered a large Indian village which had recently been abandoned by the Cheyennes. The Indians' trail from the village led the column southward and up the McClellan Creek tributary of the North Fork. Presently it grew wider and fresher.

On the afternoon of August 28, Miles left his supply wagons with two companies of infantry as a guard to follow as rapidly as possible and with the rest of the command pressed on ahead. That the Indians were fleeing in great haste was evident from the large amount of property and the many "broken down" ponies they were discarding on the trail. Crossing the Salt Fork of the Red River, Miles marched toward the Palo Duro Canyon, through which ran the Prairie Dog Town Fork (the main extension) of the Red River.

On the morning of August 30, as the command was entering a narrow defile at the head of Battle Creek and approaching a range of hills south of Mulberry Creek nearly midway between the Prairie Dog Town and Salt Forks, Lieutenant Baldwin's scouts, numbering thirty-nine whites and Delawares, who were in the lead, were "suddenly charged" by seventy-five or more Cheyennes who "came over" a hill "whooping, yelling and firing." Dismounting, the scouts "commenced pouring lead into the charging redskins, and in a few minutes they were charging back with greater rapidity than they [had] advanced.[18]

The Indians retreated two miles to "a line of high bluffs and crests" where an estimated five hundred well-armed warriors[19] were waiting to make a stand against the soldiers. While a number of skirmishers sniped away at the Indians at long range, Miles deployed the command for battle, placing the First Battalion of Sixth Cavalry under Major (Brevet Lieutenant Colonel) Charles E. Compton on the right, the Second Battalion under Major (Brevet Lieutenant Colonel) James Biddle with the scouts on the left, the artillery and a company of Fifth Infantry in the center, and Captain (Brevet Major) Wyllys Lyman's company of Fifth Infantry in reserve.

Covered by three light field guns and two or more Gatling guns,[20] the soldiers advanced to the attack against "positions which seemed almost impregnable." Unable to hold fast in the face of the hard-charging troops and their superior firepower, the Cheyennes were pushed from one crest to another. Conspicuous in a charge against "a hill covered with redskins" was Captain (Brevet Major) Adna R. Chaffee's company of Sixth Cavalry. Chaffee, who many years later would become Commanding General of the Army, led the attack shouting to his troopers, "If any man is killed, I will make him a corporal!"[21] In another notable instance, the First Battalion made a "splendid" dash "up a steep crest of 200 feet" and "carried" it "in fine order." The Cheyennes made their final stand on "a high bluff" on the north bank of the Prairie Dog Town Fork. The slope was unusually steep and rugged. Arranging his men in a double column, Captain (Brevet Major) Tullius C. Tupper, Sixth Cavalry, led them forward and upward in a mounted charge that routed the Indians from their positions.

Crossing the Prairie Dog Town Fork and finding the Indians gone, Miles halted his tired and worn command for a rest. The fight had lasted five hours and covered twelve miles. It would have been an exhausting battle under the best of circumstances, but as it was it was fought after several days of hard marching and "beneath a burning sun" in perhaps the hottest part of what had been an unusually dry summer. Although the soldiers clearly won the fight, the Cheyennes' stand bought their families enough time to burn their village in Tule Canyon and flee up Tule Creek, which emptied into the Prairie Dog Town Fork on the south.

The next day, August 31, Miles sent the scouts and part of the cavalry to follow the Indians' trail. Eighteen miles up Tule Canyon they found that the Cheyennes had climbed the rugged bluffs of the canyon walls and gone out onto the Staked Plains (Llano Estacado), heading in a southwestwardly direction. Although they had scattered over the prairie in small parties, they had come together again evidently a short distance away.

Soon after the arrival of his supply wagons, Miles with the entire expedition followed the trail for thirty miles. Several days were, however, consumed in doing so, inasmuch as the rough and broken terrain was "almost impassable" for the wagons. On September 5, Miles sent a message to General Pope at Fort Leavenworth, Kansas, the departmental headquarters, telling him that he had decided to discontinue the chase. His "transportation" was inadequate, he was running low on supplies, and he did not have water containers enough to follow the Indians through dry territory.

Miles reported his losses in the battle as one soldier and one Delaware scout wounded. The Indians' casualties he estimated at "not less than twenty-five killed and a much larger number wounded." Their loss in property was also considerable and would cause them much hardship during the remainder of the war. Presumably the Cheyennes Miles fought consisted of the entire number of those on the warpath.[22]

127

Either partly or entirely in recognition of their gallantry, Compton, Chaffee, Tupper, and Baldwin were subsequently breveted colonel, lieutenant colonel, lieutenant colonel, and captain, respectively.[23]

The Battle of Lyman's Wagon Train[24]

While Miles was on the Prairie Dog Town Fork, he placed a set of dispatches in the hands of Lieutenant Baldwin and three white scouts for them to take to Camp Supply. Baldwin's ultimate destination was Fort Leavenworth where he was to deliver verbal messages to General Pope. Leaving the camp and traveling all night, the little party made camp on the morning of September 7 in the valley of White Fish Creek, a tributary of the Salt Fork. Presently, Baldwin's picket observed the approach of more than twenty-six Indians. The scouts shot three of them off their ponies as they came near the camp.

Surrounded in a ravine and under a heavy fire from the hostiles, the men decided that their only chance "was to gain the open plain." Leading their horses up a high embankment, they mounted, drew their revolvers, and charged through the Indian encirclement. Soon, however, they found themselves surrounded again. Dismounting on a high bluff, they drove their foes back out of range of their Spencer repeating rifles. Then, mounting and drawing their pistols, they charged through the Indian lines for a second time. The Indians were, however, soon around them again, but once more the four men broke through the ring. Reaching the open plain after an eight-mile, three and one-half-hour running fight, the warriors gave up the chase. Fifteen Indians had followed the whites from the ravine; of these, eight were shot off their ponies, either killed or wounded.

At 4:00 p. m. the next day, September 8, Baldwin's party reached the high bluffs of the Washita. On the opposite side of the river was an Indian camp with pickets on lookout in the adjacent bluffs. About "one or two hundred" ponies grazed nearby. Although the pickets were "moving about as if they had discovered us," Baldwin decided not to turn back but to ride downstream as rapidly as possible. As they were moving down a ravine toward the river, the men suddenly came upon what Baldwin believed to be one of the Indians' sentinels. The surprised warrior, mounted on a mule, chose not to fight but to surrender, saying that he was a "good Comanche."

Leaving the Washita and riding northward, Baldwin at 12:30 a. m., September 9, stumbled onto Miles' supply train under Major Lyman in camp on the north bank of the Canadian River. Baldwin turned his prisoner over to Lyman and with five scouts rode on to Camp Supply, reaching there on the morning of September 10. One of his former party, Scout William F. Schmalsle, remained with Lyman. From Camp

→ *U. S. Signal Corps photograph, courtesy, The National Archives (Brady collection).*

GEN. NELSON A. MILES

→ *U. S. Signal Corps photograph, courtesy, The National Archives, Washington, D. C.*

COL. RANALD S. MACKENZIE

→ *U. S. Signal Corps photograph, courtesy, The National Archives, Washington, D. C.*

LONE WOLF
Kiowa Chief

QUANAH PARKER
Comanche Chief

→ *U. S. Signal Corps photograph, courtesy, The National Archives, Washington, D. C.*

129

→ *U. S. Signal Corps photograph, courtesy, The National Archives (Brady collection).*

MAJ. WYLLYS LYMAN

→ *U. S. Signal Corps photograph, courtesy, The National Archives, Washington, D. C.*

LIEUT. FRANK D. BALDWIN

→ *Courtesy, The Panhandle-Plains Historical Society, Canyon, Texas*

W. F. SCHMALSLE

U. S. Army Scout

→ *Courtesy, The Kansas State Historical Society, Topeka*

W. B. (BAT) MASTERSON

Scout, hunter, and lawman.

Supply Baldwin went on to Fort Leavenworth where he told the story of his recent ride through hostile Indian country to the *Leavenworth Daily Times*. "Nothing has occurred on the Plains for many years," the editor declared, "that would compare with this journey, considering the number of men engaged with no loss to his [Baldwin's] party."[25] Lieutenant Baldwin would see even more exciting action before the campaign was over.

The Indians Baldwin encountered on his ride were undoubtedly some of the Kiowas and Comanches who had recently fled westward from their agency — known as the Wichita agency — at Anadarko, Indian Territory, a short distance from Fort Sill. There on August 22 a fight broke out while General Davidson's Negro troopers of the Tenth Cavalry were attempting to disarm Red Food's band of Comanches. Kiowas under Lone Wolf, Satanta, Big Tree, and others joined the fray and they and the Comanches fled westward into the Texas Panhandle.

While they were encamped in the sand hills near the head of the Washita River, a young man named Tehan, an eighteen-year-old white captive who had evidently been taken in Texas many years before, rode out to look for some stray ponies. It was Tehan, the "good Comanche," whom Baldwin encountered and captured on September 8. When Tehan did not soon return to his village, a party of Kiowas undertook to track him down. Finding where he had been taken prisoner, the Indians followed his captors' trail. On the morning of September 9 they came upon Lyman's wagon train coming from the north. While two messengers galloped back to the village for reinforcements, the main party rode out to contest its advance.[26]

On September 1, while Miles was still in the vicinity of his fight with the Cheyennes, he sent his supply train, numbering thirty-six wagons with Company I, Fifth Infantry, and a detachment of the Sixth Cavalry under Major Lyman as escort, to the mouth of Oasis Creek on the Canadian. Miles expected it to be met there by a Mexican bull train bringing supplies from Camp Supply. Although Lyman sent Second Lieutenant Frank West, Sixth Cavalry, on ahead "to hasten" the arrival of the train, it was not at the rendezvous when Lyman reached it on September 5. Moving eastward to Commission Creek, Lyman was met on the seventh by West, the civilian train, and eight dismounted soldiers en route to join Miles. The supplies were transferred to the empty wagons "in the midst of a wild storm and rain." One of Lyman's teamsters was killed by a party of fifteen Indians while hunting near the wagon train camp.

As soon as they were loaded, Lyman started the wagons on the return journey to Miles' command, moving them in double column twenty yards apart, ready to be corralled in case of an Indian attack. The infantry, numbering thirty-nine men and officers, and fourteen dismounted cavalrymen, marched alongside the wagons. Lieutenant West with thirteen mounted troopers covered the train "as flankers." Driving the wagons were thirty-six civilian teamsters, ten of whom were armed. The total number of men counting Scout Schmalsle was one hundred four.[27]

At 8:00 in the morning of September 9, as the train was "crossing the divide between the Canadian and Washita Rivers," Major Lyman observed "single Indian vedettes . . . at a great distance on the flanks and in front." Halting, Lyman closed up the wagons and deployed his troops around the train as "skirmishers." Continuing the march, Lyman left the trail that he had made coming up and angled slightly leftward along the highest point of the terrain. The Indians did not ride immediately to the attack; instead, they hung back while a few of their number sniped at the wagons at long range.

Riding on ahead of the column, Lieutenant West with his mounted troopers cleared the Indians from a ridge. Coming to a waterhole, the command halted to water the mules and fill the canteens and water containers. Evidently the hostiles had by this time ceased firing. Soon, however, it was resumed by a handful of warriors who had taken positions in a collection of precipitous hills to the front. Since it was impossible to pass through the hills as long as they were held by the Indians, Lyman, at West's own suggestion, sent the cavalry to charge them. With "a cheer and a rush," West's troopers routed the warriors from their positions. Although "larger bodies" of Indians were milling around nearby, they made no effort to help their companions. Lyman attributed their confusion to his having left the trail and taken a new course. He had not known it at the time but apparently the Indians had planned to attack the train not far from where it had diverged to the left.

For twelve miles the wagons rolled on with its escort deployed and the nomads hanging about it at a distance. At about 2:30 o'clock in the afternoon, as the train emerged from a deep ravine about one mile north of the Washita and near the mouth of Gageby Creek, a small war party charged to within two hundred yards of West's cavalry. A rapid fire from the soldiers' rifles forced them to break off and retreat. The train no sooner "cleared" the ravine and started to form a corral than about seventy braves charged it from the rear and right side, riding to within one hundred yards of the defenders. For a few tense moments it appeared that the Indians might overrun the train. But thanks in large part to the splendid leadership of First Lieutenant Granville Lewis, Fifth Infantry, the effort failed. Lewis was shot through the left knee and Sergeant William DeArmond, Fifth Infantry, was killed during the assault. According to Lyman, Lewis' "skilful management" of the defense probably "decided the fate of the train."

Completing the corral, Lyman's men took up positions around the

132

train. West's troopers placed their horses inside the circle and joined the foot soldiers on the left of the corral. Lyman himself remained mounted, choosing to direct the defense on horseback. Dismounted Kiowas and Comanches poured in a heavy fire upon the train from several high ridges nearby. But fortunately for the whites, the reds "fired mostly too high." One bullet found its mark, however, in the stomach of the assistant wagonmaster, a civilian named Sandford, while he was carrying ammunition to the front of the corral.

Presently, part of the braves began circling "around our front" in what Lyman subsequently described as "a wonderful display of horsemanship." Sitting "erect on their ponies with shining spears and flaming blankets, and lofty fluttering head gear," they "dashed along the ridges with yells and defiant and insulting attitudes, appearing and swiftly disappearing, showing portentous against the sky in the bright sunlight." At sundown the Indians ceased to attack, and Lyman's men began digging rifle pits "close upon the wagons." Water was obtained from "a pool" about four hundred yards away.

The dawn of September 10 found the hostiles still around the train. Apparently they made no more major charges but were content to snipe at the whites from behind cover. Presumably concluding that his only hope was to obtain assistance, Lyman during the afternoon addressed a message to the commanding officer at Camp Supply telling him of his plight, and that evening gave it to a volunteer, Scout Schmalsle, to take through the Indian lines.[28] Leaving the encampment, the scout was immediately detected and pursued for some distance. His comrades would not know the outcome of the chase for several days.

The command's water having given out during the day, several soldiers and teamsters, against Lyman's orders sought, during the night, to obtain a supply from the waterhole. But the hostiles had done something that Plains Indians did not ordinarily do — they had dug rifle pits around the train.[29] And about thirty of them were in the vicinity of the pool. A volley of shots from the Indians in these pits sent all but one of the water-seekers scurrying back to the train. The exception was Tehan who had made his guard believe he was happy to be back with his race and had gone with the unauthorized party to get water. At the first opportunity he had left the group to return to his adopted people. During the night's action, Sergeant Frank Singleton, Sixth Cavalry, in one of the pits, was shot in the leg.

The siege continued on September 11 with the hostiles firing from concealment and small parties sometimes making dashes. One young Kiowa rode between the wagons and the soldiers' trenches four times without a scratch. After his fourth run, Satanta, one of the Indian leaders, embraced him declaring that "I could not have done it myself."[30] One soldier was wounded in the head during the day's fighting.

133

That night Indians sneaked up close to the soldiers' pits and shouted insults. One reminded the whites that they were surrounded by " 'heap Comanches and Kiowas.' " The "replies of my men," Lyman later declared, "were even superior in Doric strength."

On the morning of the twelfth, most of the Indians withdrew to the other side of the Washita and disappeared from view on the prairie beyond. With only a few "small parties" remaining around the train and the men and animals desperate for water, Lyman sent West with the mounted troopers and First Sergeant John Mitchell, Fifth Infantry, with fifteen infantrymen to clear the Indians from the vicinity of the waterhole. The hostiles fell back in the face of the soldiers' advance, and water was brought in from the pool. Soon afterwards a rainstorm came up, which drenched the men and turned the corral into one "great puddle."

All day long on September 13 small numbers of Indians moved "north and south along our front" out of rifle range. Late in the afternoon a large body of moving objects that looked through the mist like a column of troops was seen to the west. Lyman ordered several volleys of shots fired in an effort to attract its attention. A party of men sent out to investigate soon returned to report that it was Indians. With the siege lifted, Lyman considered trying to move out, but he decided against doing so because of "the storm," "the wounded," and the two dozen or so dead and injured animals. Food and forage was no problem since the wagons were filled with supplies for Miles.

In the meantime, Scout Schmalsle had reached Camp Supply at 8:30 a. m., on September 12, and delivered Lyman's message to the post commandant, Lieutenant Colonel William H. Lewis, Nineteenth Infantry. Gathering all the mounted personnel, scouts and cavalry, available, Lewis "started them" to Lyman's relief at noon. The party numbered fifty-one soldiers and scouts, seven quartermaster employees, a doctor, and Second Lieutenant Henry P. Kingsbury, Sixth Cavalry, who was in command.[31] Throughout the remainder of the day and the next, despite heavy rain and swollen streams, the relief force marched, until finally arriving at Lyman's wagon train at 2:30 a. m., September 14. At 9:00 o'clock that morning the train together with the rescue party moved out to join Miles. They found the advance of his column at the crossing of the Washita. Since he was in urgent need of supplies and he had received no word from the train, Miles had decided to come back and meet it. Finding the train, Miles pitched camp on the Washita.

Soon afterwards, Lyman wrote his official report of the fight. He estimated the number of Kiowas and Comanches around him as about four hundred. At least thirteen of these were killed or badly wounded. His own losses were one man killed and four wounded, one of them, the assistant wagonmaster, mortally. The Indians were armed with spears and the latest-type rifles and were led by Lone Wolf of the Kiowas.[32] Other notable Kiowa leaders whom Lyman evidently did not recognize were Satanta, Big Tree, Poor Buffalo, Maman-ti, To-hauson, and Big Bow.[33] Lyman named thirteen enlisted men who turned in outstanding performances. On the recommendation of General Miles, they were each awarded the Congressional Medal of Honor. Many years later, Major Lyman, Lieutenant Lewis, and Lieutenant West would be breveted lieutenant colonel, captain, and first lieutenant, respectively, either partly or entirely in recognition of their gallantry on the upper Washita.[34]

THE BATTLE OF BUFFALO WALLOW AND PRICE'S FIGHT ON THE PRAIRIE

While Lyman was still corralled on the Washita, another spectacular engagement was fought across the river a few miles to the southwest. On the night of September 10, a party of four soldiers — Sergeant Zachariah T. Woodall and Privates Peter Roth, John Harrington, and George W. Smith, Sixth Cavalry — and two scouts — Amos Chapman and Billy Dixon — had departed Miles' camp on McClellan Creek with dispatches for Camp Supply. Presumably the messages were concerned mainly with Miles' shortage of supplies. At sunrise, September 12, as the little group was riding to the top of a small knoll near the divide between the Washita River and Gageby Creek, it came "almost face to face" with about one hundred twenty-five Kiowas and Comanches under Satanta and perhaps others.[35] The Indians were part of those that had been around Lyman's wagon train and their meeting the dispatch-bearers was entirely accidental.

Fortunately for the surprised whites, the warriors chose initially not to charge but to circle them. Thus surrounded and badly outnumbered, the men dismounted to fight for their lives. During the first exchange of shots, Private Smith, who was holding the horses, was severely wounded. As he fell to the ground the excited animals broke away, leaving the men with no choice but to continue the fight on foot.

One by one during the morning's action the men were hit. Dixon, who was shot in the calf of his leg, and Roth were the least hurt of the wounded. Next to Smith the most seriously injured was Amos Chapman, whose left knee was shattered by a bullet. Having lived with the Indians and married an Indian woman, the hostiles knew Chapman well. And frequently they called out to him, "Amos, Amos, we got you now."[36]

Realizing that he and his companions could not survive much longer exposed as they were in the open, Dixon scanned the terrain for cover. A short distance way was a sandy, shallow buffalo wallow about ten feet in diameter! Dixon "ran for it at top speed" with bullets whizzing all around him. He was soon joined by Woodall, Roth, and

THE BATTLE OF BUFFALO WALLOW
*Drawing from Nelson A. Miles, PERSONAL RECOLLECTIONS . . .
(Chicago: 1896)*

— *Courtesy, The Kansas State Historical Society, Topeka*

Harrington. Between shots the four men threw up dirt around the edges of the depression.

Still in the open were Smith and Chapman. In response to his comrades' urgings that he join them, Chapman replied that his leg was broken. Amid a storm of bullets, Dixon ran to Chapman's side and carried him back to the wallow. No effort was made to bring Smith in since it was believed that he was dead.

Although the men had been greatly excited during the early hours of the fight, they were now, according to Dixon, "perfectly cool." Sitting upright in the wallow so as to conceal their "crippled condition" from the hostiles, the five men in the afternoon turned back one charge after another. Sometimes the reds "circled round us or dashed past, yelling and cutting all kinds of capers." Though the couriers evidently believed they killed twelve and wounded several Indians during the day's fighting, another contemporary, who received his information from Satanta, states that no Indians were killed.[37]

Without water — presumably their canteens had been on the saddles of the runaway horses — the men became "painfully thirsty." But at about 3:00 o'clock it commenced raining, filling the wallow with water. Although it was muddy and red with the blood of the wounded, the couriers evidently drank it as eagerly as if it were pure spring water.

136

The rainstorm was beneficial to the men in another way. Accompanying the rain was a strong, cold north wind. Withdrawing out of rifle range and collecting into small groups, the Indians sat still on their ponies "with their blankets drawn tightly around them." Although they had neither shelter nor coats, none of the whites, for obvious reasons, complained about the change in the weather.

Inasmuch as they were running low on ammunition, they decided that one of them should secure the six-shooter and cartridge belt belonging to their fallen companion, Smith. Roth, who volunteered for the mission, returned shortly with the news that Smith was not dead as they had thought. Together Roth and Dixon brought Smith to the wallow. Shot through the left lung and in great pain, Smith begged in vain for his friends to kill him. His suffering ended in the night, however, with his death.

The Indians disappeared at sundown, whereupon Roth and Dixon undertook to make the wallow as comfortable as possible. Tumble weeds were gathered and crushed and used as mattresses. It was decided that Roth should go to Camp Supply for assistance, but he returned two hours after he left because he could not find the Miles trail from Camp Supply.

The sun rose "clear and warm" the next morning without an Indian in sight. Dixon volunteered to go for help and had not gone a mile when he struck Miles' back trail. While he was walking along the road he spotted a large "outfit" two miles to the northwest. Soon recognizing it as a body of troops, Dixon fired his gun twice to attract its attention. The column turned out to be Colonel Price with four companies of the Eighth Cavalry from New Mexico.[38]

Price's column, consisting of two hundred sixteen troopers, eight Navajo and Mexican guides, one civilian blacksmith, thirty pack mules, two howitzers, and over forty government and civilian (Mexican) supply wagons, had left Fort Union, New Mexico, on August 24, marching southeastward toward Fort Bascom and the Canadian River. Near the White Sandy Creek tributary of the Canadian in the Texas Panhandle, Price sent First Lieutenant (Brevet Captain) Henry J. Farnsworth with the wagons and one company of cavalry on eastward toward the Antelope Hills of far western Indian Territory while Price with the main command followed a fresh Indian trail leading southeast. On September 6, Price found where Miles had pursued the Cheyennes southward toward the Palo Duro Canyon.

Picking up the trail of about forty hostiles who had been in Miles' old campsite near the Salt Fork, Price followed it southwestward. On the seventh, a Sixth Cavalry lieutenant rode up and informed Price that Miles was encamped a short distance away on Mulberry Creek. In conference with Miles, Price learned that he was "falling back . . . out of rations."

Although a heavy rain "swelled the dry aroyas [*sic*] to deep running streams," Price moved out the next day heading north presumably to find his train. Concluding that his couriers, whom he had sent to turn it southward, had "met with disaster," Price on September 12 took a northeasterly course toward the Antelope Hills, where he evidently expected to reunite with the train. At 12:00 o'clock noon, between Sweetwater Creek and the upper Washita, Price observed some one hundred fifty to one hundred seventy-five Indians riding westward across his front. Unknown to Price, these were part of the same Kiowas and Comanches that had been around Lyman's wagon train. The Indians had discontinued their siege of the train because of Price's presence in the vicinity, and they were moving their villages away from the area when this portion of them encountered Price.[39]

Both sides immediately prepared for a fight, the Indians taking positions "on the crest of a steep ridge" directly ahead and the troopers forming a skirmish line. Price had only one hundred ten men and a howitzer with which to make his attack since he had recently sent a twenty-one-man detail on General Miles' back-trail in case his wagons should come south from the Canadian. Forty or fifty warriors rode forward, as Price advanced, to harass his flanks and rear. Protecting the howitzer as it came up were twenty men under Second Lieutenant Ezra B. Fuller. The animals pulling it, however, were unable to keep up with the advance, and the Indians began "closing in" on it from adjacent ravines. Price himself led a platoon to its relief.

Although the Indians fought "very stubbornly" and bravely, often "exposing themselves by rapidly riding on every side of us and firing at short range," they were compelled to drop back to one point after another. After a running battle of about seven miles and nearly three hours, the warriors broke in the face of the hard-charging cavalrymen and "fled in every direction." Inasmuch as Price was out of provisions, he made no effort "to follow them further." His men "killed or badly wounded" eight warriors and captured a number of animals. His own loss was fourteen horses badly wounded, ten of them mortally.[40]

The next day, September 13, Price's command came upon Scout Dixon going for relief. Undoubtedly Price's appearance in the vicinity had frightened the Indians away from the buffalo wallow. Learning of the couriers' plight, Price sent his surgeon with a two-man escort to tend the wounded. As the rescue party approached, one of the men in the wallow, thinking it was Indians, opened fire, killing a trooper's horse. Hearing the shot, Dixon "ran forward" to stop his comrades from shooting at their rescuers.

Price gave the survivors some buffalo meat, which they ate raw, and sent a detail to Miles' column for an ambulance. In dire need of supplies, Price then moved on to look for his wagons on the Miles' back-trail. According to Dixon, Price refused not only to leave any men behind with the couriers, but also to furnish them with firearms. The messengers had expended most of their ammunition and their guns were of a different caliber than Price's.

At about 10:30 o'clock that evening, a rescue party with a surgeon arrived from Miles' command. The next day, Smith was buried in the wallow where he had died and the wounded were taken to Camp Supply. All of the injured survived though it was necessary to amputate Chapman's leg above the knee. On the recommendation of General Miles, each of the six soldiers and scouts were awarded the Congressional Medal of Honor. Several years later, however, the government took Chapman's and Dixon's medals away because as scouts, instead of soldiers, they were not by law entitled to them.[41]

Later on the same day as Price passed near the buffalo wallow and while he was "on the divide between the Washita and the Canadian," he heard the faint sound of several volleys of shots. His men replied to the noise by sounding a bugle. Observing three riders on a hill about two miles away, Price sent two soldiers to see who they were. The horsemen cantered away, however, as the men approached, causing Price to believe they had been Indians. Though Price "believed" that his and Miles' trains were "somewhere in the vicinity," Price chose not to leave the "road." Had he made a thorough search of the area he would have found Lyman's wagons a short distance to the southeast, for the shots he heard were those fired by the men from the train. One historian believes that Price "shied away" from what he thought was a large body of Indians because he did not want another fight with the odds in numbers so heavy against him.[42]

Price found part of his wagons on September 14 on the Canadian. His couriers had located the entire train on the ninth not far from Adobe Walls. Captain Farnsworth had then taken the government wagons with nearly all the supplies south to find Price, leaving the Mexican wagons to proceed eastward along the Canadian. But Farnsworth and Price had not made contact. Leaving the Mexican wagons, Price wandered about for several days before he finally found Farnsworth on the Canadian some ten miles west of the Antelope Hills. On September 17, Price's force was assigned to General Miles' command.[43]

With the country literally swarming with troops, their families hungry, and their ponies weak from overwork and a shortage of forage, many of the Kiowas and Comanches began to doubt the feasibility of continuing the war. Some of the Kiowas under Satanta, Big Tree, and Woman's Heart decided to turn themselves in at the Cheyenne agency in Indian Territory.[44] En route to do so late in September, they barely missed encountering Davidson's Fort Sill column, which was out looking for them. The rest of the fugitives went on to the Palo Duro

139

Canyon where they joined several small Cheyenne bands under Iron Shirt. Other Comanches and Cheyennes were at the time encamped on the Brazos River far to the south.[45]

The Second Battle of the Palo Duro Canyon

After pulling back to the Washita, Miles divided his command into four parts. One he sent back to Camp Supply with orders "to scout the region" to the north and protect the Kansas and Colorado frontiers. Two were stationed on the Canadian River and Sweetwater Creek in Texas. Miles himself remained with the fourth on the upper Washita. From the latter three camps, numerous small expeditions were sent westward to search for hostile Indians.[46]

Meanwhile, as noticed above, Davidson on September 10 had taken the field with the Fort Sill column. It consisted of six companies of Tenth Cavalry, three companies of Eleventh Infantry, a section of mountain howitzers, forty-four Indian scouts under First Lieutenant (Brevet Captain) Richard H. Pratt, Tenth Cavalry, and a number of white guides, among them Jack Stilwell. Proceeding westward "up the divide" between the North Fork of the Red River and the Washita, Davidson had his scouts sweep both sides of the rivers. His plans were to "catch" any Indians between him and Miles; if he found none he would proceed southward in an effort either to drive the hostiles down on Mackenzie and Buell who were coming up from the south or fight those Mackenzie and Buell might be driving northward.

Leaving the divide, Davidson scouted the "heads" of the North Fork and marched southward along the Caprock (the eastward facing escarpment of the Staked Plains) "to the breaks of Mulberry Creek" and the Prairie Dog Town Fork. Nothing was seen of either Mackenzie or Buell who were supposed to be somewhere in the vicinity. Running low on supplies, Davidson returned to near Fort Sill, arriving there on October 10. His entire march netted one "Kiowa Mexican" and a Cheyenne warrior captured. Not a single large Indian trail was found. The cost of the march, a hard one through "some of the most broken country" Davidson had even seen, was thirty-six horses and twenty-two mules.[47]

The effect of Davidson's, Miles', and Price's operations was to drive the hostiles down upon the Texas columns of Buell and Mackenzie. From Fort Concho, Texas, Colonel Mackenzie's column marched northward to the Freshwater Fork of the Brazos River. There, with supplies from Fort Griffin to the east, the command established its supply base. Mackenzie and General Augur at Fort Griffin completed their plans for the expedition.

Mackenzie's command, known as the "Southern Column," consisted of eight companies of the Fourth Cavalry divided into two battalions, four companies of Tenth Infantry, one company of Eleventh Infantry, three surgeons, a large party of Seminole-Negro, Tonkawa, Lipan, and white scouts, and the supply train. Leaving three companies of infantry to guard the supply depot, the rest of the command on September 20 climbed the Caprock and moved northward in the general direction of several Indian trails recently discovered by the Seminole-Negro scouts near the Pease River. During the afternoon some of the scouts had a brush with a party of Comanches. But neither a force of scouts under First Lieutenant George E. Albee, Twenty-fourth Infantry, which went in immediate pursuit, nor the First Battalion under Captain (Brevet Brigadier General) N. B. McLaughlin, which was sent after them the next day, were able to overtake them.

From the afternoon of the twentieth until the twenty-fourth, the expedition marched northward just below the escarpment of the Staked Plains, crossing the South and Middle Pease Rivers and the headstreams of the North Pease. Heavy rains impeded its movement; on one occasion the wagons became completely mired in the mud.

Leaving his wagons and the infantry under First Lieutenant Henry W. Lawton, Fourth Cavalry, Mackenzie with the cavalry, numbering four hundred seventy-one enlisted men and officers, on the twenty-fifth marched "above" the Caprock northwest to Tule Canyon. In the evening the scouts under First Lieutenant William A. Thompson came in to report that they had seen numerous Indian trails, the largest of which had been made by some 1,500 ponies going east. Mackenzie with Captain (Brevet Lieutenant Colonel) Eugene B. Beaumont's Second Battalion followed the big trail for several miles without seeing any Indians. The two cavalry battalions were reunited late the next day, September 26, a short distance south of a series of ravines known as Boehm's Canyon. Some of his scouts reporting that the Indians were gathering around him and fearing that they might try to stampede the stock, Mackenzie ordered the horses tied securely and posted, in addition to placing a heavy guard, with a number of large "sleeping parties," around them.

Mackenzie's security measures were well taken, for at about 10:30 p. m. some two hundred fifty braves, presumably Kiowas and Comanches, charged the camp in an effort to stampede the herd. Their initial attack failing, owing to the strong resistance of the troopers, the Indians for about thirty minutes circled noisily around the bivouac. Then, dropping back, they began an intermittent fire apparently at long range. It was a still, "moonlight night," and the voices of the officers directing the defense could be heard plainly for nearly a mile. Unaware of the fight, the wagon train rattled in at about midnight, surprisingly enough, unmolested.

At about 1:30 a. m. the Indians withdrew. But at daybreak they reappeared in larger numbers, firing from a ravine. Forthwith Mackenzie ordered the men to saddle-up in preparation for a counter-attack. As the troopers bore down upon them, the hostiles took to their ponies and retreated to the prairie, where they "disappeared as completely as if the ground had swallowed them." The Battle of Tule Canyon cost the Indians at least one killed and several ponies captured and wounded. The soldiers lost three horses injured.

That afternoon, Mackenzie with seven companies of cavalry proceeded southwestward and northward around the head of Tule Canyon and at sundown headed in a northwesterly direction toward the Palo Duro. The command reached the rim of the chasm near where Blanca Cita Canyon joined the Prairie Dog Town Fork just as day was breaking in the east. Several hundred feet below, sprawled out for two or three miles, stood the tipis of the Kiowas, Comanches, and Cheyennes under Maman-ti, O-ha-ma-tai, and Iron Shirt.

Hoping to strike the hostiles a severe blow, Mackenzie decided to descend into the canyon. His was not an easy decision since the only trail he could find leading down was narrow, steep, and rugged, and he had no way of knowing what preparations, if any, the hostiles had made to defend it. And once in the canyon, it would not be easy, if the Indians repulsed his attack, to fight his way out. The First Battalion under Captain McLaughlin remained on guard at the head of the path while Mackenzie with the troopers of the Second Battalion and Thompson's scouts stumbled and slid downward single-file, leading the horses.

The men were still on the path when an Indian lookout on a nearby bluff spotted them and let go a war whoop and waved a red blanket as a warning to the villagers. Those who did not hear or see his signal must have heard the shot that killed him. But the Indians were not ready for a fight, and the troopers poured unmolested onto the canyon floor. Reaching the bottom first, Thompson's scouts and Troops A and E under Beaumont, mounted and charged up the valley through the village. As soon as they could get down and form in line, Troops H and L, with Mackenzie in the lead, also charged. Chaos reigned in the camp as the Indians ran for their ponies and fled upstream or sought cover in the rocks, brush, and crevices along the canyon walls. Some of the braves tried to save the pony-herd, but after a four-mile chase they gave it up. Beaumont's men rounded up the scattered animals and drove them back down the valley.

Downstream Mackenzie had halted Troops H and L to await the return of Troops A and E. From the bluffs along the canyon walls, a number of warriors opened an enfilading fire upon them. One soldier, a bugler, fell from his horse seriously wounded. Evidently believing the command's only salvation was to clear the Indians from the bluffs, Captain Sebastian Gunther, commander of H Troop, ordered a detachment of dismounted men to charge them. But before they could do so, Mackenzie countermanded the order, declaring "Not one of them

142

would live to reach the top." Fearing that he and his companions might become trapped in the chasm, one trooper wondered aloud, "How will we ever get out of here"? Overhearing his remark, Mackenzie confidently assured him that "I brought you in, I will take you out."[48]

Observing "a movement among the Indians on the top of the bluff" and surmising that they "were going to try to block" the canyon entrance, Mackenzie sent two companies to the bottom of the trail and one to the top to prevent their doing so. But the troopers who climbed to the head of the path did not see a single Indian.

McLaughlin's battalion having descended the canyon to join the fray, Mackenzie sent part of it as dismounted skirmishers against some Indians who were moving toward a pile of boulders near the command. While McLaughlin's men drove them away, other troopers burned the Indian lodges, numbering about two hundred, together with their supplies and equipment.

Ascending the canyon, the command formed a square around the captured pony-herd and proceeded to the wagon train at the head of Tule Canyon. The next day, September 29, Mackenzie decided to destroy the Indian animals numbering 1,274 horses and 150 mules, except for 376 of the best quality, which he gave to the scouts as spoils for perilous service. Their disposal by infantry firing squads under Lieutenant Lawton took several hours. The bones of these animals would be a landmark in northwestern Texas for decades.

The Indians' casualties in the fight were at least four killed and a number wounded. Mackenzie's losses were one man wounded and thirteen horses killed or wounded. Though relatively little blood was spilled, the Second Battle of the Palo Duro Canyon was one of the most significant of the war. The Indians' loss in animals and the destruction of their village and supplies, with winter coming on, was a blow from which they could not easily recover. And there was no place for them to go where they would be safe from the bluecoats who were scouring the countryside in every direction. Thoroughly demoralized, many of them made their way back to the reservation and surrendered. Mackenzie would look for those who did not go in as well as other hostiles, with relatively minor success, in the vicinity of Prairie Dog Town Fork and on the streams to the south throughout the remainder of the fall and part of the winter.[49]

Operating east of Mackenzie, Buell's column, numbering two hundred forty-three soldiers and scouts, on October 9, attacked a small party of hostiles on the Salt Fork in Indian Territory, killing one and destroying their camp. Pursuing the reds up-river into Texas, he destroyed three abandoned Kiowa and Cheyenne villages totaling four hundred ninety lodges. With Buell in close pursuit, the Kiowas and Cheyennes, upon reaching the foot of the Caprock, turned northward. North of the

Canadian, the Indians were turned back by troops under Colonel Compton of Miles' command who were scouting between the Canadian and the Palo Duro tributary of the Beaver River. Separating, the Cheyennes fled southwestward while the Kiowas went southeastward to their agency. Although Buell was in a good position to continue the chase, he was forced, owing to a shortage of supplies, to send the bulk of his command into Fort Sill.[50]

THE WAGON TRAIN CHARGE ON McCLELLAN CREEK

Upon learning from Colonel Compton that he had driven the Cheyennes back to the plains south of the Canadian, Miles decided to place a force west of them for the purpose of driving them northeastward toward the upper Washita where they would be met by Colonel Price with three companies of the Eighth Cavalry and one company of the Fifth Infantry.

Miles himself with Compton's command, composed of three companies of Sixth Cavalry, two of Fifth Infantry, Lieutenant Baldwin's scouts, one howitzer, and the supply train, left the Canadian near Adobe Walls on October 24. Divided into three separate detachments, the command combed the countryside as it moved southwestward. Some of the Indians fled south of the Prairie Dog Town Fork but a large portion of them went eastward. After pursuing the Indians for about thirty miles beyond the Palo Duro Canyon, Miles turned his forces northeastward.[51] Baldwin commanded the right, Miles the center, and presumably, Compton the left of Miles' sweep toward Price.

Also in a position to catch the Indians fleeing before Miles was Davidson's column which had started from Fort Sill on October 21 on its second expedition of the campaign. On the twenty-fourth, a detachment of this command received the surrender of a large body of Comanches under Red Food, Tabananica, and others in Indian Territory near the Elk Creek tributary of the North Fork.[52] Since Miles' pincers movement was just getting under way at the time it undoubtedly had nothing to do with the decision of these Indians to surrender. Davidson's troops would, however, soon play a role in heading off the Indians fleeing before Miles.

Early in the afternoon of November 6, twenty-eight troopers under Captain Farnsworth, while scouting out of Price's camp on the Washita, were ambushed by about one hundred Cheyenne warriors on McClellan Creek. Taking cover in a hollow, the soldiers fought them off until sundown and then retreated under cover of darkness. Some seven Indians were killed and ten or more wounded. Farnsworth lost one man and six horses killed and four men wounded.[53] Learning of the fight, Price borrowed two troops of Tenth Cavalry from Davidson, who was bivouacked nearby, and with them and two companies of his own command started in pursuit. Near McClellan Creek on November 8 Price heard "the sound of small arms," but "for some reason" never "satisfactorily explained" to General Miles, Price moved away from it.[54]

The shooting Price heard was Baldwin's detachment in a fight with some two hundred Cheyenne warriors. Baldwin, as noticed above, had been on the right of Miles' sweep across hostile Indian country. Under his command were First Lieutenant Gilbert E. Overton's troop of Sixth Cavalry, Second Lieutenant Hobart K. Bailey's company of Fifth Infantry, a party of scouts, the howitzer, and the supply train, consisting of twenty-three wagons. Low on provisions, Miles had on November 4 ordered Baldwin to "convoy the train to the supply camp on the Washita River." If, however, he found "any considerable body of Indians," he was to "communicate with me [Miles], and attack or pursue *as you* [Baldwin] *may deem expedient.*"[55]

Leaving Miles' camp on the Prairie Dog Town Fork near the Caprock, Baldwin marched northeastward. On the evening of November 7, the little command bivouacked in a cottonwood grove on McClellan Creek. The next morning just as it was preparing to pull out, Scout Schmalsle rode in "at break-neck speed" to report that the scouts had discovered a large encampment of Cheyennes just over the divide on the north branch of McClellan Creek. They had recognized the chief's tipi as that belonging to Grey Beard.

Although the village numbered one hundred ten lodges and contained between four hundred and five hundred Indians, Baldwin decided to attack it. The element of surprise would be his and, besides, Miles was only about eight miles to the northwest in case anything went wrong. After sending Schmalsle to find Miles, Baldwin formed the train into a double column, put the infantry in the wagons, and deployed the cavalry as skirmishers. The train advanced with the two lead teams abreast of the line of cavalry, and the howitzer placed in the center of the formation.

Riding a few yards ahead of his command, Baldwin at 8:30 a. m. led it toward the village. Reaching the crest of the divide, which had separated the Indians from view, the trumpeter sounded the charge, and the men and wagons "rushed down the slope" into the camp "like a hurricane." Although the Indians were caught napping, the warriors evidently delayed the soldiers long enough for the women and children to make off on their ponies.

Retreating from the village, the braves fled westward not far behind their families. Twice they stopped to make a stand, but both times they were routed from their positions. Coming to the open plain after a twelve-mile, four-hour running engagement, the Cheyennes scattered. Because "both men and animals" were completely exhausted, Baldwin discontinued the pursuit. A troop of cavalry sent to Baldwin's relief by General Miles showed up too late to participate in the fight.

Back in the abandoned village the soldiers found two little white girl captives named Adelaide and Julia German, ages five and seven years, respectively. They with two older sisters, Catherine and Sophia, had been taken in September, 1874, by a small party of Cheyennes in western Kansas. The German family, consisting of the parents and seven children, had been traveling by wagon to Colorado over the old Smoky Hill road to Denver when they had been discovered by the Indians. After murdering the parents and three brothers and sisters, the Cheyennes had fled south, taking the remaining sisters with them. The four girls had been in Grey Beard's village at the time of Baldwin's attack, but the oldest two had been spirited away by the squaws. Adelaide and Julia were found ragged, cold, dirty, hungry, and frightened. "Be you'ns soldiers?" one of them asked her rescuers. Assured that they were, she replied: "We're so glad, we heard sisters praying all the time, that God would send the soldiers to deliver them." Both Catherine and Sophia had been forced to live with their male captors, and one of them at the time of their recovery several months later was allegedly pregnant. The four sisters were eventually reunited and raised in Kansas by Mr. and Mrs. Patrie Corney.[56]

Baldwin struck Grey Beard's Cheyennes a hard blow. An estimated twenty Indians were killed and a number wounded. Four were found dead on the field. Besides recovering the two little German girls, Baldwin captured and presumably burned the Cheyenne village. His victory did not cost him a single man.[57] For their gallantry in the engagement Baldwin would be awarded the Congressional Medal of Honor and Lieutenants Overton and Bailey would be breveted captain and first lieutenant, respectively.[58]

Because Miles' stock was "so thoroughly exhausted" by his recent operations, his command made no effort to follow the fleeing Cheyennes. Instead, he gave what information he had to Davidson, whose troops arrived upon the scene soon after Baldwin's fight, and Davidson sent his "effective force of 160 picked men and horses" under Captain Charles D. Viele, Tenth Cavalry, in pursuit. Viele followed the Indians ninety-one miles northwest to the Canadian, skirmishing with their rear-guards and pushing "them so close that they abandoned a portion of their stock and pack mules." On the Canadian, the Indians separated into two portions, one going west and the other southwest and Viele, his animals exhausted from the arduous chase, turned back to rejoin Davidson.[59]

By about mid-November most of the fight was out of the Indians. Although the campaign lasted throughout the ensuing winter, there were few encounters.[60] Day and night, however, the Indians remaining out were kept on the run. Hungry, shelterless, demoralized, and discouraged, they straggled into their agencies in large and small parties. Early in June, 1875, the Kwahadi Comanches, the last of the holdouts, surrendered their arms at Fort Sill. Collecting together the ringleaders of the uprising, the government sent them to Fort Marion, Florida, where they were imprisoned for about three years.[61] Thus ended the red man's last stand on the Southern Plains frontier.

NOTES

1. Ernest Wallace, RANALD S. MACKENZIE ON THE TEXAS FRONTIER (Lubbock, Texas: 1964), p. 119.
2. Carl Coke Rister, BORDER COMMAND: *General Phil Sheridan in the West* (Norman: 1944), pp. 154-159, 171-193; William H. Leckie, THE MILITARY CONQUEST OF THE SOUTHERN PLAINS (Norman: 1963), pp. 114-190; Donald J. Berthrong, THE SOUTHERN CHEYENNES (Norman: 1963), pp. 345-385.
3. Carl Coke Rister, BORDER CAPTIVES: *The Traffic in Prisoners by Southern Plains Indians, 1835-1875* (Norman: 1940), pp. 68-84; Zoe A. Tilghman, QUANAH: *The Eagle of the Comanches* (Oklahoma City: 1938), pp. 79-84.
4. Rupert N. Richardson, "The Comanche Indians and the Fight at Adobe Walls," *Panhandle-Plains Historical Review*, Vol. IV (1931), pp. 24-34; Rupert N. Richardson, THE COMANCHE BARRIER TO SOUTH PLAINS SETTLEMENT (Glendale: 1933), pp. 380-383. (*Panhandle-Plains Historical Review* hereafter cited P-PHR.) The Indians had planned to attack their enemies, the Tonkawas, who had often scouted for the army, but they decided not to do so because the Tonkawas lived "dangerously near" Fort Griffin, Texas, and they may have learned that their intentions had been revealed to the post commandant.
5. The old trading post had been established by Charles and William Bent and Ceran St. Vrain probably in 1842. It had been the site of a vigorous battle between Plains Indians and troops under Colonel Kit Carson in 1864. Lowell H. Harrison, "The Two Battles of Adobe Walls," *Texas Military History*, Vol. V (Spring, 1965), pp. 1-6.
6. Andrew Johnson to the *Star*, August 4, 1911, *Kansas City Star*, August 6, 1911; Robert M. Wright, DODGE CITY, *The Cowboy Capital and the Great Southwest* (n.p., n.d.), pp. 197-203; Lonnie J. White, "New Sources Relating to the Battle of Adobe Walls, 1874," *Texas Military History*, Vol. VIII (Spring, 1970), pp. 5-7.
7. "Big 50" meant any rifle of .50 caliber. But the Sharps .50 caliber was the most commonly used in buffalo hunting.
8. Clipping from *Kansas City Star*, May 10, 1913, in "Indian Depredations and Battles," Vol. I, pp. 237-238, Library, Kansas State Historical Society, Topeka.
9. W. S. Nye, CARBINE AND LANCE: *The Story of Old Fort Sill* (Norman: 1962), pp. 190-191.
10. The message he carried was presumably that from Leonard to Myers, July 1, 1874, first printed in the *Dodge City Messenger* and reprinted in the *Kansas State Record*, Topeka, July 15, 1874. It was recently published in Lonnie J. White (ed.), "Kansas Newspaper Items Relating to the Red River War of 1874-1875," P-PHR, Vol. XXXVI (1963), pp. 72-73. There is evidence to indicate that two couriers were sent. One finds it impossible to reconcile the facts that Lease and his partner, if he had one, are are supposed to have left Adobe Walls on June 28 and the message printed in the newspaper is dated July 1.
11. Nye, *Carbine and Lance*, p. 191.
12. Olive K. Dixon, LIFE OF "BILLY" DIXON; *Plainsman, Scout and Pioneer* (Dallas, Texas: 1927), pp. 155-198; George B. Grinnell, THE FIGHTING CHEYENNES (Norman: 1958), pp. 319-324; Wilbur S. Nye, BAD MEDICINE AND GOOD; *Tales of the Kiowas* (Norman: 1962), pp. 178-183; Lowell H. Harrison, "Damage Suits for Indian Depredations in the Adobe Walls Area, 1874," P-PHR, Vol. XXXVI, pp. 37-60; "J. W. McKinley's Narrative," *ibid.*, Vol. XXXVI, pp. 61-64; G. Derek West, "The Battle of Adobe Walls (1874)," *ibid.*, Vol. XXXVI, pp. 1-36; Richardson, "The Fight at Adobe Walls," *ibid.*, Vol. IV, pp. 35-38; *Kansas Daily Tribune* (Lawrence), August 9, 1874. For the best detailed secondary account of the Adobe Walls fight extant, see Dr. West's article, cited above. Dr. West's and other articles published in Vol. XXXVI of the P-PHR are reprinted in THE BATTLE OF ADOBE WALLS AND LYMAN'S WAGON TRAIN (Canyon, Texas: 1964). The Indians called the campaign of 1874 the "Wrinkled-Hand Chase" because their hands "were so wrinkled from the constant immersion in rain water." Nye, *Carbine and Lance*, p. 221.
13. This fight is also known as the Battle of Red River.
14. Leckie, *Military Conquest*, pp. 194-196; Ernest Wallace and E. Adamson Hoebel, THE COMANCHES; *Lords of the South Plains* (Norman: 1952), p. 326.
15. Nye, *Carbine and Lance*, pp. 194-200; Leckie, *Military Conquest*, pp. 196-198; Walter P. Webb, THE TEXAS RANGERS; *A Century of Frontier Defense* (Austin: 1965), pp. 312-313.

16. Sheridan to Pope, July 22, 1874, Sheridan Papers, Library of Congress; Rister, *Border Command*, pp. 192-195; Sheridan's Annual Report, October 1, 1874, Annual Report of the Secretary of War, *House Executive Document* No. 1, 42 Cong., 2 Sess., Part II, p. 27; Annual Report of the Commissioner of Indian Affairs for 1874, *House Executive Document* No. 1, 43 Cong., 2 Sess., p. 541.
17. Excerpt copies from Baldwin's diary, George W. Baird Papers, microfilm, Manuscript Division, Kansas State Historical Society; *Junction City* (Kansas) *Weekly Union*, September 26, 1874; Miles to AAG, Department of the Missouri, August 25, 1874, March 4, 1875, Joe F. Taylor (ed.) THE INDIAN CAMPAIGN ON THE STAKED PLAINS, 1874-1875 (Canyon, Texas: 1962), pp. 18-19, 197-198. Taylor's *Indian Campaign* contains the military correspondence in File 2815-1874, Adjutant General's Office, War Department, National Archives.
18. Communication of correspondent, September 4, 1874, *Wichita City Eagle* (Kansas), September 24, 1874. The head Delaware scout was Fall Leaf. Fall Leaf's Delawares had served the army before. See Berthrong, *Southern Cheyennes*, pp. 138-139, 209, 272.
19. Miles to Pope, August 31, 1874, *Leavenworth Daily Times*, September 9, 1874.
20. *Wichita City Eagle*, September 24, 1874; Pope's Annual Report, September 7, 1874, Annual Report of the Secretary of War, *House Executive Document* No. 1, 43 Cong., 2 Sess., Part II, p. 30.
21. Rister, *Border Command*, p. 194; Taylor (ed.), *Indian Campaign*, p. 22, n. 9.
22. Miles to AAG, Department of the Missouri, September 1, 1874, March 4, 1875, Pope to AAG, Military Division of the Missouri, September 11, 1874, Miles to Pope, September 5, 1874, Sheridan to Sherman, September 9, 1874, Taylor (ed.), *Indian Campaign*, pp. 21-28, 197-199; Communication of correspondent, September 1, 1874, *Leavenworth Daily Commercial*, September 10, 1874; *Wichita City Eagle*, September 24, 1874; Miles to Pope, August 31, 1874, *Daily Times*, September 9, 1874; Nelson A. Miles, PERSONAL RECOLLECTIONS AND OBSERVATIONS (Chicago: 1896), pp. 164-168; "McKinley's Narrative," P-PHR, Vol. XXXVI, p. 66; Pope's Annual Report, September 7, 1874, Annual Report of the Secretary of War, *House Executive Document* No. 1, 43 Cong., 2 Sess., Part II, pp. 29-31.
23. Francis B. Heitman, HISTORICAL REGISTER AND DICTIONARY OF THE UNITED STATES ARMY, *from Its Organization, September 29, 1789, to March 2, 1903* (Two vols.; Washington, D. C., 1903), Vol. I, pp. 185-186, 292, 319, 973; Lonnie J. White, "The First Battle of the Palo Duro Canyon," *Texas Military History*, Vol. VI (Fall, 1967), pp. 222-235.
24. This engagement is also known as the Battle of the Upper Washita. The "upper" Washita was known also as the Dry Fork of the Washita.
25. *Daily Times*, September 16, 1874; Baldwin to Baird, September 10, 1874, Taylor (ed.), *Indian Campaign*, pp. 28-31. G. D. West, "Baldwin's Ride and the Battle of Lyman's Wagon Train," *English Westerners' Special Publication No. 1* (London: 1964), pp. 3-10. There are some irreconcilable discrepancies between the newspaper account and Baldwin's official report. The *Daily Times* stated that Baldwin's party on September 8 crossed the Washita "clinging to the tails of their horses" and rode through the Indian camp.
26. Nye, *Carbine and Lance*, pp. 206-215; *Daily Times*, August 30, 1874.
27. Lieutenant Colonel William H. Lewis, the commandant of Camp Supply, understood unofficially that Lyman's command consisted of thirty-eight infantry, twenty-one cavalry, and thirty-six teamsters. Lewis to AAG, Department of the Missouri, September 12, 1874, Taylor (ed.), *Indian Campaign*, pp. 32-33. Presumably, however, these figures do not include the eight men (seven troopers and one infantryman) who met Lyman on Commission Creek, since Lyman himself states that his military force, not counting those who "joined me going to the front," consisted of thirty-eight infantry rifles and West with twenty troopers. Lyman to Baird, September 25, 1874, in Ernest R. Archambeau (ed.), "The Battle of Lyman's Wagon Train," P-PHR, XXXVI, p. 93. My own figures do not include the captured white boy, Tehan.
28. See Lyman to C. O., Camp Supply, September 10, 1874, Taylor (ed.), *Indian Campaign*, pp. 31-32.
29. See communication of correspondent, September 19, 1874, *Daily Commercial*, September 30, 1874.
30. Nye, BAD MEDICINE AND GOOD, pp. 192-194; Nye, *Carbine and Lance*, pp. 217-218.
31. Lewis to AAG, Department of the Missouri, September 12, 1874, Taylor (ed.), *Indian Campaign*, pp. 32-33.
32. Lyman to Baird, September 25, 1874, Archambeau (ed.), "The Battle of Lyman's Wagon Train," P-PHR, XXXVI, pp. 93-101; "McKinley's Narrative," *ibid.*, Vol. XXXVI, pp. 66-69; Miles, *Personal Recollections*, pp. 172-173.
33. Miles to Pope, September 14, 1874, Taylor (ed.), *Indian Campaign*, pp. 34-35; Nye *Carbine and Lance*, p. 218; Nye, *Bad Medicine and Good*, p. 190.
34. Miles to AG, U. S. Army, March 21, 1875, Taylor (ed.), *Indian Campaign*, pp. 196-197, 224-229; Heitman, *Historical Register and Dictionary*, Vol. I, pp. 630, 648, 1,020.

35. George Bent to George Hyde, February 28, 1906, George Bent Letters, Coe Collection, Yale University Library, microfilm, Kansas State Historical Society. Bent, an interpreter at the Darlington (Cheyenne and Arapaho) agency, who received his information from Satanta shortly after the fight, states that only a "few Kiowas" participated in the fight.

    Although Sergeant Woodall and Private Roth's names are spelled "Woodhall" and "Rath" in some sources, the correct spellings apparently are "Woodall" and "Roth." See note signed by T. H. Stafford, Taylor (ed.), *Indian Campaign*, pp. 44-45; [Department of the Army], *The Medal of Honor of the United States Army* (Washington: 1948), p. 222.
36. C. E. Campbell, "Down Among the Red Men," *Kansas State Historical Society Collections*, Vol. XVII (1928), pp. 654-655.
37. See Miles to Pope, September 14, 1874, Miles to AG, U. S. Army, September 24, 1874, Taylor (ed.), *Indian Campaign*, pp. 34-35, 42-44; Bent to Hyde, February 28, 1906, Bent Letters, Coe Collection, Yale University Library, microfilm, Kansas State Historical Society. I am assuming that Miles, who reported the number of Indians killed as twelve, received his information from the couriers.
38. Dixon, *"Billy" Dixon*, pp. 199-218; Miles to AG, U. S. Army, September 24, 1874, Miles to Pope, September 14, 1874, Taylor (ed.), *Indian Campaign*, pp. 34-35, 42-44; Miles, *Personal Recollections*, pp. 173-174; *Daily Commercial*, September 30, 1874; *Daily Times*, October 22, 1874; "McKinley's Narrative," P-PHR, Vol. XXXVI, p. 69; M. L. Crimmins, "Notes on the Establishment of Fort Elliott and the Buffalo Wallow Fight," P-PHR, Vol. XXV (1952), pp. 48-49. A controversial account of the buffalo wallow fight is Richard I. Dodge, OUR WILD INDIANS (Hartford, Connecticut: 1882), pp. 628-632.
39. Nye, *Bad Medicine and Good*, pp. 195-198; Nye, *Carbine and Lance*, pp. 218-219.
40. Price to Williams, September 23, 1874, Taylor (ed.), *Indian Campaign*, pp. 46-51.
41. Dixon, *"Billy" Dixon*, pp. 214-220; Miles to AG, U. S. Army, September 24, 1874, "Case of Scouts Chapman and Dixon," August 1, 1916, Taylor (ed.), *Indian Campaign*, pp. 42-45.
42. Nye, *Carbine and Lance*, pp. 218-219. Evidently Lyman had not followed Miles' back trail to the Canadian but had made one of his own which he was following, except as noticed in the text, on his return to the main command. Price said that he did not know at the time that there were two "roads" leading northward from the Washita and he took "the left hand road." Presumably, the other "road" was Lyman's. There was another road not far away — the Fort Smith-Fort Bascom road — but it seems clear from what Price says that this was not one of the two roads he was talking about. Price to Williams, September 23, 1874, Taylor (ed.), *Indian Campaign*, pp. 51-53.
43. Price to Williams, September 23, 1874, Farnsworth to Field Adjutant, Eighth Cavalry, September 23, 1876 [4], Miles to AAG, Department of the Missouri, March 4, 1875, Taylor (ed.), *Indian Campaign*, pp. 53-55, 58-61, 200.
44. A Texas court had sentenced Satanta and Big Tree to hang for leading an attack on Henry Warren's wagon train in 1871, but the governor had commuted the sentence to life imprisonment. Later they were released to their tribe evidently with the understanding that if they were implicated in future raids, they would be returned to the penitentiary. Rister, *Border Command*, pp. 174-191. For violating his parole, Santata was returned to prison in Texas where he threw himself from an upper-story window and died instantly. Big Tree was not, however, sent back because Sheridan did not consider him "guilty" of violating his parole. Taylor (ed.), *Indian Campaign*, pp. 87-100; Leckie, *Military Conquest*, pp. 218-219.
45. Nye, *Carbine and Lance*, pp. 219-221; Neill to AAG, Department of the Missouri, October 1, 1874, Taylor (ed.), *Indian Campaign*, pp. 64-68; Letters of Lieutenant Smith, October 3, 10, 1874, *Grasshopper and New Era* (Grasshopper Falls, Kansas), October 17, 24, 1874.
46. Miles to AAG, Department of the Missouri, October 12, 1874, March 4, 1875, Taylor (ed.), *Indian Campaign*, pp. 61-63, 199-201.
47. Davidson to AAG, Department of Texas, October 10, 1874, *ibid.*, pp. 69-73.
48. R. G. Carter, ON THE BORDER WITH MACKENZIE (New York: 1961), pp. 489-491. Mackenzie was called "Bad Hand" by the Indians in reference to two missing fingers from his right hand, which had been shot off during the Civil War.
49. Wallace, *Mackenzie*, pp. 124-166; Carl Coke Rister, FORT GRIFFIN ON THE TEXAS FRONTIER (Norman: 1956), pp. 110-124; Bent to Hyde, February 28, 1906, Bent Letters, Coe Collection, Yale University Library, microfilm, Kansas State Historical Society; Ernest R. Archambeau (ed.), "Monthly Reports of the Fourth Cavalry 1872-1874," P-PHR, Vol. XXXVIII (1965), pp. 141-153; James T. DeShields, "Scouting on the 'Staked Plains' (Llano Estacado) with Mackenzie, in 1874," *United Service*, Vol. XIII (October, November: 1885), pp. 400-412, 532-543; W. A. Thompson, "Scouting with Mackenzie," *Cavalry Journal*, Vol. X, (December, 1897), pp. 431-433; Charles

149

A. P. Hatfield, "The Comanche, Kiowa and Cheyenne Campaign in Northwest Texas and Mackenzie's Fight in the Palo Duro Canyon, September 26, 1874," *West Texas Historical Association Year Book*, Vol. V (1929), pp. 118-123; Sherman to Townsend, October 14, 1874, Taylor (ed.), *Indian Campaign*, p. 75; Carter, *On the Border with Mackenzie*, pp. 473-525; Nye, *Bad Medicine and Good*, pp. 216-221; Nye, *Carbine and Lance*, pp. 221-225. Dr. Wallace's study, cited above, contains the best detailed secondary account of Mackenzie's operations of 1874 in print.

Three enlisted men of Mackenzie's command were subsequently awarded the *Congressional Medal of Honor* for their gallantry in the action of September 26-28. [Department of the Army], *Medal of Honor*, pp. 220-223. Lieutenant Thompson was in 1890 breveted captain partly in recognition of his gallant service on September 27-28. Heitman, *Historical Register and Dictionary*, p. 958.

50. Buell to AAG, Department of Texas, November 8, 1874, Buell to Miles, October 18, 1874, Drum to Whipple, October 24, 1874, Whipple to AG, U. S. Army, October 30, 1874, Miles to AAG, Department of the Missouri, March 4, 1875, Taylor (ed.), *Indian Campaign*, pp. 78-83, 200-201; RECORD OF ENGAGEMENTS WITH HOSTILE INDIANS WITHIN THE MILITARY DIVISION OF THE MISSOURI, *from 1868 to 1882* (Chicago: 1882), pp. 47-48; Wallace, *Mackenzie*, pp. 152-153.
51. Miles stated that he marched eastward but actually he moved northeastward.
52. Haworth to E. P. Smith, November 14, 1874, Kiowa Agency, Letters Received, Office of Indian Affairs, National Archives; Nye, *Carbine and Lance*, p. 225; Mildred P. Mayhall, *The Kiowas* (Norman: 1962), p. 252.
53. Farnsworth to Field Adjutant, Eighth Cavalry, November 7, 1874, Taylor (ed.), *Indian Campaign*, pp. 102-103. Leckie states erroneously that this engagement occurred thirty miles from Camp Supply. Leckie, *Military Conquest*, pp. 226-227.
54. Pope to AAG, Military Division of the Missouri, November 15, 1874, Miles to AAG, Department of the Missouri, March 4, 1874, Taylor (ed.), *Indian Campaign*, pp. 107,203.
55. Alice B. Baldwin, MEMOIRS OF THE LATE FRANK D. BALDWIN (Los Angeles: 1929), pp. 70-71; Article in *Army and Navy Journal*, November 21, 1874, reprinted in *Daily Times*, November 25, 1874.
56. For accounts of the captivity of the German girls, see clipping from *Topeka Capital*, May 2, 1937, "Indian Depredations, Battles and Treaties," Vol. III, pp. 259-262, Library, Kansas State Historical Society; *Daily Commercial*, November 18, 1874; *Emporia* (Kansas) *News*, December 18, 1874; *Ellsworth* (Kansas) *Reporter*, March 11, 25, 1875; Miles to Commissioner of Indian Affairs, March 19, 1875, Cheyenne and Arapahoe Agency, Letters Received, Office of Indian Affairs, National Archives; Rister, *Border Captives*, pp. 189-193; Grace E. Meredith, GIRL CAPTIVES OF THE CHEYENNES (Los Angeles: 1927); Grinnell, *Fighting Cheyennes*, pp. 324-325; Annual Report of the Commissioner of Indian Affairs for 1875, *House Executive Document* No. 1, 44 Cong., 1 Sess., p. 771. Some sources say there were eight members of the German family, others nine. A copy of the family record found in the family bible left at the scene of the tragedy listed nine names. See Hambright to AAG, Department of the Missouri, Records of the War Department, National Archives.
57. Baldwin, *Memoirs*, pp. 70-76; *Daily Times*, November 25, 1874; Miles to Whipple, November 17, 1874, Miles to AAG, Department of the Missouri, March 4, 1875, Taylor (ed.), *Indian Campaign*, pp. 105-106, 202-203; clipping from *Winners of the West*, August 30, 1932, "Indian Depredations, Battles and Treaties," Vol. III, pp. 209-218, Library, Kansas State Historical Society; Miles, *Personal Recollections*, pp. 174-176.
58. Heitman, *Historical Register and Dictionary*, pp. 181, 185-186, 763; Taylor (ed.), *Indian Campaign*, pp. 225-226. For his outstanding performance in this fight and in the First Battle of the Palo Duro, Baldwin was also, as noticed above, breveted a captain.
59. Davidson to Carlton, November 17, 1874, Davidson to Augur, November 23, 1874, Miles to AAG, Department of the Missouri, March 4, 1875, Taylor (ed.), *Indian Campaign*, pp. 108-109, 203-204; *Record of Engagements*, pp. 48-49.
60. See *Record of Engagements*, pp. 50-53; Scout J. T. Marshall, THE MILES EXPEDITION OF 1874-1875: *An Account of the Red River War*, edited by Lonnie J. White (Austin: 1971), pp. 37-62. Two noteworthy encounters occurred after major campaigning ceased. These were the sand hill fight near the Cheyenne agency, Indian Territory, in April, 1875, and the Sappa Creek, Kansas, engagement of the same month.
61. Berthrong, *Southern Cheyennes*, pp. 396-405; Leckie, *Military Conquest*, pp. 228-235; Nye, *Carbine and Lance*, pp. 229-239. The story of the Indians' imprisonment in Florida is told by their jailor, Richard H. Pratt, in BATTLEFIELD AND CLASSROOM: *Four Decades with the American Indian, 1867-1904* (New Haven and London: 1964). Grey Beard was shot and killed while attempting to escape from the railroad car conveying the Indian prisoners to Florida. Pratt to AG, U. S. Army, May 23, 1875, Taylor (ed.), *Indian Campaign*, pp. 285-287.

THE WAGON BOX FIGHT

T HE TRAGIC FETTERMAN DISASTER OF DECEMBER 21, 1866, was the worst defeat the United States Army had suffered on the frontier up to that time. Conversely, the battle of the "Hundred in the Hands" was a great victory for the Sioux and their allies, one which proved to be the capstone of Red Cloud's successful two-year struggle to expunge the military from the Powder River country.[1] On August 2, 1867, less than eight months after Fetterman's command had perished on the frozen slopes of Massacre Hill, the Army erased some of the stigma and humiliation of that disaster in an encounter known as the Wagon Box Fight. Though it was strictly a defensive victory, and had no effect on the ultimate status of the Army in the Powder River country, the Wagon Box Fight continues to attract the attention of writers and students of the Indian wars.[2]

This apparent fascination with an encounter of such little real military significance is due, in part, to the dramatic way in which a handful of soldiers, armed with new breech-loading rifles, turned back repeated attacks by an overwhelming force of hostile Indians. Then, too, the collection of myths and half-truths promulgated by early accounts of the fight has provided a fertile field for the serious student of the Indian wars. Stories of wagon boxes lined with boiler iron, reports of fantastic casualties in the hostile ranks, and, finally, a minor controversy as to the exact location of the fight, have all provided grist for a continuing study of the affair.[3]

The immediate aftermath of the Fetterman disaster produced a wave of apprehension among the garrison and families at Fort Phil Kearny, who feared that the hostiles would try and follow up their victory of December 24 with an attack on the post itself.[4] However the winter of 1866-1867 settled down over the Powder River country with unusual severity, and when it became apparent that the Indians had no intention of conducting winter operations, the fear of an attack gradually subsided.[5]

Nevertheless, it was a long winter for the inhabitants of Fort Phil Kearny. The arrival of a relief column in January, 1867, increased the strength of the garrison by nearly three hundred men, but created a shortage of food and animal forage.[6] The arrival of spring, and the first bull trains up from Fort Laramie alleviated the supply problem, but the warmer weather also heralded a renewal of the hostiles' harassment of the Bozeman Trail forts.

On July 3, 1867, a civilian contractor, J. R. Porter, representing the firm of Proctor and Gilmore, arrived at Fort Phil Kearny with a supply train, carrying in addition to the usual items, a shipment of seven hundred Springfield-Allin breech-loading rifles and 100,000 rounds of 50-70-450 Martin bar-anvil-primed cartridges.[7] Long overdue, these new weapons represented a dramatic improvement over the old .58-caliber Civil War muzzle-loaders, with which the infantry companies of Fort Phil Kearny had previously been equipped.

The breech-loading rifle was not in itself new, however. During the Civil War, the Army had used a variety of models with considerable success. Notwithstanding, by the end of the war, the .58-caliber Springfield muzzle-loader remained the primary infantry weapon.[8] In view of the breech-loader's success, and because of the great variety of such weapons introduced during the Civil War, the Army was faced with the necessity of effecting a transition to the breech-loading principle in a practical and economical way. Accordingly, in 1865, Erskine S. Allin of the National Armory in Springfield, Massachusetts, was authorized to develop a method of converting muzzle-loaders to breech-loaders.[9] Allin's efforts resulted in the development of a single-shot, breech-loading system, which he patented in September, 1865. The Army approved, and subsequently authorized the armory to convert a number of muzzle-loaders to the new system.[10]

However, in March, 1865, a military board had determined that the standard infantry rifle should be reduced from .58 to .50-caliber. This modification required the newly converted breech-loaders to have their bores reamed to accept .50 caliber liners, which were then brazed into place.[11] It was this new model 1866 Springfield-Allin breech-loader, with the .50-caliber liner, which arrived at Fort Phil Kearny on Porter's bull train.[12]

Issuance of the new weapons commenced on July 10, pursuant to an order from Fort Phil Kearny's new commanding officer, Colonel John Eugene Smith, who had arrived with Porter's train and officially assumed command on July 5. Coincidentally, Colonel Smith's second-in-command was Major Benjamin Smith. The two officers were not related, except by way of professional calling. Each had served with distinction in the Civil War, Colonel John Smith having been breveted major general of volunteers, while Major Benjamin Smith had received the brevet of brigadier general of volunteers.[13]

Throughout the month of July, the hostiles continually harassed the hay-cutting parties around Fort Phil Kearny, and made repeated attempts to drive off the animal herds grazing in the vicinity of the post, but met with little success.[14]

Providing protection for the wood-cutting operation was somewhat more difficult, because of the distance separating the cutting area from the fort. The source of the timber supply was a place called Piney Island, some five miles northwest of Fort Phil Kearny. The area featured a heavy growth of first-rate trees, with many running "ninety feet to the first limb, and as straight as an arrow."[15] Early maps showed the area as being enclosed by North and South Piney Creeks, thus presenting an island-like configuration: Hence the name Piney Island.[16]

The logging camps were called "pineries," the "upper pinery being located near the South Fork Canyon of South or Big Piney Creek, while the "lower pinery" was situated near the month of Little Piney Creek Canyon. Both sites served as bases for smaller "side camps."[17]

Upon his arrival at Fort Phil Kearny, Porter was awarded a contract by the post quartermaster, Captain George B. Dandy, to supply the fort with logs for the sawmill and fuel for the coming winter. The contract stipulated that the quartermaster would supply wagons, while the contractor furnished the necessary complement of civilian wood-cutters and herders. It was also understood that the Army would provide guard and escort details for the operation.[18]

Early in July, the contractors, in an effort to protect their stock from night raids by the hostiles, erected a corral of wagon boxes on an open plain near Piney Island. The cut timber was hauled to the fort on the running gear of the wagons, an arrangement which left the tops, or boxes, available for other use.[19] The corral itself consisted of fourteen of these boxes, placed end-to-end, so as to form an oval-shaped enclosure approximately seventy feet wide and one hundred twenty feet long. The space between each box was wide enough to permit a man to pass through, but not large enough for any of the stock to escape.[20]

One wagon box with the canvas still attached to its bows, and in which was stored the rations for the civilian workers, was located on the east end of the enclosure. A second such box, containing the military rations, was positioned on the south end. One fully complete wagon, containing reserve rations and bedding for the civilians, was located some ten feet from the west end of the corral. Both the civilians and the soldiers slept in tents pitched around the outside of the enclosure.[21]

One of the earliest misconceptions of the Wagon Box Fight was that these boxes were lined with steel or boiler iron, had loopholes, and were therefore bullet-proof and all but invincible. The men who participated in the fight have stated categorically that the boxes were not lined with anything, and were, in point of fact, constructed of nothing more than ordinary pine wood about one inch thick.[22]

The corral was positioned so that both "pineries" were under visual control. Powell reported that the position was "well selected for defense, and the best security that the country afforded for the stock."[23]

During the month of July, Company A, Twenty-seventh Infantry, had drawn the guard and escort assignment for the wood-cutting operation, but experienced little trouble from the hostiles.[24] The fact that there had been no concerted effort to harass the wood-cutting operation during the early part of the summer, was probably due to the hostiles' preöccupation with their annual Sun Dance.[25]

However, with the conclusion of the Sun Dance, about the last week in July, the Sioux and some of their Cheyenne allies began discussing plans for an effort against the Bozeman Trail forts, but were unable to agree on a unanimous target. One group favored attacking Fort Phil Kearny, while another group thought the objective should be Fort C. F. Smith, some ninety miles northwest of Fort Phil Kearny.[26] The end result was two war parties, one which attacked Fort C. F. Smith on August 1, in the famous Hayfield Fight, and the other which struck Fort Kearny's wood-cutting operation on the following day.[27]

The Fort C. F. Smith contingent was composed mainly of Cheyennes, while the party which attacked the wagon box corral consisted primarily of Sioux: Oglalas under Crazy Horse, Miniconjous under High Hump and Sans Arc led by Thunderhawk.[28] The Fort Phil Kearny contingent, numbering approximately one thousand,[29] departed from their Rosebud River camp, probably about July 31, and reached a point some five miles north of Fort Phil Kearny on August 1, where they camped and made preparations to attack the wood-cutting operation on the following day.[30]

A favorite Indian tactic was to have a small group lure an army unit into an unexpected encounter with a much larger force. This tactic had worked particularly well against Fetterman, and the hostiles apparently planned to use the same device in attacking the wood-cutters and their escort.[31]

On July 31, about the same time that the Sioux war party was departing its camp on the Rosebud, Company C, Twenty-seventh Infantry, Captain James Powell commanding, departed Fort Phil Kearny with rations for thirty days, and orders to relieve Company A. Powell's command numbered fifty-one enlisted men, and one other officer, Lieutenant John C. Jenness.[32]

James Powell was a veteran of nineteen years, having entered the army as a private in 1848. At the outset of the Civil War he was promoted to second lieutenant, Eighteenth Infantry, the regiment in which he served throughout the war. He was brevetted for gallant and meritorious service at Chickamauga and at Jonesboro during the Atlanta Campaign, where he was severely wounded. Powell was one of Carrington's original officers, having come west with his regiment in June, 1866. Under the Army's new plan of reörganization, effective January 1, 1867, the second battalion, Eighteenth Infantry, which included Powell's Company C, became the new Twenty-seventh Infantry.[33]

Powell's second-in-command, First Lieutenant John C. Jenness, was a native of Vermont, and also a Civil War veteran who had come up through the ranks. Nothing much seems to be known about Jenness, other than that he was apparently well liked and respected as an officer.[34]

Arriving at the wagon box corral, Powell discovered that the contractor's operation necessitated an undesirable division of his command. One non-commissioned officer and thirteen men were given the job of escorting the wood train to and from the fort. Another non-commissioned officer and twelve men were assigned to guard the wood-cutting camp, located "about one mile distant in a southwesterly direction, on a commanding point across the Little Piney Creek, at the foot of the mountains." This last group was further divided, with nine men being assigned to the main cutting party, and four to the "side camp." These dispositions left Powell and Jenness with twenty-four men at the corral.[35]

Late in the afternoon of August 1, a fully loaded train came in from the pinery and camped at the corral, so as to be ready for an early start back to the fort.[36] Reveille was sounded early on August 2. By sunrise breakfast had been served, and shortly thereafter, the train and its escort departed for Fort Phil Kearny. At the same time, an empty train headed back to the pinery.[37]

So the day began in rather routine fashion. Powell, reportedly, went down to the Little Piney to take a bath. Private Sam Gibson was made acting lance-corporal for the day, and placed in charge of the picket post on the Little Piney, which was, evidently, closer to the "side camp" than to the main cutting party. Gibson's companions in this assignment were Privates Nolan Deming and John Garrett.[38] Sam Gibson recalled that upon arriving at the picket post, he stuck willows in the ground, and fashioned a make-shift canopy with his poncho as protection against the sun.[39]

About the time reveille was sounding at the corral, a civilian teamster, R. J. Smyth and a partner, left Fort Phil Kearny to hunt deer in the nearby hills. Shortly after daylight, they "discovered a lot of Indian smoke signals on the hills, and decided that we had better get back to the fort." They soon found, however, that it would be safer to try and reach the wood train, then enroute to the fort. But this idea, too, was quickly vetoed when they discovered that Indians were between them and the train. The pair finally elected to try for the wagon box corral, which they managed to reach, and none too soon.[40]

Gibson and Deming, meanwhile, had been relaxing in the shade of their lean-to, when Garrett suddenly spotted Indians and immediately shouted an alarm.[41] Off to the west, the three pickets counted seven mounted Indians, moving in single file, and at a dead run toward the Little Piney. Not yet having had an opportunity to try out his new breech-loader, Gibson carefully adjusted the sights to seven hundred yards, laid the weapon on a stone breastwork, took careful aim and fired.

155

According to Gibson, the bullet struck a stone in front of the lead rider's pony and ricocheted off, wounding the pony, which in turn threw its rider, who was immediately picked up by one of his companions.[42]

Now, as the three pickets turned their glances in the direction of the corral and beyond the Big Piney, they saw more Indians than they had ever seen before. Gibson directed Garrett to watch for signals from the corral, advising them to return, and sent Deming across the Little Piney to warn the choppers in the "side camp."[43] While Deming was gone, Gibson and Garrett watched the Indians swarming over the hills "like a big swarm of bees." Gibson was becoming concerned because they had not received any signal to return to the corral.[44]

Meanwhile, the "side camp" was already under attack, the hostiles having set fire to the wagons, forcing the four choppers and their four-man escort to beat a hasty retreat toward the mountains.[45] One of the choppers, J. I. Minnick, recalled that the biggest Indian in the group grabbed the whiskey jug, and for this dastardly act was promptly shot by the leader of the choppers, a man named Jones. According to Minnick, the big Indian's death "and the loss of the 'firewater' seemed to make the other Indians quite angry and eager for revenge."[46]

As Minnick's group fled toward the mountains, one of the soldiers was unable to keep up with the others, and fell behind. Minnick and another chopper tried to assist by providing a cover fire, but it was to no avail, as the soldier was caught and killed. Minnick was about to remind his companion that they would have to move quickly in order to save their own "skins," but when he looked over, he found his companion had not waited to be so advised and was already gone, having left his boots and rifle behind![47] Alone now, Minnick wasted no time heading up the Little Piney. Presently he heard a whistle, and was much relieved to see a friendly hand waving to him from behind a mass of large rocks.[48]

The other three choppers and one soldier had managed to escape and take refuge in these rocks. Minnick took up a position next to this surviving soldier, whose curiosity soon proved to be his undoing. Raising his head just above the rocks, the soldier immediately drew rifle fire from the hostiles, one bullet striking uncomfortably close. Jones warned the man to keep his head down, but the soldier persisted, and shortly thereafter was rewarded with a bullet between the eyes.[49]

Fortunately for Minnick's little group, the hostiles apparently became more interested in directing their efforts toward the destruction of the wagon box corral, and made no further attempts to disturb the four choppers.[50]

In the meantime, Deming had returned to report on the action at the "side camp," bringing a civilian herder along with him. Gibson concluded that the situation was critical, and decided to abandon the picket post without orders. Accordingly, Gibson, Garrett and Deming, accompanied by the herder from the "side camp," started back to the corral, but had hardly proceeded more than seventy-five to one hundred yards when hostiles began swarming up out of the Little Piney in groups of two and three. Gibson recalled that one was waving an old Spencer carbine at his companions, urging them on. He and Gibson exchanged shots, with Gibson finally scoring.[51]

The herder, who was leading his horse, asked Gibson to prod the animal with his bayonet to get him moving. Gibson told the man to forget the horse and start shooting, as the hostiles seemed to be emerging from the surrounding country like a "flock of birds."[52] Decked out in their finest war regalia, with bodies painted white, green and yellow, Gibson remembered that it made them appear "hideous in the extreme."[53]

By now the four men were running for their lives. Even the herder's mount, its rump and flanks bristling with arrows, seems to have decided that speed was of the essence. The hostiles attempted to cut Gibson's party off from the corral, and Gibson remembered that the fate of Fetterman's men was on their minds.[54] At this juncture, a young German immigrant, Corporal Max Littman, seeing the plight of Gibson's party, ran out from the corral, dropped down on one knee, and coolly began to deliver a most effective covering fire, which enabled Gibson and company to reach the corral, exhausted but safe.[55]

Gibson, who was only eighteen at the time, was much relieved to be back at the corral, but also very much concerned at what might happen because he had deserted his post without orders. He reported to Powell, explained his reasons for abandoning the post, and was assured by the captain that he had done exactly the right thing.[56] By the time Gibson's group reached the corral, Powell and Jenness had already assembled the rest of the company. Ammunition had been distributed, and the men instructed to take up positions and be prepared to fight for their lives.[57]

Some confusion exists as to the exact time the fight began. In his official report, Powell says that "About 9 o'clock in the morning two hundred (200) Indians attacked the herders in charge of the herd, driving them off: at the same some five hundred (500) attacked the train at the foot of the Mountains, driving off the men belonging there and burning it . . ."[58]

Both the choppers in the main cutting camp, and the personnel accompanying the wood train apparently fled to the safety of the mountains, as did Minnick's group. The herders, however, were cut off, and at this point, Powell, allegedly sallied out with a small detachment and attacked the hostiles from behind, thus creating a diversion that enabled the herders to reach the corral.[59]

So the stage was set. Powell had started the day with a total of fifty-three men, including himself. Better than fifty percent of his command — twenty-seven enlisted men — had been detached for guard and escort duty, and were not available. He had been reinforced by the addition of six civilians, but there was still a net loss of twenty-one, so that the force in the corral now numbered two officers, twenty-four enlisted men and six civilians, a total of thirty-two.

Inside the corral, Powell instructed his men to take up positions and prepare for the onslaught. Some got inside the wagon boxes, others behind them, and still others found positions between the boxes. Evidently each man simply selected the spot that suited him best. For once there was an adequate supply of ammunition and plenty of weapons. While most of the weapons were the new breech-loaders, the teamster, Smyth, reported that he had two Spencer carbines and two Army Colt revolvers. He also recalled that the soldier next to him had a "needle gun," a Spencer rifle and one or two revolvers.[60]

Sam Gibson recalled that after picking out his spot, he walked around the enclosure and observed the men standing around in groups, some were apparently outside the corral, others were inside, all watching the Indians assemble. According to Gibson, there was little in the way of conversation, and he noted expressions of "intense earnestness" on the faces of many.[61] Gibson also noted that many of the old-timers had fastened their shoestrings to the trigger of their weapons, so as to reserve the final shot for themselves, in the event the position was overrun.[62]

Fetterman had had more than twice as many men, and had been wiped out. The defenders of the wagon box corral must have weighed the odds, and despite the presence of a more effective weapon, and a better defensive position, anticipated the same finale. Powell, in fact, later told his wife that he never expected to get out alive.[63]

The hostiles appeared to be everywhere. Many were dashing back and forth on fleet war ponies, chanting war songs. Lieutenant Jenness watching the activities of a group of hostiles through field glasses, thought he identified Red Cloud, and called Powell's attention to the fact.[64] The interim period was of brief duration. Powell reported that within fifteen minutes after the attack on the mule herd and wood train, he "was surrounded by about eight hundred mounted Indians. . . ."[65]

Their preparations complete, the hostiles launched the first attack against Powell's defenders. Powell instructed his men to "shoot to kill," and evidently issued few, if any other orders throughout the remainder of the fight, probably feeling the situation required little in the way of a running commentary.[66]

Confusion also exists as to both the method and direction of the initial attack. Gibson's account states that it was a mounted charge from the open plain between the Big and Little Piney, which would mean from some point on the compass between south and west. Max Littman, however, stated that the first attack came from the north, and was made by warriors on foot. In point of fact, Littman claims that *all* of the attacks he witnessed were made by warriors on foot.[67]

Powell, it will be recalled, stated that they were surrounded by eight hundred mounted Indians, which, if taken literally, would mean that both Gibson and Littman were correct as to the direction of the attack. It is possible, too, that from his position, Littman may have witnessed activity on the part of dismounted warriors. But in view of the fact that Powell had witnessed some of the Civil War's heaviest fighting, and thus was a practiced observer in such matters, coupled with the fact that his report was written forty-eight hours after the fight, rather than forty-odd years, would seem to pretty well confirm his observation that the impetus of the initial attack was provided by mounted warriors.

It should be noted, too, that the terrain had a very definite influence on the conduct of the battle, in that all but the north side of the corral, and particularly the south and west approaches were well-suited to mounted charges. On the north, the land extends no more than one hundred yards, before dropping off into the valley of the Big Piney. Along this north edge there was also a ditch or trough which extended out into the northwest perimeter, and which later in the fight would provide excellent cover for the Indian snipers who inflicted most of the damage on Powell's command.[68]

There does not seem to be any evidence that Powell attempted to use controlled fire in repelling the hostile attacks. Some accounts suggest, too, that only the better marksmen actually fired, while the others kept loaded weapons ready.[69]

Sam Gibson recalled that the attackers rode back and forth, each time coming a bit closer, and some actually got close enough to throw spears.[70] Surprised by the continuing volume of fire which poured forth from the corral, the hostiles pulled back to reconsider. "Finding they could not enter the corral," Powell wrote, "they retired to a hill about six hundred yards distant and there stripped for more determined fighting . . ."[71]

As was frequently the case, the hostiles' attempt to employ the decoy trick failed completely because some of the impetuous young warriors were unable to restrain themselves. Had the Indians pressed home this first attack, they would, in all likelihood, have simply overwhelmed the defenders by sheer weight of numbers.[72]

During the lull, the defenders replenished their supplies of ammunition, crawling on hands and knees to the various locations around the corral where it had been placed. Gibson remembered the silence as being "uncanny." A few of the men also maintained a desultory sniping fire during this interval.[73]

There is nothing to indicate just how long the first attack lasted, but it was probably of brief duration. In connection with this, one implication that has been maintained has been the notion that the Wagon Box Fight consisted of one massive head-on assault after another, when, in all probability, the three major efforts lasted a total of perhaps one hour at the very most, and the rest of the time was spent in threatening demonstrations by the hostiles, and harassing fire by both sides.

In any event, it was now approaching the time of day when the heat of the sun began to be felt. Many of the defenders were using their caps to hold cartridges, and as a result were bareheaded and beginning to feel the effects of the sun.[74]

The Sioux and Cheyennes had come down from their camps confident of another great victory, and had brought some of their non-combatants along to watch from the surrounding heights. Apparently some of the warriors also acted as observers, at least for part of the fight, as Powell reported the ". . . hills in the immediate vicinity were covered with Indians who merely acted as spectators, until they saw how fruitless were the efforts of their comrades near my corral when they also moved up, and seemed determined to carry my position at all hazards and massacre my command . . ."[75]

Having reëvaluated the situation, the hostiles now launched their second attack. An estimated seven hundred warriors, on foot, advanced from the north and west. Simultaneously, a body of mounted warriors appeared to be readying for a charge from the south.[76] As the hostiles advanced someone suddenly noticed that the tents outside the corral were in the line of fire. Why these tents were not taken down before the attack commenced is a good question, but in any event, Gibson, Private John Grady and some others now made a dash for the tents and managed to "drop" all but the one used by Powell.[77]

With the tents out of the way, the defenders had a clear field of fire, and proceeded to pour a steady stream of lead at the oncoming hostiles. Gibson recalled that many gun barrels became over-heated from the intense firing.[78] During this second attack Indian snipers secreted in the ditch along the northwest perimeter killed Lieutenant Jenness with a bullet in the head. Privates Henry Haggerty and Thomas Doyle were also killed by the same snipers.[79]

By now, the heat of the day, combined with the smell of burned powder and the odor from smoldering piles of hay and manure inside the corral, had created an almost unbearable stench and a great thirst among the defenders.[80] There was a partially filled barrel of water some twenty feet from the west end of the corral, but it had been pierced by bullets several times, and the contents had nearly all leaked out. However, under the covered wagon, also on the west end, were two camp kettles, containing the breakfast cooking water. Once again Gibson and

160

Grady volunteered. They were given covering fire, but even at that the hostiles made it a risky proposition. The two volunteers managed to bring the kettles back without being hit themselves, but when Gibson looked at his kettle, he found it leaking from two bullet holes! Fortunately, there was sufficient water remaining in both kettles to last the remainder of the fight.[81]

Among those attackers who came on foot, displaying their personal prowess and bravery, was an unusually large Miniconjou Sioux named Jipala, who came at the defenders, brazenly brandishing a spear, buffalo hide shield and chanting a war song. Presumably he was also armed with bow and arrows, because as he advanced, Jipala moved about in a dodging fashion, now and then leaping into the air, and releasing an arrow from the apex of his leap. A number of the defenders tried unsuccessfully to get him, but it was young Max Littman who finally brought Jipala down. Littman remembered this as a personal duel between Jipala and himself.[82]

Meanwhile, Colonel Smith had somehow been made aware of Powell's plight. Whether someone from the wood train or the cutting party had managed to get back with the news, or whether the firing was heard at the fort, is not clear. At any rate, Major Benjamin Smith was immediately ordered to proceed to the pinery with a relief column.

> Yesterday about Guard Mounting, hostile Indians made their appearance on all sides of the Post. At first just a few but gradually increasing to several hundred. About 11 o'clock developments indicated that the Wood Party and its guard, five miles in the Pinery were in imminent danger. Bvt. Maj. Gen'l John E. Smith Commanding, directed me to proceed to their relief with Lieutenants Connolly, Paulus and McCarthy of the 27th Inf. and one hundred enlisted men of the same Regiment from Companies A and F. I also took a Mountain Howitzer and ten ox wagons, the citizen teamsters being armed. My command started about 11:30 a.m. and proceeded cautiously to the Pinery with skirmishers and flankers thrown out.[83]

By now it was nearing the noon hour, and thus far Powell's men had repulsed two major efforts and kept the hostiles at arms-length for nearly three hours. Major Smith's relief column was on the way, but of course the defenders were not as yet aware of that happy fact, although there must have been many frequent and hopeful glances in the direction of Fort Phil Kearny.

Suddenly the men heard a strange sound that gradually grew in intensity. On the open plain to the south and west, mounted warriors galloped back and forth, some brandishing spears, others firing on the defenders. All the while this strange sound grew louder, and then suddenly, from the trough along the northwest perimeter, a large body of warriors burst onto the plain. Led by a magnificently war-bonneted individual, said to have been Red Cloud's nephew, shouting their songs

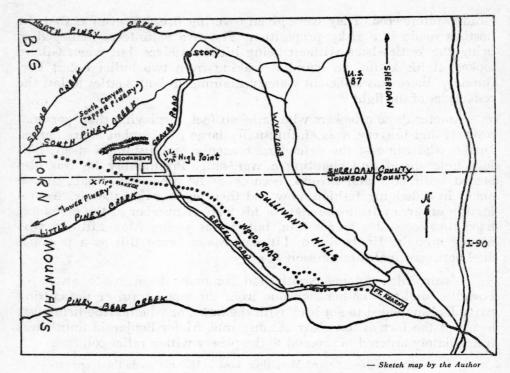

— Sketch map by the Author

LOCATION SKETCH MAP OF THE WAGON BOX FIGHT

of war and filled with determination. Sam Gibson vividly recalled that
the sight "chilled my blood."[84]

Powell's men responded to this third attack by again firing as fast
as they could work the mechanisms of their new breech-loaders, pouring
a concentrated stream of fire into the hostile ranks. Many fell, including
the one alleged to have been Red Cloud's nephew, but still the attackers
came on, seemingly oblivious to the heavy volume of fire. Then, just
when it appeared that this new assault might turn the tide, the hostiles
broke off and withdrew.[85]

Retiring to the shelter of the trough, the hostiles continued a desultory fire on the corral, while attempting to retrieve their fallen comrades. Some crawled forward behind the protection of buffalo hide
shields, and dragged the dead and wounded back with them. Others, in a
superb display of horsemanship, dashed in, grabbed a wounded comrade
by the hand or wrist and carried him to safety.[86]

It was now about thirty minutes past noon, and some of the defenders noted that several hostiles on one of the nearby hills suddenly
dispersed and came streaking down across the valley. Then from the
east end of the corral a shout went up, announcing the arrival of the

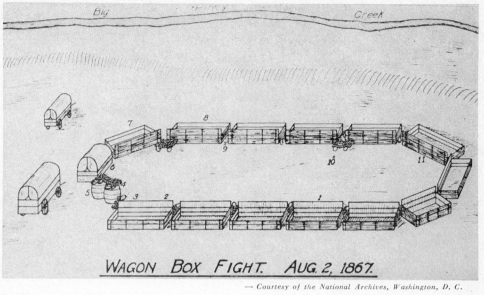

WAGON BOX FIGHT. AUG. 2, 1867.

— Courtesy of the National Archives, Washington, D. C.

Two Artists' Conceptions of the Wagon Box Fight Scene

The sketch above was drawn by Grace Raymond Hebard from data supplied by Sergeant Sam Gibson. The sketch below, by an unnamed artist, shows the scene from a directly opposite viewpoint. For orientation see the author's sketch map of the area, reproduced on the opposite page.

— Courtesy of the University of Wyoming Library, Laramie

163

— Courtesy of the University of Wyoming Library

CAPTAIN JAMES POWELL

— Courtsy Library of Congress

RED CLOUD
Oglala Sioux Chief

SERGEANT SAM GIBSON
*From a photograph taken at Camp Proctor
on the Yellowstone River,
in September, 1891.*

CORPORAL MAX LITTMAN

MONUMENT COMMEMORATES THE WAGON BOX FIGHT
The late Maurice Frink, historian, is shown standing next to the Monument.

relief column. Then the boom of Smith's mountain howitzer rang out across the plain, scattering the hostiles, who very quickly dispersed, having no wish to contest the issue further, now that more soldiers and one of the hated "medicine" guns had arrived on the scene.[87]

In his official report, Major Smith described the arrival of his relief column.

> On nearing the corral of the Wood Party and about a mile and a half from it, I discovered that a high hill near the road and overlooking the corral of the Wood Party was occupied by a large party of Indians, in my estimation five or six hundred were in sight, many more probably concealed. The grass was burning in every direction. The Indians appearing disposed to make a stand I turned off the road to the right, some few hundred yards, to occupy the extreme right point of the hill, which was flanked on that side by a steep precipice, with the intention after securing it to follow the ridge to the corral of the Wood Party, commanded by Bvt. Maj. Powell, 27th Inf. Before turning from the road, in obedience to my instructions. I fired a shot from the Howitzer, as a signal to inform Bvt. Maj. Powell's command that assistance was near. The shell fired was in the direction of the Indians, but fell short, as I anticipated, but seemed to disconcert them as a number of mounted Indians who were riding rapidly toward my command turned and fled. Upon my ascending to the crest of the hill all had disappeared from it and were seen across the creek, on an opposite hill about ¾ of a mile away leaving all clear to Bvt. Major Powell's corral."[88]

To say that Powell's men welcomed the relief column would be a decided understatement. They jumped into the air, shouted, hugged each other, laughed and cried, such had been the strain. The post surgeon, Doctor Samuel P. Horton, who had accompanied Smith's column, received Powell's permission to give each man a drink of whiskey; there is no evidence to indicate that anyone refused the surgeon's offer.[89]

Shortly after Smith's arrival, four choppers and fourteen soldiers came to the corral, having hidden out in the woods during the fighting. Smith then sent a company under Lieutenant Connolly to check for other survivors in the pinery, and the latter returned to report that the wagons were all burned and the men gone.[90]

The four surviving choppers from the "side camp" remained in hiding until late that night, by which time they were so overcome with thirst that they decided to risk sneaking back to the fort. Minnick was the only one who had kept his boots, and by the time the four men reached Fort Phil Kearny, at five o'clock the following morning, the other three men had such sore feet that they were barely able to walk for several days.[91]

Not wishing to give the hostiles an opportunity to launch another attack, Smith and Powell wasted no time in returning to Fort Phil Kearny. Upon reaching a high point east of the corral, the men looked back and saw a line of Indian ponies carrying off dead and wounded.[92]

Apparently, the Indians were unable to retrieve all of their dead and wounded, however, because some of the soldiers returned to the fort with scalps, and one Indian head, which Surgeon Horton subsequently sent back to Washington for examination.[93]

Powell had suffered a loss of three killed and two wounded in the corral, and four others killed in the fight at the "side camp." Indian losses are almost impossible to determine with any degree of accuracy, and range from an absurd low of two to an equally absurd high of fifteen hundred.[94] Powell estimated that "there were not less than sixty Indians killed on the spot and one hundred twenty severely wounded." Gibson, Littman and other participants imply that Powell's estimate was extremely conservative. And, at least one Indian account, that of Fire Thunder, an Oglala Sioux participant, stated that there were "dead warriors and horses piled all around the boxes and scattered over the plain."[95]

Historians who have written of the battle from the Indian point of view have agreed, unanimously, that the accounts of Indian casualties are wildly exaggerated and completely unrealistic.[96] In view of the fact that Powell's men had had no opportunity to test fire their new breech-loaders, and allowing for the fact that most were highly excited, and probably fired wildly, it is entirely possible that even Powell's estimate was too high.[97] But whatever the number of casualties, Powell's force did inflict enough damage to hold off their attackers until help arrived, and in the final analysis, that was all that really mattered.

That the presence of the Springfield-Allin breech-loader meant the difference between victory and defeat, also seems irrefutable. Major Smith stated that "If Powell's men had been armed with muzzle-loaders instead of breech-loaders, his party would have been massacred before my arrival."[98]

In retrospect, then, it would seem that the significance of the Wagon Box Fight was two-fold: first, it proved that a few well-positioned defenders, armed with breech-loading weapons, could enjoy tactical superiority over a much larger force of hostile Indians; second, the fight restored a measure of prestige and confidence to a frontier army badly in need of an impressive victory.

But perhaps the most intriguing aspect of the entire affair is the controversy regarding the exact location of the corral. Two sites are involved: by far the most prominent and official-looking is the fenced enclosure, containing a large rock monument and small stone marker, located in Sheridan County, approximately one mile south of the little community of Story. The access road to this site is also the boundary between Sheridan and Johnson Counties, and just across the line in Johnson County is a four-inch diameter iron pipe, which, supposedly, also marks the site of the Wagon Box Corral.

The Wagon Box Fight

In 1908, Sam Gibson came out to Sheridan to participate in ceremonies dedicating the Fetterman Monument. Desiring to revisit the scene of the Wagon Box Fight, Gibson, in the company of a local citizen, Charles E. Bezold, rode out to the area, but time ran out before they were able to complete the trip. They did get close enough, however, for Gibson to point out various landmarks, and advise Bezold that if he would look in a certain spot, he would find shell casings which would identify the location of the corral.[99]

Bezold was unable to undertake a search for two weeks, at which time he returned to the area, and did, indeed, find shells just as Gibson had predicted. Bezold evidently did nothing with the shells at the time, but several years later he sent them to Doctor Grace Raymond Hebard at the University of Wyoming, who was then state secretary of the Historical Landmark Commission. Doctor Hebard, in turn, sent the shells off for examination, and was subsequently advised that they were of the type used in the Wagon Box Fight.[100]

It was then decided to invite Gibson back to Sheridan to take part in dedicating a permanent marker to be placed on the spot where Bezold had found the shells. However, because of World War I, the visit had to be postponed, and it was not until 1919 that Sam Gibson was able to return to the area.[101]

Meanwhile, in 1916, in conjunction with a celebration commemorating the fortieth anniversary of the Battle of the Little Big Horn, an interested group met in Sheridan, Wyoming, for the purpose of visiting historical sites in the area.[102] One of the group, W. M. Camp, of Chicago, had previously obtained separate interviews with both Sam Gibson and Max Littman, regarding the site of the Wagon Box corral. With Camp using his notes as a guide, the group carefully examined the area, and finally selected the spot where the pipe marker now stands. Three days later, on the morning of June 30, Mr. H. C. Benham, president of the Sheridan Commercial Club, and Mr. H. H. Tompson, editor of the *Teepee Book*, returned to the site and planted the four-inch iron pipe, capped with a six-inch brass plate which reads: "Site of the WAGON BOX FIGHT Aug. 2, 1867."[103] In 1916, Max Littman also visited Sheridan, and while in the area, reportedly identified the site where the large rock monument now stands, as having been the location of the corral.[104]

In 1919, Sam Gibson returned to Sheridan, and this time he and Bezold went over the entire area very carefully. Gibson again pointed out landmarks, and vividly recalled the battle that had occurred fifty-two years earlier. Gibson's choice as to the correct location is, today, marked by the large rock monument inside the fenced enclosure.[105]

In addition to the pipe marker, there had been at least one other site, thought by some to mark the location of the corral. This third site consisted of the remains of a large circular entrenchment, south and west of the site marked by Gibson. When asked about this third site, Gibson pointed out that there had been no entrenchment on August 2, 1867, that this particular site had been fortified and used as the main camp right after the Wagon Box Fight, a fact which is confirmed by another veteran of the Fort Phil Kearny saga.[106]

When asked about the pipe marker, Gibson explained that he had given the information to Camp in Omaha, while the latter was enroute to Sheridan, and had attempted to describe the location of the corral as best he could from memory and diagrams. Gibson remarked that he was pleased that his information had enabled Camp to come so close to the actual location.[107]

In 1936, seventeen years after Gibson's identification of the site, the large rock monument was erected by the Civilian Conservation Corps, under the direction of the Sheridan Chamber of Commerce. The monument stands at what was then the west edge of the corral, which actually extended to the east, beyond the present enclosure.[108]

But that was not the end of the controversy. In an article appearing in the September, 1950, issue of the *Chicago Westerners Brand Book*, the late T. J. Gatchell, a Buffalo, Wyoming, druggist, an authority on early Wyoming history, stated that Camp, with the help of survivors Max Littman and John Hoover, had correctly identified the pipe marker as the site of the corral. According to Gatchell, Camp visited the site with each man separately, and each agreed that this was the correct location. Gatchell also indicated that even before Camp marked the site, he had personally visited the area with one Frank Peach, a bullwhacker who had participated in the fight, and Peach, too, verified the pipe marker site as being correct. Some years after the erection of the large marker, Gatchell again visited the area with his friend, Medicine Bear, a Cheyenne chief. When Medicine Bear asked Gatchell if he wished to know where the soldiers or the Indians had been located, Gatchell replied that he wished to know about the soldiers, whereupon Medicine Bear climbed through the fence, and promptly proceeded to within some ten feet of Camp's pipe marker![109]

With the selection of both sites being the result of personal recollections made nearly half-a-century after the event, it would seem that one choice is nearly as valid as the next, except for one other factor: Empty shells have been found at both sites, but those found at the pipe marker were not manufactured until after the Wagon Box Fight. The shells found in the vicinity of the large rock monument were of the Martin bar-anvil type, while those found around the pipe marker featured the Benet-cup primer, which was not produced until 1868.[110]

Based on this evidence, which is simply irrefutable, there does not appear to be any question but what the present rock marker represents the actual site of the Wagon Box corral.

NOTES

1. Mari Sandoz, CRAZY HORSE, p. 199; James C. Olson, RED CLOUD AND THE SIOUX PROBLEM, pp. 51, 76.

2. Stanley Vestal claims that only the Battle of the Little Big Horn has received more attention than the Wagon Box Fight, a statement which may be suspect, but which nevertheless, points to the fact that the Wagon Box Fight has received an unusual amount of attention from writers and historians. See Stanley Vestal, WARPATH, p. 70.

3. The best examples of these exaggerated accounts is contained in Colonel Richard Irving Dodge, 33 YEARS AMONG OUR WILD INDIANS, pp. 480-489, and Fred M. Hans, THE GREAT SIOUX NATION, pp. 500-506. For accounts of the controversy regarding the correct site of the Wagon Box Fight, see *The Chicago Westerners Brand Book*, Volume VII, No. 7, September, 1950; *Old Travois Trails*, Vol. II, July-August, 1941; and *The Teepee Book*, July, 1916.

4. Dee Brown, FORT PHIL KEARNY: *An American Saga*, p. 191.

5. *Ibid.*, p. 205.

6. Robert A. Murray, MILITARY POSTS IN THE POWDER RIVER COUNTRY OF WYOMING, 1865-1894, p. 87.

7. *Ibid.*, p. 67; Grace Raymond Hebard and E. A. Brininstool, THE BOZEMAN TRAIL, Volume II, pp. 40-43.

8. Kenneth M. Hammer, THE SPRINGFIELD CARBINE ON THE WESTERN FRONTIER, p. 1; Francis A. Lord, THE CIVIL WAR COLLECTORS ENCYCLOPEDIA, pp. 237-243.

9. Hammer, *Springfield Carbine*, p. 1.

10. *Ibid.*

11. *Ibid.*

12. Murray, *Military Posts*, p. 93.

13. *Ibid.*, pp. 92-93.

14. *Ibid.*, pp. 94-95.

15. Hebard and Brininstool, *Bozeman Trail*, Vol. II, p. 93.

16. Piney Island is, today, the site of Story, Wyoming. During the 1860's the area was mistakenly referred to as an "island," due to an error in mapping. See PINEY ISLAND: *A Guide To The Story Area*, p. 24.

17. Charles D. Schreibeis, "The Wagon Box Fight," *Old Travois Trails*, Vol. III, May-June, 1942, p. 7.

18. Schreibeis, "The Wagon Box Fight," p. 7; Hebard and Brininstool, *The Bozeman Trail*, Vol. II, p. 43.

19. Schreibeis, "The Wagon Box Fight," p. 7.

20. Sam Gibson stated that the wagons were of the same type as those used during the Civil War, and Frederick Claus, another participant, said that they were of the common prairie schooner type. Since the bed of the average prairie schooner was about fifteen feet long, it would seem that 70' x 120' would be a reasonable approximation of the size of the corral. See Hebard and Brininstool, *The Bozeman Trail*, Vol. II, pp. 43-44, 50, 51, 84; Shreibeis, "The Wagon Box Fight," p. 7, and Foster Harris, THE LOOK OF THE OLD WEST, pp. 151-162.

21. Hebard and Brininstool, *The Bozeman Trail*, Vol. II, p. 44.

22. Colonel Richard Irving Dodge probably laid the foundation for this misconception in his 33 YEARS AMONG OUR WILD INDIANS, p. 481, first published in 1882. The story was repeated in Jacob Dunn, MASSACRES OF THE MOUNTAINS, p. 430, published in 1886, and again in George A. Forsyth, THE STORY OF A SOLDIER, p. 191, published in 1900. For accounts stating that this had no basis in fact, see Hebard and Brininstool, *The Bozeman Trail*, Vol. II, pp. 50-51, 75, 84-85; C. T. Brady, INDIAN FIGHTS AND FIGHTERS, p. 66. Roy E. Appleman's recent and very fine account of the battle suggests that some

of the wagon boxes may have had loopholes, but this, too, has been denied by Gibson and Littman. See Roy E. Appleman, "The Wagon Box Fight," in GREAT WESTERN INDIAN FIGHTS, p. 150.

23. Captain James Powell, Letter to Adjutant, Fort Phil Kearny, August 4, 1867; Appleman, "The Wagon Box Fight," p. 152.

24. Hebard and Brininstool, *The Bozeman Trail*, Vol. II, p. 43; Murray, *Military Posts*, pp. 94-95.

25. George Hyde, RED CLOUD'S FOLK, pp. 158-159.

26. *Ibid.*

27. *Ibid.*

28. *Ibid.* According to Vestal, the principal chief was "Flying-By." Red Cloud reportedly accompanied, but did not exercise any authority. See Vestal, *Warpath*, pp. 71-72.

29. The size of the attacking force, as with the number of casualties later reported, varies tremendously. Grinnell believed that there were only 300 Sioux and 75 to 100 Cheyennes, while Vestal and Hyde seem to agree that the force numbered about 1,000. Brady, on the other hand, put the figure at 3,000. See George Bird Grinnell, "The Wagon Box Fight," *Midwest Review*, Vol. IX, Feb.-March, 1928, p. 5; Hyde *Red Cloud's Folk*, p. 159; Vestal, *Warpath*, pp. 71-72; Olson, RED CLOUD AND THE SIOUX PROBLEM, pp. 64-65; Brady, INDIAN FIGHTS AND FIGHTERS, p. 48.

30. Vestal, *Warpath*, p. 71; Appleman, "The Wagon Box Fight," pp. 152-153.

31. Vestal, *Warpath*, p. 72.

32. Captain James Powell, Letter to Adjutant, Fort Phil Kearny, August 4, 1867; Hebard and Brininstool, *The Bozeman Trail*, Vol. II, pp. 43-44.

33. Francis Heitman, HISTORICAL REGISTER AND DICTIONARY OF THE UNITED STATES ARMY, Vol. I, p. 802; Murray, *Military Posts*, p. 51.

34. Heitman, *Historical Register*, p. 572; Brady, *Indian Fights and Fighters*, p. 67.

35. Captain James Powell, Letter to Adjutant, Fort Phil Kearny, August 4, 1867; Appleman, "The Wagon Box Fight," p. 149; George Geier, "The Side Camp," *Old Travois Trails*, Vol. II, July-August, 1941, p. 14. South Piney Creek is sometimes referred to as Big Piney, and is located to the north of the wagon box site, while Little Piney is to the south. Appleman says the wood-cutting camp was across Big Piney, but Powell's report says Little Piney, and Gibson described all the action as taking place at the "lower pinery," which was across Little Piney Creek. See also, Hebard and Brininstool, *The Bozeman Trail*, Vol. II, pp. 43-45.

36. Hebard and Brininstool, *The Bozeman Trail*, Vol. II, pp. 45-46.

37. *Ibid.*

38. *Ibid.*, pp. 46, 73, 83.

39. *Ibid.*, p. 46.

40. Brady, *Indian Fights and Fighters*, p. 66.

41. Hebard and Brininstool, *The Bozeman Trail*, Vol. II, p. 46.

42. *Ibid.*, p. 47.

43. *Ibid.*

44. *Ibid.*

45. Geier, "The Side Camp," p. 14.

46. *Ibid.*

47. *Ibid.*, p. 15.

48. *Ibid.*, p. 15.

49. *Ibid.*, p. 15-16.

50. *Ibid.*

51. *Teepee Book,* August, 1915, p. 9.

52. Hebard and Brininstool, *The Bozeman Trail,* Vol. II, pp. 48-49.

53. *Ibid.*

54. *Ibid.,* p. 49.

55. *Ibid.*

56. *Ibid.,* p. 50.

57. *Ibid.,* pp. 73, 83-84.

58. Captain James Powell, Letter to Adjutant, Fort Phil Kearny, August 4, 1867. Brady says that a private letter from Powell, written some years after the fight, put the time at seven a. m. See Brady, *Indian Fights and Fighters,* p. 46.

59. It seems reasonable to assume that Powell would have attempted some such maneuver, but it also seems strange that he did not make mention of the fact in his report. See Brady, *Indian Fights and Fighters,* p. 47; Captain James Powell, Letter to Adjutant, Fort Phil Kearny, August 4, 1867.

60. Hebard and Brininstool, *The Bozeman Trail,* Vol. II, pp. 51-52; Brady, *Indian Fights and Fighters,* p. 67.

61. Hebard and Brininstool, *The Bozeman Trail,* Vol. II, pp. 51-53.

62. *Ibid.*

63. Brady, *Indian Fights and Fighters,* p. 50.

64. Hebard and Brininstool, *The Bozeman Trail,* Vol. II, pp. 52-53.

65. Captain James Powell, Letter to Adjutant, Fort Phil Kearny, August 4, 1867.

66. Hebard and Brininstool, *The Bozeman Trail,* Vol. II, p. 53.

67. Captain James Powell, Letter to Adjutant, Fort Phil Kearny, August 4, 1867; Hebard and Brininstool, *The Bozeman Trail,* Vol. II, pp. 53-54, 76.

68. Appleman, "The Wagon Box Fight," pp. 151-152.

69. *Ibid.,* p. 155; Hebard and Brininstool, *The Bozeman Trail,* Vol. II, pp. 53-54.

70. *Ibid.*

71. Captain James Powell, Letter to Adjutant, Fort Phil Kearny, August 4, 1867. Vestal says too much emphasis has been placed on the Indians' reaction to the volume of fire from the new breech-loaders. He says they were probably impressed, but nothing more. Grinnell, on the other hand, says the Indians were mystified, and referred to these weapons as "Medicine Guns." See Vestal, *Warpath,* p. 82; Grinnell, "The Wagon Box Fight," p. 4.

72. Hyde, *Red Cloud's Folk,* p. 159.

73. Hebard and Brininstool, *The Bozeman Trail,* Vol. II, pp. 57-58.

74. *Ibid.,* p. 59.

75. Captain James Powell, Letter to Adjutant, Fort Phil Kearny, August 4, 1876.

76. Hebard and Brininstool, *The Bozeman Trail,* Vol. II, p. 59.

77. *Ibid.,* pp. 59-60.

78. *Ibid.,* p. 60.

79. *Ibid.,* p. 61.

80. *Ibid.,* pp. 62-63.

81. *Ibid.,* pp. 62-63.

82. *Ibid.,* p. 77; Vestal, *Warpath,* p. 77.

83. Major Benjamin F. Smith, Letter to Adjutant, Fort Phil Kearny, August 3, 1867.

84. Hebard and Brininstool, *The Bozeman Trail*, Vol. II, p. 66.

85. *Ibid.*, p. 67.

86. Appleman, "The Wagon Box Fight," p. 159.

87. Hebard and Brininstool, *The Bozeman Trail*, Vol. II, p. 68.

88. Major Benjamin F. Smith, Letter to Adjutant, Fort Phil Kearny, August 3, 1867.

89. Hebard and Brininstool, *The Bozeman Trail*, Vol. II, p. 68.

90. Major Benjamin F. Smith, Letter to Adjutant, Fort Phil Kearny, August 3, 1867.

91. Geier, "The Side Camp," p. 16.

92. Hebard and Brininstool, *The Bozeman Trail*, Vol. II, pp. 69-70.

93. Brady, *Indian Fights and Fighters*, p. 69.

94. Olson, *Red Cloud and the Sioux Problem*, pp. 64-65.

95. Captain James Powell, Letter to Adjutant, Fort Phil Kearny, August 4, 1867; Hebard and Brininstool, *The Bozeman Trail*, Vol. II, pp. 56, 66, 67, 70, 78; Brady, *Indian Fights and Fighters*, p. 68; John G. Neihardt, BLACK ELK SPEAKS, p. 16.

96. Vestal, Grinnell, Hyde, and Olson have all advanced convincing arguments refuting the claim of heavy Indian casualties. See Vestal, *Warpath*, pp. 79-81; Grinnell, "The Wagon Box Fight," p. 6; Hyde, *Red Cloud's Folk*, p. 159; and Olson, *Red Cloud and the Sioux Problem*, p. 65.

97. Murray, *Military Posts*, p. 96.

98. Major Benjamin F. Smith, Letter to Adjutant, Fort Phil Kearny, August 3, 1867.

99. Vie Willits Garber, "The Site of the Wagon Box Fight," *Old Travois Trails*, Vol. II, July-August, 1941, p. 17.

100. *Ibid.*, p. 18.

101. *Ibid.*

102. *The Teepee Book*, July, 1916, p. 35.

103. *Ibid.*, p. 38.

104. Sheridan, Wyoming, *Press*, July 15, 1964.

105. Garber, "The Site of the Wagon Box Fight," p. 18.

106. Garber, "The Site of the Wagon Box Fight," p. 19; Elsa Spear, BOZEMAN TRAIL SCRAPBOOK, p. 11.

107. Garber, "The Site of the Wagon Box Fight," pp. 19-20.

108. *Sheridan* (Wyoming) *Press*, March 21, 1936; J. W. Vaughn, Letter to the author, July 6, 1966.

109. *Chicago Westerners Brand Book*, Vol. VII, No. 7, Sept., 1950.

110. Hammer, *The Springfield Carbine*, pp. 1-2; J. W. Vaughn, Letter to the author, July 6, 1966.

GENERAL CROOK AT CAMP CLOUD PEAK:

"*I Am at a Loss What to Do*"

I N THE BATTLE OF THE ROSEBUD, on June 17, 1876, General George
Crook's Big Horn and Yellowstone Expedition was attacked by a
force of Sioux under Sitting Bull and Crazy Horse, with their
Cheyenne allies. After that conflict, Crook's column retreated from
the Rosebud River to its supply base at Goose Creek, on the headwaters
of the Tongue River in Wyoming. There he remained from June 19 to
August 3, awaiting reinforcements, resting his command and accumu-
lating supplies, while a few days march away the Indians met and an-
nihilated the Seventh Cavalry detachment under George A. Custer.

Crook's long delay at Goose Creek has provided the basis for much
controversy, both then and since. It has had its defenders — notably the
general's friend and aide-de-camp, John G. Bourke. To others, however,
it seems a bit puzzling, and to still others the general's behavior is down-
right reprehensible. One recent work, for instance, speaks of Crook's "dal-
lying" on a "pleasant vacation" while the Indians had their way with
Custer. Even one of Crook's own couriers believed that the general's
"actions deserve criticism," and General William Tecumseh Sherman,
who publicly approved the retreat to Goose Creek, privately branded it
"a terrible mistake."[1]

Crook's encampment on Goose Creek, however, was not quite a vacation. Nor was it, as Bourke tries to make it appear, the result of an explicit order by Crook's superior, Philip H. Sheridan, Division of the Missouri commander. And if it was "a terrible mistake," it was one which
arose rather understandably from the conditions surrounding the so-
called Sioux War of 1876. The situation was one in which three and
then two separate commands, communicating poorly if at all, were
groping in the dark for each other and for a hostile force which was an
unknown and unpredictable quantity, worried at what they might find.

Crook's column was operating as one of three sent into the field to
force non-treaty Sioux and allied Cheyennes into reservations which had
been established for them in Dakota Territory. Crook, commanding the
Department of the Platte, had made the earliest start, beginning his
campaign in March, 1876, with Colonel J. J. Reynolds in command of
the advance of his expedition. Reynolds encountered the Indians on the
Powder River on March 17, but after capturing their village he was
counter-attacked, and he retreated under conditions which led Crook to
bring court martial proceedings against him and two of his subordinates.[2]

Chagrined at the failure of an expedition which had been so widely heralded as one certain to cow the haughty Sioux, Crook had moved back to Fort Fetterman, where he soon began preparations to return to the field. The primary result of the campaign had been to further embolden the hostiles. Indeed, even the agency Indians were poking fun at the Army; so good a Sioux friend of the white man as Spotted Tail, when told by an officer that Crook was planning to move out after the hostiles again, remarked, "If you don't do better than you did the last time, you had better put on squaw's clothes and stay at home."[3]

Crook, a quiet, unprepossessing veteran of twenty-four years of Indian wars and the Civil War, had never before fought the Sioux or Cheyennes. He was accustomed to the kind of victories he had won in recent conflicts with the Apaches in the Southwest and in earlier wars with the Indians of the Pacific Coast. He had expected stout resistance from the Plains Indians. They were well-supplied, were superb horsemen and were operating in territory they knew well. They out-numbered the Army on the Plains, and Crook was well aware of their tendency to mount an attack in cases where the Apaches might refuse to be drawn into battle. If Crook, as has sometimes been asserted, was in fact guilty of "supreme" over-confidence at the beginning of the campaign, he betrayed little of it to his old friend Rutherford B. Hayes; "I don't feel very sanguine of success," he had written in March, "as they have so much advantage over us."[4] Nevertheless, Crook certainly had not counted on the prompt defeat of his first expedition. In order to reduce the chances for blunders, he had taken personal charge of the refitted command when it resumed its operations late in May. His new expedition included fifteen companies of cavalry, five companies of infantry and at least one hundred seventy-five Crow and Shoshone allies.

By the time Crook had moved out, the other two columns — one commanded by Colonel John Gibbon, the other by Brigadier General Alfred H. Terry, commanding the Department of Dakota — had also taken the field. Gibbon, marching southeast from Fort Shaw, by the end of May had taken position along the Yellowstone to guard against the hostiles' escaping across that river. Terry, moving west from Fort Abraham Lincoln towards the Yellowstone, soon would reach the river and establish communication with Gibbon.[5]

Crook's line of march took him from Fort Fetterman to the forks of the Powder River and, after he had established a supply base on Goose Creek, then north to the valley of the Rosebud River. There the hostiles, having observed the expedition's progress for several days, attacked it on June 17. The battle has been treated extensively elsewhere[6] and need not be recounted in detail here; the conflict raged for almost five hours over rough, broken ground, until the Indians left the field.

There is some evidence that their withdrawal may have been an

176

attempt to lure Crook's command into a trap, although it is possible that the Indians were simply tired and hungry and decided to go home.[7] Crook's forces had expended more than twenty-five thousand rounds of ammunition and had sustained casualties of ten killed and twenty-one wounded. The command camped on the battlefield that night, and the next day — because, Crook stated, he was short of rations and his wounded needed attention — it turned about and returned to the supply camp at Goose Creek.[8] There he and his officers "made very brief reports of the battle," as Anson Mills recalled, "having little pride in our achievement."[9]

Crook's column had been halted in its tracks, its offensive posture suddenly changed to the defensive. Pleased with the results of the battle, the Indians moved on to the Little Big Horn for four nights of war dances.[10] Yet Crook stubbornly refused to admit that he had been defeated. He acknowledged to Sheridan that the Indians had "displayed strong force at all points," and that he had attempted but failed to reach their village (which he mistakenly believed to be only a short distance away), but he insisted that the soldiers "drove the Indians back in great confusion." Although he did not specifically claim victory for his command either in his preliminary report or in his formal report of the following day, he certainly implied it, and he later flatly asserted that the Indians had been defeated.[11]

Since the battle was the reason for Crook's return to Goose Creek, and because it helped to condition his decision to remain there, some aspects of the conflict deserve notice. First of all, Crook had been struck a blow much harder than he had believed the Indians capable of delivering. The Indians had been spirited and courageous. "The old method of hovering, circling at a safe distance, and taking little risk was gone," writes George E. Hyde; "a new spirit had been born in them, and they came on with their ponies at a dead run, often breaking in among the troops and fighting hand-to-hand encounters."[12] The reports of all the field-grade officers bear witness to the severity of the battle. Crook found it impossible to estimate the enemy's numbers during the battle, but he noted in his report, apparently in some astonishment, that "they anticipated that they were strong enough to thoroughly defeat the command."[13] It is difficult to know the exact size of the Indian force at the Rosebud, but the best guesses estimate it at about one thousand, or roughly equal to Crook's own command.[14]

The battle at once became a topic of conversation and debate in the camp at Goose Creek, adding to the bad feeling and dissension dating to the court martial charges against Reynolds and before. According to one young lieutenant, some of Crook's enemies asserted that he had been out-generaled. The lieutenant admitted that Crook's success was "incomplete," but he commended the general's "timely caution" which "may have prevented a great catastrophe." Lieutenant Bourke saw the

177

battle from a different perspective: "This engagement gives us the 'morale' over the boastful Dacotahs," he wrote; "It is the prelude to the campaign in which we hope to destroy every village they have."[15]

As things turned out, however, the battle was more directly the prelude to many long weeks of relative inactivity. Lieutenant H. R. Lemley asserted that the inactivity was partly the fault of Crook's Indian allies. The general was still full of fight just after the battle, according to Lemley's story, and he proposed to his Crow and Shoshone scouts "a night march with a daylight attack upon the Sioux village," but the scouts had declined because "they had taken thirteen scalps during the day and they were satisfied."[16] This story seems to receive some support from Bourke's statement that Crook spoke with the Indian scouts near sun-down on the day of the battle "to learn their ideas relative to the prosecution of operations."[17] If Crook in fact made such a proposal and received such a response, it is odd that he failed to mention it in his report, in which he observed that he had followed the second of two options — "to follow the retreating Sioux without rations, dragging our wounded after us on rough mule litters, or return to our train where they could be cared for."[18]

From his base camp, which he named "Camp Cloud Peak" for the nearby mountain rather than the inelegantly-named Goose Creek, he notified Sheridan of the battle and informed him that reinforcements of five companies of infantry had been ordered from within the Department of the Platte. Until those reinforcements arrived, Crook would "not probably make any extended movement." (The Crow and Shoshone allies in the meantime had left for home, but had promised to return soon for more fighting.)[19] With dispatches going by courier between Crook's camp and the telegraph at Fort Fetterman some one hundred seventy-five miles to the southeast, communications were slow, and Crook could expect no answer to his report for about a week.

A courier came into camp on the morning of June 23, bearing a number of dispatches. One informed Crook of the disquieting reports that some eighteen hundred young warriors had left the Red Cloud agency to join the hostiles. Adding point to the report was Lieutenant W. S. Schuyler, who had accompanied the courier and who related that his party of three had struck a Sioux trail. The trail was large, and new enough that Schuyler's party had sought safety in rocks until nightfall, when they continued their ride into camp. To make matters worse, the agencies were buzzing with rumors (which at that time were not based on fact) of a sharp conflict between Terry and the hostiles. Another dispatch, from Sheridan, offered the more reassuring news that a fourth column, made up of eight companies of the Fifth Cavalry under Lieutenant Colonel Eugene A. Carr, was taking the field to move from Fort Laramie northwest to the Powder River. "I think," Sheridan wrote, "that this will stir things up and prove advantageous in the settlement of the

Indian question." Yet unaware that Crook had met the hostiles and that things had been stirred up a bit already, Sheridan added confidently that "with Terry operating probably up Powder River and you down that river and Carr from this side . . . good results must follow."[20] Still buoyantly optimistic, Lieutenant Bourke was encouraged by the news and felt that if Crook would order three more companies of cavalry into the field "the Sioux will be crushed 'ere the Summer solstice."[21]

Crook seemed unable to share in Bourke's enthusiasm. He had no way of knowing where Terry and Gibbon were and was distressed by the lack of news from either. In the hope of seeing some physical evidence of them, the general decided to make a scout up to the crest of the Big Horn Mountains. With six officers, four newspaper correspondents, and a few pack-mules, Crook left camp on July 1. The party did a little hunting and some exploring, but as Crook scanned a sweep of almost one hundred miles of flatlands with his glasses, he could see no sign of Terry or Gibbon — or of the Indians either, for that matter. Just before Crook's party returned on July 4, a courier had arrived in camp. Sheridan had received Crook's report of the Battle of the Rosebud and his instructions were to "hit them again and hit them hard." Crook read the telegram and remarked glumly, "I wish Sheridan would come here himself and show us how to do it. It is rather difficult to surround three Indians with one soldier."[22]

There had been little recent indication of any hostile Indian presence in the vicinity of Crook's camp. Bourke believed this to be clear evidence of the "severe handling the Sioux received" at the Rosebud. "Were they victorious or had the day been even undecided," he wrote, "our camp would long since have been beleaguered by their sharpshooters." The general, however, suspecting that the hostiles might still be nearby, on July 6 sent Lieutenant F. W. Sibley, with twenty men, Scout Frank Grouard and newspaper correspondent John F. Finerty, to scout towards the Little Big Horn in an attempt to see what the enemy was doing.[23] The next day, Crook himself led a small hunting and scouting expedition into the mountains, planning to be gone about four days. Their hunting was spectacularly successful, but the general peered fruitlessly through his field-glasses for some sign of the other columns. "The failure to hear from Terry or Gibbon distressed Crook a great deal more than he cared to admit," Bourke recalled some years later; "he feared for the worst, obliged to give ear to all the wild stories brought in by couriers and others reaching the command from the forts and agencies."[24]

"The worst" had already happened to Terry. Stunned by the Custer disaster on June 25, he had heard nothing from Crook and he appealed to Sheridan for information. "If I could hear [from Crook]," he wrote, "I should be able to form plans for the future much more intelligently. I should very much like instructions from you, or, if not instructions, your views of the situation based as they must be on what has taken place elsewhere as here."[25] Sheridan sent the confirmation of Custer's defeat — which had already been rumored in the newspapers — to Sherman, who advised Sheridan to have Crook and Terry join forces, and to reinforce and resupply both columns. The commanding general suspected that the two conflicts of the summer had inflicted enough injury on the hostiles that they would attempt to go in to the agencies. "I am sure," he wrote Sheridan, "both Crook and Custer have killed many of the best warriors in actual conflict and Sitting Bull's camp must be encumbered with wounded and families."[26]

None of this news, of course, was yet known at Camp Cloud Peak. While the scouting parties were out, Bourke had organized a fishing party near the camp, and there had been little to disturb the picnic-like atmosphere enjoyed by the command. Then, early on July 9, Lieutenant Sibley's detachment returned, haggard and exhausted from a two-day march on foot over rugged mountain trails. Attacked by a force of hostiles between three hundred to four hundred strong, they had abandoned their horses and fled over the mountains. The attacking force, declared Frank Grouard, was only a small part of the hostiles in the area; "The whole country," he said, "was covered with them." Moreover, a war party of Sioux was seen moving towards Camp Cloud Peak. Bourke sent the news to Crook by courier, and later, with his usual optimism, confided to his diary that the scout had been "successful at least in demonstrating the enemy's presence and power." He added his belief that "Within a week, we may expect to have an engagement in force." Late that night, the hostiles fired on a section of the camp, but caused more excitement than damage.[27]

At daylight the next morning, Courier Ben Arnold and Scout Louis Richaud rode into camp with a large number of letters and dispatches. Included was a telegram from Sheridan reporting the Battle of the Little Big Horn. As it raced through the camp, the news — as Bourke related in his ornate style — made "every lip quiver and every cheek blanch with terror and dismay." The mood of the entire command was affected: "Grief, Revenge, Sorrow and Fear stalked among us." Even Bourke had lost his optimism. He began to ponder the weaknesses imposed by a niggardly Congress on the Army, which was "so depleted and fettered," he felt,

> . . . that a regiment doesn't equal a Battalion, a company cannot muster more than a squad. Our men are so occupied with the extraneous duties of building posts and cantonments, no time is left for learning military evolutions. They are all willing and brave enough, but are deficient in experience and military intelligence.

And where was Crook? His party had not yet returned, and the countryside might be swarming with hostiles. Lieutenant Colonel William B. Royall, commanding in the general's absence, had sent a search party out during the day. Uneasy at the thought that the party might find only the mutilated corpses of Crook's small group, Bourke indulged in a rare criticism of his commander's behavior: "The General," he wrote, "has set an example of recklessness that cannot too strongly be condemned. This rashness must be foregone in the future."[28]

The Indians had set fire to the dry grass in the valley during the morning. The smoke was towering like a massive column in the sky when, late in the afternoon, the general at last appeared, escorted in by the search party. Welcomed with immense relief by his officers, Crook went to his headquarters tent, where he found a number of recent dispatches. One of them was a communication from Sheridan, which provided news of Terry's location and which — while it did not order Crook to combine with Terry — strongly indicated Sheridan's hope that he might do so. Above all, he hoped that, if the Indians were still concentrated, "you will be able to give them a good hard blow." He offered Crook the column of Fifth Cavalry, now under command of its new colonel, Wesley Merritt, and towards the end of the letter Sheridan repeated for emphasis, "As soon as you feel strong enough strike them hard."[29] Considering the mood of the camp that day, Sheridan's obsession with attack must have caused some perplexity in Crook's command.

Couriers had also brought newspapers containing accounts of the Battle of the Rosebud and its aftermath. Crook's conduct was being warmly debated by the national press. Most of the correspondents with the command had reported the conflict as a victory for the Army, but one, the *New York Herald's* R. B. Davenport, had informed his readers that the so-called victory had been something less than that. He accused the general of sending conflicting orders to Royal, of ordering a "disastrous" retreat of the right wing, and of not properly supporting the advance of his Crow Indian allies. The *Herald,* in an editorial comment on the dispatch, spoke of the "serious check" Crook had sustained and proclaimed the hostiles the victors. The paper declared itself not yet ready to blame Crook for the outcome — "Whether he blundered in the fight we do not presume to say until he has been heard from at length."[30]

It would be some time, however, before Crook was heard from, even briefly. Indeed, the long silence from Camp Cloud Peak gave rise to uneasiness and rumors. Rutherford B. Hayes, now the Republican nominee for President, inquired anxiously for some news of his friend, and newspapers began to speculate on the likelihood of Crook's command having met the same fate as Custer's. Sheridan assured General Sherman that there was nothing to worry about; "Crook never sends a courier," he wrote, "unless he has something important to say or wants something."[31]

Crook at last broke his silence on July 12. The knowledge that there were other military operations in the area, regardless of success, seems to have heartened him, and he had begun to think in terms of a victory which might redeem the entire campaign. He informed Sheridan that, although he was certain that he could defeat the hostiles with his present force, he feared that the victory might "be one barren of results." He had ordered the Fifth Cavalry to join him and would defer the attack until the regiment had arrived. Then he would "end the campaign with one crushing blow." From the reports of his scouts, Crook estimated that the enemy now had three men to his one. Although George E. Hyde feels that this estimate may have been too high, he nevertheless asserts that during July the hostiles had the power to defeat either Terry or Crook separately, had they cared to do so. That the hostiles did not attack in force was apparently due to the fact that they were engaged in their usual summer housekeeping tasks — dancing, feasting, bringing lodge-poles from the Big Horn Mountains — and paid only occasional visits to Crook's front to raid or to observe.[32]

Sheridan was disappointed in Crook's decision to delay, although he admitted in his reply to Crook's message that he was too far away to issue explicit orders or even to make suggestions. The division commander, however, did observe again — "for what it is worth" — that it might be well for Crook to unite with Terry and strike the Indians before they left the Little Big Horn Valley.[33]

By now Crook had heard from Terry, whose couriers twice before had been turned back by the Indians. Terry had no idea of the present location of either Crook or the Indians, but he wanted desperately to unite with Crook or at least to coöperate closely. Hoping that Crook might work out a plan for the campaign, Terry assured him that should the two columns unite, Crook would still be free to pursue his own course despite Terry's seniority in rank.[34]

The letters from Terry and Sheridan intensified Crook's desire to move away from his base, but he could not yet bring himself to risk another reversal. Reinforcements were coming in, however. A force of more than two hundred Shoshone warriors, led by handsome old Chief Washakie, had arrived on July 11, and they were followed on July 13 by a supply train and seven companies of infantry under Major Alexander Chambers. Crook was expecting Merritt and the Fifth Cavalry to arrive towards the end of the month. Unknown to the general, however, Merritt had set out to intercept a party of warriors leaving Red Cloud Agency, and the receipt of Crook's orders had been delayed for several days.[35]

On July 16, Crook replied to Terry's dispatch. He had planned to attack just after the arrival of his supply train, he told Terry, "but about that time I learned that the hostiles had received reinforcements and also learned at the same time that I could get the eight companies of the Fifth Cavalry, so I concluded to defer the movement until the arrival of those companies." When both columns were in the field, Crook believed, the first one to strike the Indians should hold them until the other column

182

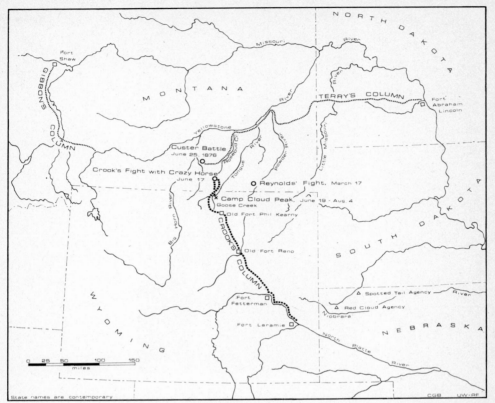

— *Map by Carol G. Barrett, Department of Geography, University of Wisconsin, River Falls*

CROOK'S MARCH TO GOOSE CREEK, SUMMER OF 1876

— *Courtesy of the National Archives, Washington D. C.*

GENERAL GEORGE CROOK
Photograph was made circa 1875.

— Courtesy of the National Archives, Washington D. C.

GENERAL CROOK'S FIELD HEADQUARTERS, 1876

This camp was on Whitewood Creek.

185

— *Courtesy of the National Archives, Washington D. C.*

WASHAKIE

*Chief of the Shoshones, Washakie was
General Crook's ally in 1876.*

could come up. Crook left the matter of a juncture up to Terry, but suggested that the latter might move in the direction of Crook's supply camp, which would provide some security should the columns pass each other in the field.[36]

Soon after the arrival of the Shoshones, Crook conferred with Washakie, who sustained the general's decision to await the Fifty Cavalry. In the meantime, scouting continued. Washakie led one expedition, which found the deserted site of a huge hostile camp in the valley of the Big Horn River, but none of the enemy was in evidence. Scout Louis Richaud also led an expedition to the Big Horn and was also unopposed.[37]

Days passed, but the Fifth Cavalry failed to appear. Crook became increasingly anxious and irritable. Always noted for his taciturnity, the general now was practically incommunicative. "For ten days," Finerty wrote with keen insight, ". . . Crook, nervous and unhappy, kept vibrating like a pendulum between the divers branches of Tongue River and Goose Creek. He felt instinctively that the Indians were playing him a trick, and he was puzzled what to do. To attack them with an inferior force, after the tragedy on the lower Big Horn, was too much to risk, and to wait for the promised reinforcement was both tedious and unheroic."[38]

The general's reply to Sheridan's recent dispatch seethed with frustration. He lashed out at the *New York Herald's* "villainous falsehoods" in its coverage of the Rosebud fight, and declared himself "immeasurably embarrassed by the delay of Merritt's column." He was "in constant dread of an attack" — particularly one in which the Indians might fire the tinder-dry grass and drive the command out of the country. His Indian allies were restive and eager to get moving, but he feared that if he took the offensive without the additional cavalry, he "could do but little beyond scattering" the hostiles and thus lose all hope of the one crushing blow he had hoped to strike. "I am at a loss what to do," he wrote unhappily. Quite missing the point, Sheridan remarked that Crook "seems to be a little demoralized by the attacks of the *New York Herald*" as he sent the dispatch on to Sherman. "Assure General Crook," Sherman replied curtly, "that he need not mind the *Herald* provided he do good execution on the enemy."[39]

For the enemy, however, the fighting season apparently had passed. "Sitting Bull's war was now over," Hyde has written, "and the Indians had no intention of doing any further fighting." The great encampment was beginning to break up into smaller groups to go off into winter camps and into the agencies.[40] Crook was informed of the movement on August 2 by a somewhat inaccurate report from Omaha that the entire body of Indians had started south towards the agencies. Among dispatches that same day was one from Sheridan, advising him that Merritt, by now, would be approaching Crook's camp. The division commander stressed that the behavior of both Crook and his command had been "ap-

187

proved all the way through" by both himself and Sherman, but that he had now sent all possible reinforcements, and that Crook must now take the field and, if necessary, unite with Terry.⁴¹ Crook needed no further urging. The next morning he marched out to meet Merritt, and the following day, against a sky blackened by the smoke of prairie fires, the general led his command back into the field.

The "one crushing blow" which Crook had hoped to deliver was not to be struck, either by Crook or by other forces in the field. The great Indian encampment had vanished. For another month Crook stayed in the field, soon meeting Terry, and then parting from him to engage in a further search for the hostiles. On what has been called the "Horsemeat March" or the "Starvation March," Crook's column fought and defeated a band of Sioux under American Horse at Slim Buttes, but that was the only glimmer of success in the campaign. Sitting Bull, after a clash with Colonel Nelson A. Miles, took some two hundred lodges of his people across the Canadian border during the winter, and Crazy Horse was eventually induced to surrender.

So ended the Sioux war of 1876. Looking back on the operations from the following winter, Sheridan believed Crook and Terry to have been "each abundantly strong to have met and defeated the Indians," as he wrote privately to Sherman, and he had concluded that their campaigns "will not bear criticism." Sherman agreed. He was convinced, moreover, that had Crook remained at the Rosebud "and kept up the pressure on the enemy," calling his wagon train up to him rather than returning to it, the Custer disaster would have been avoided.⁴² Grand strategy no doubt appeared much clearer to Sherman and Sheridan in their headquarters than it did to George Crook on Goose Creek, out of touch with any other column in the field and facing an enemy of unpredicted power and skill. For all Crook then knew, there was no other military force within one hundred fifty miles, and it would be three weeks before he was informed of Terry's location. By that time, reports of hostile strength and activity were enough to encourage a prudent commander to await all possible reinforcements before taking the field. On the other hand, it is possible that Crook's very desire for a smashing victory kept him awaiting those reinforcements for so long that the victory was snatched from him.

Whether Crook should have moved out several weeks earlier than he did must be judged in light of the inclination of several thousand warriors to remain concentrated and to fight as they had at the Rosebud and the Little Big Horn, and that is a question open to the widest speculation. It may be that Crook's command should have remained in contact with the hostiles. It may also be that, had he attempted to do so, the Indian-fighting Army's greatest disaster might have carried the name of Crook rather than Custer.

188

NOTES

1. J. G. Bourke, On the Border with Crook (New York: Charles Scribner's Sons, 1891), p. 336; John Upton Terrell and George Walton, Faint the Trumpet Sounds (New York: David McKay, 1966), p. 431; Sherman to P. H. Sheridan, February 17, 1877, Sheridan Papers, Library of Congress.
2. These operations are treated in J. W. Vaughn, The Reynolds Campaign on Powder River (Norman: University of Oklahoma Press, 1961).
3. J. G. Bourke Diary, May 12, 1876, USMA Library, West Point.
4. Crook to Hayes, March 1, 1876, Crook Papers, R. B. Hayes Library, Fremont, Ohio, *Cf.;* J. W. Vaughn, With Crook at the Rosebud (Harrisburg: Stackpole, 1956), p. 168.
5. Good coverage of these operations is in E. I. Stewart, Custer's Luck (Norman: University of Oklahoma Press, 1955).
6. Vaughn, *With Crook at the Rosebud.*
7. *Ibid.*, p. 147; G. B. Grinnell, The Fighting Cheyennes (Norman: University of Oklahoma Press, 1956), p. 329; Martin F. Schmitt, General George Crook: *His Autobiography* (Norman: University of Oklahoma Press, 1960), p. 195.
8. Crook to AAG, Military Division of the Missouri, June 20, 1876, Letters Received (LR), Military Division of Missouri, National Archives and Records Service (NARS) Records Group (RG) 98.
9. Anson Mills, "On the Battle of the Rosebud," *Proceedings of the Annual Meeting of the Order of the Indian Wars*, Washington, D. C., 1917, p. 31.
10. Grinnell, *Fighting Cheyennes*, p. 344.
11. Crook to Sheridan, June 19, 1876, and Crook to AAG, Military Division of Missouri, June 20, 1876, Letters Sent (LS) B. H. & Y. Expedition; Annual Report for Department of the Platte, September 25, 1876, LS Department of the Platte, NARS RG 98.
12. G. E. Hyde, Red Cloud's Folk (Norman: University of Oklahoma Press, 1937), p. 264.
13. Crook to Sheridan, June 19, 1876, NARS RG 98.
14. Grinnell, *Fighting Cheyennes*, p. 332n; Hyde, *Red Cloud's Folk*, p. 263.
15. H. R. Lemley, "The Fight on the Rosebud," *Proceedings of the Annual Meeting of the Order of the Indian Wars* (Washington, D. C., 1917), pp. 40-41; Bourke Diary, June 17, 1876.
16. Lemley, "Fight on the Rosebud," p. 42.
17. Bourke Diary, June 17, 1876.
18. Crook to AAG, Military Division of Missouri, June 20, 1876, NARS RG 98.
19. Crook to Sheridan, June 19, 1876, NARS RG 98.
20. Bourke Diary, June 23, 1876; Sheridan to Crook, June 18, 1876, LS Military Division of Missouri, NARS RG 98.
21. He added that the three additional companies were "not essential to the successful pursuit of the campaign," but that as many troops as possible should be allowed "to share in the glory of the good work." Bourke Diary, June 23, 1876.
22. *Ibid.*, July 1-4, 1876.
23. *Ibid.*, July 6, 1876.
24. Bourke, *On the Border with Crook*, p. 333.
25. Terry to Sheridan, "Confidential," July 2, 1876, copy in R. C. Drum to Sheridan, July 6, 1876, LS Military Division of Missouri, NARS RG 98.
26. Sherman to Sheridan, July 7, 1876, LS Army of US, NARS RG 108.
27. Bourke Diary, July 9, 1876; the Sibley scout is related in J. F. Finerty, War-Path and Bivouac (Norman: University of Oklahoma Press, 1961), Ch. XIII.
28. Bourke Diary, July 10, 1876.
29. Sheridan to Crook, July 10, 1876, LS Military Division of Missouri, NARS RG 98.
30. *New York Herald*, June 24, 1876.
31. Sherman to Hayes, July 12, 1876, LS Headquarters Army of US, NARS RG 108; George Crook Scrapbooks, Military History Research Center, Army War College, Carlisle Barracks, Pa.; Sheridan to Sherman, July 12, 1876, LS Military Division of Missouri, NARS RG 98.
32. Crook to Sheridan, July 12, 1876, LS B. H. & Y. Expedition, NARS RG 98; Hyde, *Red Cloud's Folk*, pp. 273-274.
33. Sheridan to Crook, July 16, 1876, LS Military Division of Missouri, NARS RG 98.
34. Terry to Crook, July 9, 1876, copy in LS Military Division of Missouri, NARS RG 98.

35. Bourke, *On the Border with Crook,* pp. 334-336; Finerty, *War-Path and Bivouac,* pp. 146-148.
36. Crook to Terry, July 16, 1876, LS B. H. & Y. Expedition, NARS RG 98.
37. Bourke, *On the Border with Crook,* p. 342.
38. *Chicago Times,* September 22, 1876.
39. Crook to Sheridan, July 23, 1876, copy in Sheridan to Sherman, July 27, 1876, LS AGO, NARS RG 94; Sherman to Sheridan, July 27, 1876, LS AGO, NARS RG 94.
40. Hyde, *Red Cloud's Folk,* p. 275.
41. Sheridan to Crook, July 28, 1876. LS Military Division of Missouri, NARS RG 98.
42. Sheridan to Sherman, Feb. 10, 1877, Sherman Papers, Library of Congress; Sherman to Sheridan, Feb. 17, 1877, Sheridan Papers, Library of Congress.

THE BANNOCK - PIUTE WAR OF 1878:

Letters of Major Edwin C. Mason

INTRODUCTION

THE OUTBREAK OF THE BANNOCK-PIUTE[1] WAR in 1878 marked the third consecutive summer of Indian wars in the Northwest. The cause was a common one; failure of the federal government to deliver food and other supplies promised to Indians confined on reservations where they could not provide for themselves. The desperate Bannocks of Fort Hall, Idaho, began with a dash westward to join equally unhappy Piutes in southeastern Oregon, who, in turn, forcibly recruited some fellow tribesmen from Nevada.[2]

In the ensuing campaign, Major Edwin C. Mason had an important part, although he has not been prominent in the accounts of the war. Born in Ohio in 1831, he entered military service thirty years later as a captain of infantry in the Ohio Volunteers. He served throughout the Civil War, and by brevet promotions reached the rank of brigadier general. He saw much action, and was wounded three times. He remained in the Army and spent most of the 'seventies in the West. As a member of General Edward Canby's staff, he narrowly escaped when that officer was slain in the Modoc War. In 1876 he was assigned as inspector general for the Department of the Columbia, at Fort Vancouver.

As in the Nez Perce affair of 1877, Mason served as General Howard's chief of staff, and on both campaigns, he wrote frequent letters which his descendants have preserved. These letters and supporting papers were made available by his grandson, Colonel Kenneth M. Moore. They are complete and legible, presenting no problems beyond the necessity of using only about one-third of the material. The omitted sections mostly deal with family matters and other concerns not directly related to the war. Care was taken to include all portions which cast light on the strategy of the campaign, and particularly on the performance of General Howard. Major Mason shows a warm personal regard for his commanding officer, but was often distressed by the general's poor judgment, often alternating between rash impatience and wavering indecision.

A SUMMARY OF THE CAMPAIGN

Mason was also called upon to write the summary of the campaign in the Department's official report, designated General Field Orders Number 9, dated October 4, 1878:

Before the fatigue incident to the arduous but successful campaign against the hostile Nez Perces had been forgotten, or even the remount of the cavalry of that expedition had been effected, another outbreak on the extreme southeastern boundary of the Department called the troops again into the field.

The Bannock Indians, leaving their reservation at Fort Hall, swept rapidly across the southern part of Idaho, murdering and robbing as they went, gathering at the same time a constantly increasing force, until they numbered at Stein's [Steen's] Mountain[3] a band of six or seven hundred warriors — Bannocks, Piutes, Klamaths, and Columbia River renegades, with their women and children — a body of people not far from two thousand souls.

Rapid as had been their movement, not less speedy was the pursuit. Within a few hours after the news of the revolt was received at Fort Boise, the garrison of that post was in the field, and by forced marches of extraordinary length, overtook the hostiles at Stein's [Steens] Mountain,[4] and despite the disparity of numbers, (not less than 7-to-1) unhesitatingly charged and drove the Indians from their camp, killing and wounding many, and destroying a considerable amount of their property. Captain Reuben F. Bernard, 1st Cav., and the officers and men of that regiment with him in that engagement, are deserving of high commendation for the gallant and dashing manner in which they inaugurated the campaign. By this time the infantry, which had been brought forward with wagons to aid in accomplishing the long marches daily made, joined in the pursuit from Camp Curry, from which place the Indians turned northward. The troops followed their obscure and difficult trail through the fastnesses of the Blue Mountains. The embarrassments of such a march can be appreciated only by those who have experienced them.

On the seventh day of July a concentration of troops from front, rear and flank, was effected in the vicinity of Pilot Rock, near which place the combined cavalry under the command of Captain Bernard, in the presence of the General Commanding, struck the enemy, well posted in a chosen position in the mountains, defeated him, drove him from his camp, and filled the forests of the Blue Mountains with fugitives.

The hostiles made soon another attempt to carry out their original plan of crossing the Columbia River, which was defeated by the gunboats under the prompt and vigorous command of Captain John A. Kress, of the Ordnance Corps, and Lieutenant Melville C. Wilkinson, aide-de-camp.

Turning now toward the Umatilla Reservation, they are met by the Artillery, Infantry and one company of Cavalry under command of Captain Evan Miles, and again defeated and scattered. All the approaches to the Columbia and Snake Rivers are closed, and turn where they may, they find a force confronting them. Disheartened and demoralized, they turn upon their trail and fly, at first faster than the troops can pursue them. Lt. Col. Forsyth, 1st Cavalry, in this pursuit strikes them once in an ambuscade; a severe skirmish ensues, when they again run. Intent now only on escaping, they scatter in small parties and hide in the mountains and forests, whence they are hunted up and made to surrender. A few, stealing horses as they run, are driven by the cavalry beyond the limits of the Department.

The campaign has been brought to a satisfactory close. Within 90 days a formidable force of hostile Indians was repeatedly met, in every encounter defeated, and finally captured or dispersed, and with the exception of a handful, forced to surrender, until scarce a hostile Indian is unaccounted for. Success has characterized every movement, and it is an added source of gratification that all has been accomplished with so small a loss of life on the part of the troops.

To the officers and men who have been engaged, thanks are due for their excellent conduct throughout. Gallantry in action has been displayed by those whose good fortune it was to meet the enemy, while all have borne uncomplainingly the privations and hardships inseparable from so active a campaign.

By command of Brigadier General Howard:

> EDWIN C. MASON,
> Major 21st Inf.,
> Acting Asst. Inspector General

Thus did Major Mason summarize the Bannock-Piute War after it was over. Sometimes during the campaign, he saw it differently, as reflected in numerous letters to his wife, their three small daughters, and his mother. From the outset, he must have been impressed with the similarity of this development to the Nez Perce episode, as he started out in the identical way, ascending the Columbia River from his Vancouver station to join General O. O. Howard and assist in getting the campaign underway. The first letter home from Walla Walla assures the ladies that the affair will soon be over, and that he misses them and loves them dearly. These general themes pervade most of the succeeding letters.

From Boise, on June 12, he writes of the general's plan to establish headquarters at "Sheep Ranch," near the Owyhee River. "We are of the opinion that it is only a big spree among the Indians and that a month's good work will knock the bottom out of it."

June 13 brought the report that General Howard had advanced to Sheep Ranch, leaving the major in Boise; also this bit of news: "Sarah Winnemucca, a noted Indian woman, has gone out from Bernard's camp to try to induce her people, the Piutes, to come in and surrender. I have little idea she will succeed." Later, he had more to tell about Sarah.

Mason was still at Boise on June 18, handling messages to and from the forces in the field, and trying to relay the latest information to General Howard, whose nervous movements made him hard to find. Captain Bernard, who was nearest to the hostiles, reported them going north, which Mason interpreted as evidence of a plan to move through the Salmon River country. The next day's letter has him working day and night, hoping to get away soon to join Howard. Meanwhile he is helping Colonel Cuvier Grover to organize a column aimed at an eastward sweep, to push the Bannocks back toward Fort Hall, while other forces engage the Piutes and local allies in central Oregon. Overwork shows in Mason's usually good spelling: "We have no Indian news worth telling — the people over about Harney are so scart they can't think straight. I don't beleave . . ." We will never know what it was that he did not "beleave." A note dated June 20 cuts in, saying he has been ordered to join the general immediately, which he did at Malheur City. They then moved to Malheur Agency and Camp Harney, whence his letter of June 24 fills in some details of travel:

> We drove until it was so dark we could no longer see, then without any other supper than a poor cup of coffee, we laid down on the ground with the sky for covering, until 3 a. m. when we pushed on, arriving at the Agency about 10 a. m. For two hours I was on the jump — arranging the troops into two battalions — and other things. This was the first time I had seen our companies since leaving Umatilla. We started at 12 noon and moved out on the Harney road. We camped on the Malheur River about 15 miles from the Agency. I went to bed about half-past nine. At 11 a messenger came, saying Bernard had struck the Indians and had a fight. I was up immediately and hard at work in a few moments. We had breakfast at 1 a. m. Then the General, myself and staff started for Harney.

They made it in twelve hours, fifty miles over "mountains and rocky roads." Here and on following occasions, Mason pays tribute to his horse "George," for enduring these arduous rides. George was really Mrs. Mason's horse, her husband's gift and a souvenir of the Nez Perce chase. The major acquired him after his original rider, Bugler Brooks, became a casualty at the Camas Meadow fight in eastern Idaho. George survived that campaign and like his owner, had barely recovered when this newest war broke out. Mason impulsively had him brought along, and now took possession of him when they were all united at the agency. George seems to have been an exceptional animal; a well substantiated account tells of his intelligent effort to get the mortally wounded bugler to remount and be carried to safety.[5]

A note dated June 26 reports an advance to Camp Curry, sixty miles accomplished from early morning of the day before to 3:00 o'clock p. m. of the next day. His statements are obvious ones: he was tired but still working hard, had only a moment to write while the courier was waiting, and they were expecting to resume pursuit early in the morning and to catch the Indians within a few days. The next letter was newsy enough to call for extensive quotation:

> Camp Laurence Babbitt
> June 27, 1878   6 p. m.
>
> My dear wife and mother,
>
> We started this morning in direct pursuit of the Indians, following their trail which leads through mountainous country northeast toward the John Day River, thence through the Umatilla country. They say they are going to "Moses," thence to "Sitting Bull" — we will see about it.[6] They have about 700 warriors — about 1,500 people in all. Bernard says there were just acres of them, when he saw them in his battlefield. We are camped in the woods tonight — it's raining, too, by way of a change. I am well fitted for the rain with my rubber coat and leggins. Bernard's

194

— Courtesy of Colonel Kenneth M. Moore

MAJOR EDWIN C. MASON
*This photograph of the author of the letters
was taken two years before the outbreak
of the Bannock-Piute War.*

— Courtesy of Colonel Kenneth M. Moore

FRANCES KINGSBURY MASON

This studio portrait of Major Mason's wife was taken circa 1876. Major Mason wrote to her often during the campaign of 1878.

fight was a most successful affair, considering his small force. We have with us 5 companies of cavalry and 8 of foot.

Saturday, June 29. Camp Bernard, 8 p. m.[7]

We left Camp Babbitt in a rain storm. It soon began to grow cold and then the snow came down thick and fast — all day we marched in a driving snowstorm — I suffered with the cold, as I am only dressed for the summer. We got to camp about 1 o'clock and waited till dark for the wagons to come in — we are trying to bring our wagons through these mountains. . . . We have made a good march and are now only one day behind the enemy. Bernard has gone on, and may strike them. We are high up in the mountains where it is cold all the time. We forgot to put the rubber gloves in, so my hands were both wet and cold yesterday. My coat is splendid, and will keep me dry in the hardest rain. . . . Must stop, for it's getting too dark to see.

Sunday, 3 p. m.

I would tell you where we are, did I know. The truth is, we don't know just where we are. We started into these mountains with our wagons on the representations of our guide that we would find no trouble in getting through. We have had trouble from the start, and this morning have almost been obliged to abandon them. Since 7 o'clock the General, Wood and myself — with the orderlies — have been scouring the country, up one mountain slope only to plunge down another. We have ridden about 30 miles, and are now resting until the troops come up. We will cut loose from the wagons and push on, leaving Spurgin to work his way with the train into John Day Valley. This thing of following an Indian trail with wagons won't do. We should have pack trains. I got all the pack animals in Boise I could hire — but they are not with us. We must drop our wagons in John Day Valley even if we have to carry our rations on our backs. We are now trying to work our way down to the South Fork of "John Day." This place where we are resting is a grassy nook, well shaded by big pines, with good water near at hand. I am writing on my knee, finding it rather an awkward desk. We have with us Sarah Winnemucca and her sister (her brother's wife, Mattie). Sarah is a remarkable woman — a full-blooded Piute Indian, yet well educated, speaks the best of English, and can read and write as well as anybody.[8] She was educated by the Catholics. She is very much more of a lady in her manner and address than many white women I know. She did a bold thing in going into the hostile camp at Steen's Mountain and bringing out her people. She rides a side-saddle — but Mattie, a man's saddle. It would interest you to see them go anywhere with a dash few men could excel. Mattie will not talk English although Sarah says she understands it. They mess with us[9] and have a tent at headquarters. Sarah is deeply interested in this war and feels bitter toward those who have led her people astray. Do you remember while we were in Frisco hearing that Lt. Bartlett — a brother of Mrs. General Schofield's — married an Indian woman? Well, Sarah is the woman! So we have Mrs. General Schofield's sister-in-law for an interpreter! Not the least interesting part of the story is that Sarah asked for the divorce. She told Gen. Howard he was too bad a man for any woman to live with!

Monday July 1st.

Camp Duncan on the S. Fork of John Day. 6 p. m.

I have been in the saddle most of the day. We are working our way out of the mountains, but it's hard work . . . I am well but dirty as a pig, and get very tired every day. Unless we get out of these mountains very soon, we might as well give up the pursuit of the Indians. We were close on their heels a few days ago —now, we must be far in the rear. . . .

> Yours with much love,
> EDWIN

It was July 5 before Major Mason could write again, this time from the junction of John Day River and its south fork, at present Dayville:

We marched yesterday over the most broken country I have ever seen wagons taken over. We marched for miles and miles down the bed of a stream. We were 13 hours in the saddle. This is the main stage road from The Dalles to Canyon City, from which point we are distant about 37 miles. . . . Our wagons of course did not arrive. We expected to go without supper and sleep in the sagebrush, but found, much to our gratification, three houses within a few miles of each other. We took the best one, finding it deserted but full of provisions — it had been deserted in a hurry, for the table was set and supper on it. Wood and I climbed in through an open window and explored. In a few minutes Sarah Winnemucca and her sister were in the kitchen putting things to rights, and in due time a good supper was on the table — coffee, biscuits, spring chicken, eggs. Sarah is a good cook, and as bright and cheerful as possible. We worked until midnight getting up despatches. For a time I expected to go to The Dalles and thence to Walla Walla. . . . The General wanted me to go up to Wheaton and [undecipherable] him. We finally gave it up, sending despatches instead. . . . From here, we take what pack animals we have and push on after the Indians on their trails. I will be glad to get rid of the wagons, for it's mighty hard work to follow Indians and make road also. I have no idea where this thing will end, but rather think we will have another chase to the British line. The Indians crossed this road about 3 miles from here on Sunday. They were all day passing, from early morning until late at night. There must be 1,500 souls with an immense herd of horses, some 3 or 4 thousand. I doubt whether they will stand and fight us. If they had wanted a fight, they could have had it any day by just waiting for the troops to come up.

In the first days of July, Howard and his staff moved ahead of the slow wagons, leaving them in the John Day Valley and pressing on to overtake Bernard's cavalry. Mason explains this in a letter dated July 6 from Camas Prairie:

This will be a brief note, for a courier goes in a few moments to Hetner [sic, Heppner] a small post office on the Dalles and Umatilla stage road. My last letter was from John Day Valley. We left there Thursday morning and traveled 42 miles through the mountains to overtake Bernard with the cavalry. The infantry we left behind to come on by shorter marches. We didn't find Bernard until yesterday after marching 25 miles more. Today we have marched about 25 miles and are now near the head of Butter Creek, some 50 miles from Pendleton. What a big swing we have made! Here we are, almost back to the stage road we passed over going to Boise a few weeks ago. This has been a wild and picturesque country, so high in the air it has been very cold every night. It takes all the clothes I have to keep me warm. I want some more clothes,

The Bannock-Piute War of 1878

but don't know just how to get them — one pair of heavier pants (those
soldier pants I used last summer), those army sox and army mittens. The
soldier's blouse, if you could stitch in an extra lining, it would make it
much more serviceable. Our operations are likely to be in the mountains
where it will always be cold at night and if we have to follow these
hostiles to the British line again it will be cold weather before we are
through.

A postscript adds that "George is doing fine," ridden only occasionally as he has another horse. That same evening, Mason starts another
letter, to have it ready when the next courier departs.

You have doubtless seen by the papers that the Indian outbreak is
very general. . . . If we had an army, we could very soon dispose of the
question — but we have not got an army, only the frame of one. Little
squads of men instead of companies and regiments. . . . Two summers running of Indian wars is too much of a good thing. While you are about it,
you had better send my buckskin undersuit — this may look like preparation for cold weather long in advance, but it is well. Put in the rubber
gloves also.

July 7th, evening

We marched from Camas Prairie to this place — Pilot Knob or
Pilot Rock, about 30 miles. . . . Tomorrow we expect to move toward the
Columbia River via Butter Creek. We hope to find the Indians on the last
named place. We are near them and if we have good luck may strike
them. We expected to find Wheaton here, but he has not left Walla Walla.
Oh no, not he. I wish *I* could stay at home in that way and have it all
right, as others seem able to do.

Another letter, started that same evening, resumes his complaints
about Wheaton's slowness in getting a gunboat patrol on the Columbia
to prevent the Indians from fleeing across the river. "He doesn't seem
to 'take in' the situation. A man in Indian warfare must have plenty of
'go' in him." As it was to develop, these armed river steamers did get into
action in time, and played a big part in foiling the Indian plans for
escaping northward. Writing the next evening, Monday, July 8, Mason
had something definite to report:

Well, we had a lively fight today. We had only been out about two
hours when we got word from our scouts that the Indians were in force
in our front — soon we saw them, clustering like bees on the hillside
about two miles away. They took a strong position on the top and rocky
sides of a high hill. Bernard had seven companies of the 1st Cav. which
he handled in the best manner possible. I have rarely seen men handled
in better style. They moved to the attack without a moment's hesitation,
firing as they advanced, leading their horses up the steep and rocky hill
without a particle of cover, for the country is treeless. After the enemy
had been driven from the first hill, he retreated to a second one — Capt.
Winters charged this hill, pistol in hand, the enemy flying in haste before him. It was beautifully done — the cavalry has redeemed itself in
these two fights.[10] It's all owing to Bernard's splendid soldiership. We
have seven companies of cavalry which is ample to whip these Indians,

199

I know. Well, to go on with my story — we drove the Indians back over the hills to the wooded mountains behind. We followed them fast and hard, giving them a crack every few moments. Finally we went into camp at this place, which is on the very road we marched over yesterday. The flight of the Indians was for some miles up this mountain. Finally they took their way up a deep and rocky canyon. Our loss was none killed,[11] a number wounded — a good many horses killed. The Indians lost a number killed — how many wounded we do not know, about 200 head of horses, and a large amount of plunder of all sorts. The foot troops, Throckmorton and Burton, were not in this fight, having been sent another way. The other foot troops under Miles are about one day's march in our rear. We will start again tomorrow on the chase.

Mason began still another letter the next day:

> In the field near battle ground
> July 9, 1878
>
> My dear wife and mother,
>   This morning we moved camp about 2 miles in order to get nearer water. We are awaiting the report of scouts to decide which way to move. It looks as though the Indians have divided into several bands. . . . I was so sleepy this morning I took a nap and didn't wake up in time to get a letter ready. We have reveille at 3:30 every morning, and it's from 9 to 10 every night before we get to rest . . . not a night passes without couriers coming in and waking everybody up. . . . Tell the little girls I have one of their skipping ropes with me — it was in the tent bag, got in there I expect the last day they played in the tent. I have it safe and will bring it home with me. Your horse George stands the campaign well, I only ride him part of a day and not always every day.
>
> July 11.
>   Yesterday we marched from 6 a. m. to 6 p. m., twelve hours in the saddle. We arrived at Cayuse Station. It was just one month to the day since we had been at the same station, going from Walla Walla to Boise. 7 p. m. I am now in camp 15 miles from Walla Walla, having left Cayuse Station at 2 p. m. The General has gone ahead — I will follow in the morning. We are going as fast as we can travel to Lewiston to head off the hostiles.
>
> Wallula, 1 p. m., Friday 12.
>   I rode all last night and got into W. Walla just in time to take the cars here. We are now on the steamer going to Lewiston. I have not had anything to eat today and am feeling rather hungry. As I am too busy to write and not in a very good humor, I will close.

He started a new letter the next day, still aboard the steamer *Northwest* which he had boarded at Wallula and which was now ascending the lower reaches of the Snake River.

> We have been making slow time up this rapid river. The boat is small and crowded to its last foot of room. About 50 animals and four companies, with Headquarters, makes a big load. . . . The heat has been terrific — this boat must have large boilers to generate steam enough to push against the strong current. Consequently the boat is like an oven, the deck so hot it almost burns our feet. This, with the shaking of the boat, has kept me from writing.

The Bannock-Piute War of 1878

Sunday, July 14, Lewiston.

We were crawling up the river all night and have just arrived (6 a. m.). We will leave at noon and go on up the Snake on this boat. We hope to get as high as the mouth of the Grande Ronde or the Salmon. It will save a hard march through the mountains and will also save time. I am in hopes this movement to head them off will result favorably — else we may expect a long tramp across the continent to Sitting Bull. I was not in favor of this movement just at this time. I think we had the promise of better results by following up the enemy with cavalry. The General didn't ask my opinion, so I didn't give it.

On Monday, July 15, he commenced a new letter, still aboard the *Northwest* now tied up at the mouth of the Grande Ronde:

We left Lewiston at noon and crawled up to this point, about 40 miles in 7 hours. At one place we were obliged to land the men, and man a rope, and thus aid in climbing a rapid. We have been waiting today for our pack-train to come overland from Lapwai. We will however move the men out about 6 miles on the trail tonight. This morning we received telegrams from Wheaton at Walla Walla giving an account of Miles' fight at Canyon Station. I am indeed sorry we did not stay there — it was against my judgment making this move. . . . I have made up my mind that in case we have any more campaigns in the Dept., I will go out in command of my Regiment. I have not had any trouble with the General — not the least — but I have not enough to do at Headquarters to make it worthwhile for me to stay. I could be of much more use with the troops. . . . I could have handled the battalion more satisfactorily than it has sometimes been managed. Don't say anything about this to anyone. . . . The steamer will leave this place as soon as the pack string is over the river. We march toward Summerville, at the head of the Grande Ronde Valley. We hope to intercept the Indians en route. . . . I must close, as the boat is going one way, and I am going another.

On July 17 he reported on the command's march since leaving the boat late on the previous afternoon. They checked the head of the Im-naha Valley, ascertaining that the Indians had not come that way, then turned toward the Wallowa, in order to meet them if coming from that direction. Time was to show that the hostiles were breaking into small bands and generally retreating toward the south, back to their points of origin and away from the Columbia. Those still in the field were being compressed in a tightening coil as the army units drove inward to the Blue Mountains.

Mason tells of a short bout with indigestion — "half-cooked beans are a little too much even for my stomach to manage." With questionable judgment he goes on to describe "the General and the girls standing around the campfire, laughing and talking. . . . George is just as well as ever and is looking finely. I don't ride him much — once in every 3 or 4 days for a few hours." One suspects that Mrs. Mason was more pleased to hear about George than about "the girls." Under date of July 18, Mason wrote:

We made a march of 25 miles today and are camped in the Wallowa Valley. . . . This is a wild, picturesque valley and has an interest to us as the home of Joseph, the place he wanted, but no — the few miserable squatters now here, being white men, must have it, and it cost a million dollars and 500 lives to give it to them. We have not seen a trace of the hostiles and are satisfied they have not come this way. . . . I expect we will get some news during the night.

The major wrote next from La Grande two days later, after a forty-mile, thirteen-hour ride, followed by a final jaunt in a wagon, for another eighteen miles:

We found Gen. Wheaton here. I got to bed at midnight, was up at 1 a. m. to read despatches, up again at 3 to write despatches, and up again at 6 to go to work and have been hard at it. We leave in a few minutes to join the cavalry 50 miles in advance — in hot pursuit of the hostiles. I think the end is coming fast. Eagan, the big chief, has been killed and the Indians appear to be perfectly demoralized.

Mason concluded with a promise to write more from the next camp. He missed doing so, but resumed the following evening from a location described as in the mountains west of Canyon City. "We are camped on a mountain 8,100 feet in the air (by the barometer).[12] We have had a grand game of snowball, for the snow is all about us." Mrs. Mason could draw whatever conclusions she liked about who was snow-balling whom. Surprisingly, Mason reports sending George back to Walla Walla, and wiring Headquarters at Vancouver to send a soldier to take him back home. "The good old fellow could not much longer stand these mountains and I could not bear the idea of leaving him on the trail as I was fearful I would be obliged to do — so concluded to send him home." He closes with the announcement that he must stop and sew a button on his pants, explaining that "It's rather cold up here." Reasonable enough.

On July 22 it was 4:00 p. m. before he got to writing. "We have marched 20 miles and are now in camp on Granite Creek near the mining camp of Granite City." That was the extent of the news, but he started another letter that evening and extended it the next day to say that they were camped on Burnt River about forty-five miles from Baker. His big news was receipt of portraits of the family. He writes at length of the sensation among the friendly Umatillas and even the captive Bannocks, at seeing the pictures of the nicely dressed women and children of the Mason household.

Letters of the next couple of days resume the military theme, as General (actually Lieutenant Colonel) James W. Forsyth arrived to take over the cavalry, relieving Bernard from an unusual command of seven companies, rather much for a captain. In reporting the disintegration of the fleeing enemy, Mason writes on July 25:

We have picked up a few squaws in the past few days, and one baby,

202

actually abandoned by its mother in the haste of leaving camp during the last attack.[13] The baby is about 6 months old, cries like any other baby, and probably, being an Indian baby, will get through. It has not a rag of clothes — it's wrapped in an old shawl. The old squaw to whom we turned it over for care and protection takes good (Indian) care of it. The hostiles are, we think, near Ironsides Mountain, which is just before us. . . . I do not remember if I told you that the infantry had been left in camp near La Grande. The general wanted to bring them on, but I objected and wanted to mount them before sending them into the field again. I carried my point, so the 21st. Inf. owes its exemption from the hard stern chase to myself. We have just sent a scout to locate the camp of the hostiles. If we can do so, we will attack tomorrow.

Mason briefly gets his dates confused, but this seems to have been written on the morning of Friday, July 26:

We have only marched about 4 miles this morning, going into camp on the Canyonville and Baker City road. We are waiting for supplies, as the command is entirely out of rations, indeed have nothing at all to eat. The men got their last mouthful for breakfast and must live in the recollection of that meal until they can get another. We are close on the heels of the Indians and dislike losing a day by waiting. I hope we will induce the Piutes to surrender and thus reduce the hostile force two-thirds. Sarah and Mattie with Capt. Wilkinson and a small force, and the Nez Perce scouts, have gone to the Malheur Agency which we find is about 25 miles to the northeast.[14] They hope to find some of the Piutes there with whom they can communicate . . .

Apparently written from the same place later in the day, Mason reports:

The General and I had a long talk about the situation and I have written a long order in conformity therewith. We will go first to the Malheur Agency, then to Boise City, establishing Headquarters in that place. I think that the General is coming to the conclusion that he is "de trop" in the field with another man's command. I know if I was Forsyth, I would not want my superior about.

Sunday, July 28, 8 a. m.

We marched 25 miles yesterday, coming to the Malheur Agency. It is deserted and the buildings have been dismantled. It is a lonely place, like all the reservations I have seen, located in a treeless valley, a barren, desolate place. We must stay here until our rations come up. We have sent to Harney for supplies. We could have had them by waiting about 6 hours when we were back on the Baker City road, but the General was impatient and would not wait, so we have been without rations for 3 days, the men living on beef part of the time and on inferior flour found here. It is on questions of this sort that the General and I always differ, for I never let my impatient [sic] run away with my judgment, and he frequently does. This opinion of my C. O. is, of course, confidential. We are up a stump as regards our Indian friends. The trails have scattered so it is no easy matter to tell where they have gone. Col. Green is probably on the main Bannock trail and has followed it toward the Snake River. I am disappointed at finding that the Piutes had not stopped in the reservation. . . . We will leave a small garrison here to pick up all who may come in.

. . . Capt. Marcus Miller, 4th Artillery, has just arrived from Baker City with supplies. . . .

That evening, hastily closing the above, Mason tells that they are about to move toward Camp Lyon (far to the south) and that "the project of going to Boise is busted up." General Howard was again yielding to the impulse to stay in the field and try for one more glorious, conclusive victory. On July 30, Mason describes a two-day march: "no road, no trail, no nothing — hot rocks! rocks! rocks! up one mountain and down another." In the heat of this desert, Howard and Mason did their own scouting, riding a mile or more in advance of the column, seeking the trail of the main body of hostiles but never finding traces of more than twenty-five or so. Howard's eagerness led to this rash action, which brought comment from another officer that the danger of ambush was worse than the risks during a pitched battle. Mason ends this letter early the next morning, announcing that they were about to strike across country to the Owyhee River. August 2 brings an account of this miserable trip across a waterless desert that had been represented as twenty miles wide but was closer to fifty-five. Next day found them moving toward Boise and encamping about twenty-five miles west of Silver City. They observed the Sabbath on August 4 by sleeping until 7:00 a. m. Mason finished his letter after a "fearfully hot" march, writing from "Trout Creek Station on the Winnemucca Stage Road." Howard was responding again to the temptation to catch more Indians, this time a group of Bannocks fleeing back toward Fort Hall, and was actually planning a dash of one hundred fifty miles to the vicinity of Twin Falls. Mason himself writes, "I am anxious to hurry these Indians past Ft. Hall into the buffalo country."

The next day, after a thirty-mile advance which brought them near Silver City, the general again reversed himself and re-instated his plan to take up station in Boise. Always impulsive, he dashed on ahead, leaving Mason in charge of the camp, to follow him a day later. The major commented:

> I have had a long talk with the General, his way of doing things, scouting with a small column — while Wheaton was really running the campaign. I didn't propose to go into the subject. It is sufficient to say that HQ will be for a time where the Dept. Commander can control matters, and the captains will be permitted to exercise their legitimate commands. For a time? How long? I don't know.

Monday, August 7, he was in Boise at last, after another hot ride of thirty miles. He found the general still planning on staying there, and Mason applauds, ". . . if he sticks to it. The work of picking up the stray Indians will be left to detachment commanders. Green will follow the main band out of the Department."

The letters of the next few days betray anxiety lest Howard again decide to take the field, as Mason gently persuades him to go home, all the way to Vancouver, to prevent any such turn. Meanwhile, they are "camping" on the river and renting a furnished house for headquarters. The big break comes on August 11 — General Howard resolves to start for Vancouver as soon as possible. Mason writes twice on the following day, quite early anticipating Howard's departure at 4:00 p. m., and again in the evening, to report that the general had really left! He himself can come on as soon as Colonel Forsyth arrives to take charge in Boise. He mentions that the campaign has been more fatiguing than the Nez Perce affair. "I trust we will get through this summer without an outbreak in the north. I am so disgusted with the vile, low people on the frontier — I have no heart to fight for them."

The letter dated August 13 tells that some fifty Piutes led by one of their last remaining chiefs had surrendered at Malheur Agency, signalling the end of the fighting in Oregon. Now he can really plan on heading for Vancouver.

> Good bye. I want to go home bad!! I am worser than a schoolboy. Kiss the dear children,
>
> > Every yours,
> > EDWIN

Thus, much as it had begun, the Bannock-Piute War of 1878 came to its end.

NOTES

1. The spelling here follows Mason, also Howard and Sarah Winnemucca, although Paiute seems to be the preferred form recently.
2. The war is treated at length in George F. Brimlow, THE BANNOCK INDIAN WAR OF 1878 (Caldwell, 1938), and briefly in Brigham D. Madsen, THE BANNOCK OF IDAHO (Caldwell, 1958).
3. Mason had spelled "Steens" correctly in his letters.
4. The site of the battle was on Silver Creek, west of Burns, Oregon.
5. Mark H. Brown, THE FLIGHT OF THE NEZ PERCE (New York, 1967), p. 296.
6. Chief Moses was the leader of militant elements north of the Columbia River. Sitting Bull was lingering along the eastern Montana border in Canada with remnants of the force that had destroyed Custer in 1876.
7. It was the army practice to designate temporary camps by names of outstanding military men, frequently one in the local command who had recently distinguished himself.
8. All accounts of this war take note of her. She tells her own story in Sarah Winnemucca Hopkins, LIFE AMONG THE PIUTES (Boston, 1883).
9. Mrs. Mason would understand this term in its military sense.
10. The cavalry had been under a cloud after its poor showing in the 1876 and 1877 campaigns.
11. One wounded man died the following day.
12. Elevations above 8,000 feet are not uncommon in the area.
13. This incident is described with varying details in Brimlow, *The Bannock Indian War of 1878*, p. 143., and Abe Laufe, ed., AN ARMY DOCTOR'S WIFE ON THE FRONTIER (Pittsburg, 1962), p. 350. Sarah W. Hopkins, *op. cit.*, relates how the child was restored to its mother.
14. His directions are reversed; they were northeast of the agency.

SOLDIERING AND SUFFERING IN
THE GERONIMO CAMPAIGN:

Reminiscences of Lawrence R. Jerome

THE INDIAN WARS of the post-Civil War period of American history have lived in countless movies, novels, and television shows as a romance of high adventure. In this morass of glamor, the hardships and suffering of both soldier and Indian have largely been forgotten. Both were caught in a vicious fight for survival under conditions not of their own making or choosing. For the soldier, it was a fight to contain the aborigines so that the land could be exploited by civilians, while for the Indian it was a fight for his traditions, his beliefs, and his customs of untold generations.

After the Civil War, the Army of the United States changed greatly. It was reduced to 25,000 enlisted men and officers, many of whom were sent to the Western frontier to suppress Indian uprisings. Hard work, poor equipment, low pay, and slow, if not impossible, promotion characterized this Indian-fighting army. The military was strictly volunteer, composed of men seeking steady employment and the lure of adventure, as well as of men wanted for crimes who found it expedient to travel. A recruit enlisted for five years and received thirteen dollars a month. No matter how abominable conditions were, he rarely transferred from his regiment. Often the soldier sought diversion in drinking, gambling, or fighting; and punishment for men who deserted or otherwise broke army regulations was unusually severe. Deserters were marched double-time around the parade ground, branded with a "D," suspended by their wrists for hours, or confined to the guard house for days. Stephen B. Elkins, Secretary of War, estimated that losses through desertion, between 1867 and 1891 inclusive, averaged one-third of all enlistees.

Isolated from polite society and politics, officers also found soldiering difficult, promotion slow, living conditions execrable, pay miserable, and society far from appreciative. Moreover, each officer had his opinion of the Army, and frontier commanders had their own philosophy of solving Indian problems. Nevertheless, the Army could only carry out congressional policies.

The people these soldiers had to contain likewise found their lot difficult to bear. The Apaches reacted to governmental policy by leaving their reservations and attacking settlements in southern Arizona. In truth, the hostiles were not raiding and wreaking havoc on the countryside without provocation; for many years the government of the United States had refused to recognize Indian culture or to relate governmental policy to the Indian's needs.   Yet, the Apache Indian remained a fierce, tireless, formidable warrior, who very early in life was taught to hunt and fight, often defying death and defending his honor.   Every aspect of Apache society reinforced these traditions, and, as settlement progressed westward into Apache hunting grounds, it became more evident that settlers neither respected nor understood the Indian way of life.   In search of solutions, the government moved yet more tribes to the southwest, crowding them together on reservations and ordering them to become farmers.   Weak in theory, the reservation philosophy was even weaker in practice, and often was run by corrupt agents.

The San Carlos Reservation in southwestern Arizona was typical of this reservation system.   During the period 1871-1875 and 1882-1886, when General George Crook commanded the Department of Arizona, some reforms in the system were made — but none so effective as to convince renegades such as Chatto, Natchez, Juh, and Geronimo to live as wards of the government.   Although General Crook worked for a peaceful solution, he also trained the Army for rapid pursuit.   Along with the use of Indian scouts, these new tactics gave the Army the mobility to follow and capture marauding Indians.   After the Apache outbreak of 1881, the renegades led by Geronimo and Natchez avoided capture for two years, finally to meet with Crook and discuss surrender.

This agreement of 1884 placed five hundred fifty men, women and children of the Chiricahua and Warm Springs tribes at Turkey Creek, part of the San Carlos Reservation.   Once back on the reservation and bored with confinement, the warriors drank, gambled, and loafed, depending on the government for their livelihood.   Excessive drinking of a native beer called *tiswin*, along with wife beating, an ancient tribal custom, prompted Crook to interfere in reservation life.   By May 15, 1885, the Indians, already primed for a confrontation, decided to test the Army.   They informed Lieutenant Britton Davis, who had immediate charge of them, that the Apaches intended to continue drinking and would practice their tribal customs, including wife-beating. In addition, they asked Davis what action he proposed to use to stop them. Wisely, Davis took no punitive action; instead he wired Crook for instructions.   Unfortunately, the telegram was not delivered to Crook, but was lost for three months.   Fearing Army reprisal, the Indians became increasingly restless, and on the afternoon of May 18 Geronimo, Natchez and one hundred thirty-two Chiricahua and Warm Spring Apaches, men, women, and children, fled to Mexico.

Geronimo's band led the Army on a chase of several hundred miles both in Mexico and the United States.   Although Crook received orders to force an unconditional surrender from the Indians if possible, he finally offered to negotiate a settlement.   Therefore, on March 25, 1886, a peace conference was held at Cañon de los Embudos, just south of the Mexican border.   Knowing that the Indians would not surrender unconditionally, Crook promised them only two years' imprisonment in Florida, after which they would be returned to their native Arizona. On these terms Geronimo surrendered, and his band was led towards the United States' border. En route the party encountered Bob Tribollet, an itinerant bootlegger, who sold the Indians whiskey and told them they would be shot upon arrival in Arizona. Under cover of darkness and a cold drizzling rain, Geronimo and Natchez, along with nineteen warriors, thirteen squaws, and six children, fled in the direction of their hideout in the Sonoran Mountains.

The news of Geronimo's escape reached Washington with a deafening roar, and cries for Crook's head were heard in prominent political circles and even were printed in many newspapers. Because of this harsh criticism, Crook asked officials in Washington for a vote of confidence by offering his resignation — only to have it accepted. On April 2, 1886, a disillusioned Crook was relieved of command of the Department of Arizona, and nine days later General Nelson A. Miles arrived at Fort Bowie to assume command. He conferred with the departing officer, but General Miles' philosophy for solving Indian problems differed greatly from the former commander's. Where Crook had attempted to solve Indian problems through negotiation, his replacement believed the only solution was to run the renegades until they collapsed or surrendered unconditionally.

General Miles had no interest in a colorless or peaceful solution — such a settlement was unlikely to win national publicity. Miles' method of securing the unconditional surrender of the renegades was to select approximately one hundred of "the best atheletes in our service." Their task would be to pursue the hostiles so relentlessly that they would tire — and accept terms dictated by Miles. The man he selected to lead this chase was Captain Henry Ware Lawton, described as a brave, ambitious, and resolute officer — adjectives Miles would have applied to himself. Through the reminiscences of Trooper Lawrence R. Jerome, an anonymous member of "B" Troop in Lawton's Fourth Cavalry, an insight has been provided to the hardships involved in pursuing the hostile Indians in the barren and trackless lands of northern Mexico and southern Arizona. Lawton and his "athletes" proved unsuccessful in forcing the renegades to surrender. Ironically, Miles was forced to return to Crook's policy of negotiation, for on July 9, 1886, he sent Lieutenant Charles B. Gatewood, guided by two Apache scouts, to meet with Geronimo and secure terms of capitulation: two years in Florida and then a return to Arizona. Yet Miles and the government did not adhere to the agreement Gatewood signed with the Apaches, for they were held as prisoners of war at different locations until 1913 — and never allowed to return to their native Arizona.

The original of the Jerome manuscript, reproduced below, is in the Gatewood Collection of the Arizona Historical Society in Tucson.

THE GERONIMO CAMPAIGN

As Told by a Trooper of "B" Troop of the 4th U. S. Cavalry,

LAWRENCE VINTON

(Lawrence R. Jerome)

GENERAL CROOK was in command of the Department of the Southwest in 1886, and had captured Geronimo and his band of hostile Indians in Old Mexico and was on his way with them to the reservation.[1] General Crook camped for a short time at the San Bernardino Ranch with his scouts and Indian prisoners. This ranch is situated on the border line between Mexico and Arizona. James Triblett had the contract for providing beef to the troops in the field, and was most desirous of seeing the campaign continued. He gave the hostile Indian prisoners mescal (Mexican whisky), on which they got drunk and again went on the warpath, leaving in General Crook's hands the decrepit warriors and a few squaws.

The scouts refused to follow on the trail of the escaped renegades and they made good their way back into the Sierra Madre Mountains of Mexico. General Crook was relieved of his command by the War Department, and Brigadier General Nelson A. Miles was appointed to take his place.[2] Miles had never fought the Apaches but had a long and varied experience with the hostile tribes of the northwest, especially with the Sioux and Nez Perce Indians. Miles said he would have Geronimo and his band captured within three months, but he knew little of the country and the Apaches he had to deal with. A treaty was made between our government and that of the Republic of Mexico, allowing our troops to follow the hostile Indians onto Mexican soil.

Two troops of the Second Cavalry were also brought into the territory from California. Therefore, General Miles had at his disposal in Arizona the Fourth Cavalry, the Tenth (colored) Cavalry, the Eighth Infantry and two troops of the Second Cavalry. General Miles chose Captain Lawton and his troops (B of the Fourth Cavalry) to take the trail of Geronimo and keep it, wherever it might lead. Captain Lawton also had two large pack trains and thirty Indian scouts under him.[3]

We started out from Fort Huachuca on the morning of the first of April, 1886, and crossed the mountains to Nogales, a town that is situated half in Mexico half in the United States.[4] On our arrival at Nogales we got our first report of the Indians from a man named Peck, who came in from the mountains with the story that he and his partner, Thomas Watson was a short distance from their ranch and had a calf roped and were about to brand it, when they were jumped by a band of Indians.

Watson, trying to make his escape, was shot and killed. Peck said Geronimo (Peck had met Geronimo before) told him that he, Peck, was a good man, requested him to remove his boots and also told him not to return to his ranch. While the conversation was going on Peck recognized, as the band of Indians passed, his little girl, who was about twelve years old, riding on a mule behind a squaw.[5]

Peck, contrary to his instructions from Geronimo, did go to his ranch, only to find that his wife had been killed and mutilated, as well as his infant child. At the time there was considerable doubt as to the truth of Peck's story, but later it was verified. During the night of the first of April two cow-punchers rode in with the report that Captain Lebo of the Tenth Cavalry had encountered the Indians in Hell's Canyon, Mexico, south of Nogales, and that the Indians had whipped the soldiers, killing several of them.[6] We started before daybreak to help Lebo and met him about noon. He had lost four men killed and had with him several wounded. The Indians besides had captured quite a number of his horses.

Lebo and his troop kept on towards Nogales, while we took up the pursuit of the Indians. The hostiles did not stop to give us a fight, but led us a chase over the very roughest country. Both men and horses suffered severely as we were fat and soft. Our scouts kept us hot on the trail. Sometimes we would press the Indians so closely that they would be compelled to kill the lame and tired horses. During this chase we found evidence of Peck's little girl being with them. A child's shoe, a little sunbonnet and a piece of ribbon were picked up by some of the men.

The fourth day found us at a little settlement on the border line called La Noria.[7] The Indians had doubled back into Arizona again. We camped at La Noria. The next few days reports were circulated of Indians in half-a-dozen different places one hundred miles apart. We could not account for it at the time, but later found out that the wiley old Geronimo had split his band into several small parties and, stealing fresh horses from the well-stocked ranges, made forced marches, killing prospectors and attacking isolated and unprotected ranches. It was but a few days when, by a probably pre-arranged plan, the hostiles joined their several bands together and once more headed for the Sierra Madre Mountains of Mexico.

Captain Hatfield of D Troop of the Fourth Cavalry was on their trail.[8] He jumped their camp early one morning, captured a number of horses, reloading outfits and a lot of plunder, but the Indians got away. Captain Hatfield had no Indian scouts with him, but took up the trail in pursuit. His command consisted of fifty soldiers and a pack train. Twenty men were sent in advance and he followed with the remainder. At some waterholes he stopped to water the stock and the advance guard gained a very considerable distance on the rear column. The Indians were in an ambush up a narrow ravine. They permitted the advance guard to enter unmolested, but when Captain Hatfield came up with the rear column, they opened up on him with their Winchesters. The Captain's first words were, "My God, we are ambushed!" The men, most of whom had never smelled gunpowder, were in single file on the side of a precipitous mountain. One man was killed and three wounded at the first volley. The pack train stampeded and, to tell the truth, so did most of the men. Some never stopped until they reached Santa Cruz, a small town in the valley.

Hatfield and a few of the cooler men made a stand. The Indians, however, recaptured their own horses, also a number of cavalry horses. When Geronimo finally surrendered he was wearing the Captain's blouse, which was tied to the saddle when Hatfield lost his horse. This made the second time the Indians had whipped the troops, both black and white.

As I stated, we were camped near La Noria, which is only a few miles from Santa Cruz. A courier brought us the news of Hatfield's defeat. Instantly we were off on a gallop to the scene of action. Our Indian scouts found the trail which we took and followed. We kept on the hostile trail with as much haste as the nature of the country would permit, our Indian scouts in front, the troop following in single file and the pack train bringing up the rear. When it got too dark to follow the trail with any certainty, we made camp, a dry camp with no fires allowed. A ration of raw salt pork constituted supper and breakfast. Those who had drunk their water had to go without, and, after a swift march, most of the time on foot dragging your horse over the very steepest of mountains, and to top it off a piece of the driest and saltiest bacon, made many of the men suffer considerably. We were new to the business then but got used to it before the Indians surrendered six months later.

I forgot to state that Dr. Wood, the present General Wood, governor of Cuba, accompanied us throughout the campaign in the capacity of surgeon. Dr. Leonard Wood was a man who was well liked and respected by all the command. When it came to marching and roughing it he had no equal.[9]

To resume: With the earliest streak of light we were again underway, hot on the trail. The usual program was to breakfast on a piece of bacon, a slice of bread and a cup of coffee before daylight; as soon as there was light enough to take up the trail and follow until it was too dark to see, never stopping for dinner. Two meals a day. Sometimes this had to be changed on account of water and feed for the stock.

The Indians led us a merry chase for two weeks or more, doubling and twisting along the backbone of the various mountains, occasionally descending into the valleys to make a killing of some defenseless Mexican miner or rancher, and to kill a beef and to steal fresh horses. We never allowed them to rest. At times we were so close to them that we found their camp fires still burning; again they would lead us by a considerable number of miles. There was no way of heading them, as their direction and destination were unknown; all we had to do was to patiently follow on the signs they left in their wake.

Eventually they headed for the Sierra Azul (Blue Mountains), a massive range. We were pressing them very closely and, on arriving on the summit of the Sierra Azul, they killed all their stock, a hundred or more of horses and mules, and branched out in several small parties on foot. Here, on top of this range of mountains, there was every evidence to show that a permanent camp had been maintained. There was an abundance of water and no party could approach within twenty-five miles without being seen. The hostile Indians were equipped with the best of field glasses stolen from cow ranches in Arizona.[10]

The question arose now, which small band to follow. Finally it was decided to follow a party of about ten. Day after day we kept on the trail. It was not long before the hostiles were again well mounted on fresh stock stolen from Mexican ranches. Continually we found dead Mexicans. Now it would be a couple of prospectors and again a lonely wood-chopper. Be it understood that up to this time we had not got into the real fastnesses of the Sierra Madre range, where no one lives, but were in a sparsely settled country with an occasional town in the valleys. There were no roads or wagon travel and transportation was done on horseback over trails. The Indians would sometimes follow these trails for a distance and then strike out and pick a way of their own.

After days and days of continuous marching, our Indian scouts informed us that the band we had been following had been augmented by some ten more, making in the neighborhood of twenty hostile Indians that we were now following. They knew this by reading the signs of the trail. Nature and practice have given the red man a wonderfully keen perception, and he is rarely at fault in sign lore. These two bands had united undoubtedly on a preärranged plan, made weeks before on top of the Sierra Azul. We now felt confident that they would eventually come together at some appointed rendezvous.

I will now relate an instance where the wily hostile Indian is at fault and makes a serious mistake himself. A few days after these two bands had joined forces, they came onto moccasin tracks and the signs of unshod horses, and they must have thought that they were about to meet some of their own kin. They were mistaken, however, for suddenly they ran into a "round-up" or rodeo. The Mexicans were camped in a narrow valley and the hostiles were right on top of them before they knew it. Peck's little girl, the girl I made mention of as having been carried off by the Indians in the first part of my story, was with this band of Indians and was riding a mule. The mule stampeded to join the

—Map by Don Bufkin, Tucson, Arizona

ROUTE MAP

Course Lawton oommand followed in pursuing Genronimo.

— *Courtesy Arizona Pioneers' Historical Society*

REGULAR ARMY AND APACHE SCOUTS

— *Courtesy Arizona Pioneers' Historical Society*

APACHE RENEGADES IN THE GERONIMO CAMPAIGN

— Courtesy Arizona Pioneers' Historical Society

APACHE CHIEF NATCHEZ

— Courtesy Arizona Pioneers' Historical Society

APACHE SCOUT CHATTO

Mexican herd. The squaw who had the little girl in charge tried to cut the mule out, that is, turn it back to the Indians. The squaw was unsuccessful; she made a good fight, however. Emptied both her six-shooters, killing one man and wounding another before she, herself, was killed. A general fight now ensued, between the Mexican cowmen and the Indians; the latter retreated, the former following, until they had lost three men killed, which cooled their ardor and they returned to camp.

We came up four hours after this had happened. The above is hearsay, but the dead squaw and the four dead Mexicans, besides the recovery of Peck's little girl, was all the evidence necessary for the truth of their story.[11] The little girl had an interesting story to relate, both her eyes were discolored, blackened and swollen from the effects of a blow given her by a buck the day before because she was crying. The little girl was with the party under Natchez. Natchez was the heriditary war chief. Most people are lead to believe that Geronimo was the leader, but such was not the case. Geronimo was the medicine man of the Chiricahua tribe, the same as Sitting Bull was of the Sioux tribes. This encounter took place not far from the town of Cinnocepia [Sinoquipe] and there Peck's girl was taken by the Mexicans and eventually was returned to her father at Nogales.[12]

The Indians revenged themselves for the loss of the little girl and the death of the squaw, who by the way was Geronimo's daughter, by killing a number of wood-choppers on the surrounding hills, killing and mutilating them. It was only in this neighborhood that the Indians mutilated the dead; all the other corpses we came across were not mutilated, not even scalped. General Miles had sent Lieutenant Benson[13] with a company of the Eighth Infantry to Opusure, a town over two hundred miles south of the United States border, to establish a supply camp. Not since the time of General Scott and the Mexican War had a permanent camp, under the Stars and Stripes been maintained so far south in Mexico.

The Indians, after leaving the neighborhood of Cinocepia, headed south into the little known parts of the great Sierra Madre Mountains. I could easily fill a volume with reminiscences of what we suffered. Our clothes, what we had, were in rags. No one seeing us would have taken us for United States soldiers. The weather now changed; the rainy season commenced and every night we were drenched. We had no tents, no shelter, no overcoats, only our saddle blankets. The rain improved the grass, however, and our horses fared some better. We had sent back to Fort Huachuca all those who had shown weakness, and now we numbered only twenty-five. The last little Mexican settlement, Nacori by name, was left behind. The next nearest town was Suaripa [Sahuaripa], one hundred and fifty miles distant. Captain Lawton, with his six feet four inches of brawn and muscle, had to succumb for a few days to the effects of hardship and exposure and was taken along on an improvised travay [travois]. It was not the largest men who stood the marches the best; on the contrary, it was the medium sized men.

Our own Indian scouts, as well as our four white couriers, were equally ignorant of the country we were now in. The hostiles had cut away from the regular traveled paths and were making a virgin trail over these bold mountain ranges. There was no such thing as stop now, no matter how badly one felt, one was compelled to keep on. Most of us were suffering from diarrhea. It was only pure American grit that kept us going at times. After several weeks of this seeming never-to-end chase, we came to the Río Arras [Río Haros].

About four o'clock in the afternoon of the day we came to the river, a messenger from Lieutenant [Leighton] Finley, in command of our scouts, came to us with the news that the Indian scouts had located the hostile camp on the river. Lawton sent word to Finley to keep quiet until he came up, but Finley could not control the scouts. They rushed into the hostile camp, shouting and firing their guns. They hit no one, and in my opinion they did not wish to. The hostiles were taken completely by surprise and had time only to grab their guns and flee into the cane brake which grew along the water's edge.

We came up a few minutes later and had our hands full keeping the scouts from killing each other over the division of the captured plunder, some eighty or ninety head of horses and mules, about three thousand pounds of jerked beef, ammunition, saddles, jerked beef, etc. etc., in fact all they had stolen along the road. The scouts could not be made to take up the trail of the retreating enemy. Night came on and the following morning the scouts, after an examination of the signs left by the hostiles, stated that the band had crossed the river. Right here a great mistake was made. Instead of turning loose or killing the captured stock it was given to the scouts, and all they cared for now was the preservation of the animals given them. Instead of trailing afoot as they did previously, they were mounted and could not do as satisfactory work.

Captain Lawton dispatched two white couriers to Laurarepa [?] to make inquiries and to put them on their guard for Indians. We could not cross the pack train over the river as it was wide, very swift and brimming. Camp was established and a raft had to be built. There was but one ax and no nails; considerable time was lost in cutting down palms, for when taken to the water they were found to have no buoyancy.

With much difficulty dry weed and dead timber was secured and lashed together. On top of this, cane was placed and it served the purpose of taking the ammunition and provisions to the other side of the River Aris. While in this camp, Lieutenant Gatewood, Tom Horn and two of Geronimo's braves came to us.[14] The two Indians had been sent by Geronimo back to the reservation in Arizona to tell Lieutenant Gatewood that he and the hostiles were willing to hold a powwow and surrender.

Gatewood, under the guidance of these two Indians, had started south, took up our trail, and it was here in this camp that we had just jumped that the Indians thought to find Geronimo and the rest of the band. The two Indians from the hostiles did not know where to look for the rest of their crowd. With great trouble the stores were rafted over the river, the men, horses and mules having to swim. We met the two couriers returning from Laurarepa, one day's march from the Río Aris. They reported that the Indians had attacked a Mexican pack train, routed the Mexicans and were again mounted and headed north. Lawton, on hearing this news, sent for Billy Long, a courier, and myself.[15] He gave into our hands some dispatches which were to be delivered to Lieutenant Benson at Oposura, our supply camp. Lawton told us the necessity of the dispatches reaching their destination; that in case one of us should be killed or play out, the other should push on at all hazards. We were instructed to make inquiry whenever it was possible concerning Indian news, to procure fresh horses if necessary, and also empowered to hire Mexican couriers to take to him any news of importance we might hear. Lawton said that he was going to recross the river and that we would find him north of the Aris and south of Nacori. Stating again the importance of a speedy delivery of the dispatches, he ordered us to start.

Dr. Wood, the present governor of Cuba, was standing alongside of Lawton during this conversation. I asked the doctor if he could give me something for diarrhea. I was very ill at the time. He gave me the few remaining opium pills he had left, with instructions how to use them, and it was owing to them that I was able to make the journey.

We heard nothing at Nacori, but when we reached Guasaguas [Huasabas], I fortunately met a man by the name of George Woodward, a Californian, a nephew of Woodward of Woodward's Gardens in San Francisco.[16] He had married a Mexican woman and was engaged in the cattle business. Woodward had had considerable experience fighting Indians and he told us that Indians had been seen quite lately in the adjoining mountains, and that he had lost some horses himself. Woodward got me two Mexicans, who he vouched for, to carry news to Lawton. Woodward, after hearing my story about jumping the hostile camp on the Río Aris, and of Lieutenant Gatewood's coming to us with two of the Indians remarked that the hostiles would now undoubtedly head for the Terrace Mountains, Cochise's old stronghold. I sent a dispatch to Captain Lawton, telling what I had heard, also stating Woodward's prediction.

Woodward's two Mexicans, with my dispatch, started the next morning. They found Lawton north of the Aris River; and Lawton acted on the advice of my dispatch. Woodward was right in his surmise, for later Lawton did get the hostile Indians in the Terrace Mountains, had a parley with them and they surrendered.

219

After seeing the Mexicans off, we continued our journey, reached Oposura and delivered Lawton's dispatches to Lieutenant Benson. We made immediate preparations for a return and the next morning found us travelling south to rejoin Lawton, Lieutenant Benson accompanying us. We got to Guasaguas in the evening and stopped at Woodward's ranch. We left Woodward's at nine o'clock the same night; rumors of Indians were rife and as there was good water and grass on top of the divide the Lieutenant thought it would be safer to cross at night. We had to swim the river in the valley before heading for the mountains, and we were delayed some time trying to find the main trail, as it was an excessively dark night. We were probably half way up the mountain when it began to storm, as it only can in that country. The rain descended in torrents, the lightning was incessant, ball, fork and chain, and the thunder one continuous peal as it reverberated from one massive rock wall to another. Riding up close to the lieutenant I told him I had to stop for a moment. It was customary at night, and especially such a dark night, if one stops for all to stop. The lieutenant's answer was, "You cannot."

I said, "I must."

He then ordered Billy Long to take my horse, and I like a fool permitted him to do so. But as I dismounted I took my carbine from its holder. The lieutenant ordered Long to follow him and bring my horse, and they left me alone, sick in a foreign country, afoot on such a night and surrounded by hostile Indians. I could not believe he meant to desert me. He did, however. I soon hastened to follow and discharged my carbine, but the report of the gun was lost in the louder detonations of thunder.

Wet and chilled to the bone, weak and exhausted, I crawled under a projecting rock and waited for day. The storm passed over and long before day I was toiling up the trail in pursuit. A little before sunup I reached the top of the divide; by the fast brightening day I made out some ponies. They must have "winded" me, for they threw up their heads and the same time up popped an Indian's head, another and another. I had seen sufficient. I lay very close to the ground and was not discovered. The ponies resumed their grazing. I remained where I was until I was positive I had not been noticed, then cautiously crawled back along the trail until out of sight. Once out of sight I straightened up and made for the valley at my best gait and that was not slow. The trail where it debouches into the valley from the mountains is quite a distance from Guasaguas, and not far from a little town by the name of Granados.

I met a man riding near the foot of the mountains and told him of the Indians, and he invited me to accompany him to Granados and report to his brother who, he said, was the presidente. He also told me that the inhabitants of Granados had lost a number of horses. On entering the town I was invited into a house and offered food. I ate heartily, thanked the donor, and stepped out of the house and was confronted with a dozen or more shoeless individuals, dressed in dirty linen, having in their hands old fashioned rifles, and all these guns pointing directly at me. I was ordered to give up my carbine and pistols and to consider myself a prisoner. It is unnecessary to say that I obeyed. I was brought before the presidente, told my story and was in turn told that I would be held pending an investigation.

The third day of my detention, during an interview with the presidente, in which I stated that I was a United States soldier, etc., etc., I happened to mention Woodward's name. Immediately there was a change. I was asked if I knew Woodward. Answering in the affirmative, I was told I might go up the river towards Guasaguas and if Woodward would vouch for me they would return me my guns. I found out later that it was about this time that there were complications between the two governments over the so-called "Cutting affair" at El Paso, Texas; that the relations between Mexico and the United States were anything but pleasant; also that the treaty that allowed us to be in Mexico either expired or had been annulled. Had actual trouble existed I would undoubtedly have been shot.[17]

I walked up the river to Woodward's ranch, told my story, and he sent a letter to Granados; the messenger returned with my arms. Woodward kindly invited me to stay with him as long as I wished, but that was not to be thought of; I belonged to Uncle Sam. The second day at Woodward's a man coming in reported that he had seen a dozen or more United States soldiers with a pack train going north headed toward Agua Caliente spring. I made up my mind then and there to follow them. There was no time to waste. The soldiers had been seen several hours before.

I started out on foot. About sundown I reached Agua Caliente springs, and in the sands saw signs of about a dozen shod horses and the same number of mules. It was a moonlight night and a plain trail. I made all haste possible, as I knew if I was to overtake them I must do it that night. About three o'clock in the morning I saw a camp fire. Scouting cautiously, to make sure I was coming on to friends, to my joy I recognized a soldier in United States uniform, and I was sharply challenged. I answered and was advanced. I had come onto a detachment of K Troop of the Fourth Cavalry, in command of Lieutenant [James B.] Richards, who was chasing Lawton with instructions to him to get out of Mexico, as trouble was brewing between the two governments, and the treaty allowing us on Mexican soil was annulled.

Lieutenant Richards heard my story and gave me an extra horse he fortunately had. But I had to ride him without saddle or bridle. We made about sixty miles the first day, fifty the second, and the third day we came up with Captain Lawton below Fronteras. I reported to the captain. He said he had received my dispatches. Lieutenant Benson had told him a lot of lies, but Lawton was too just a man to condemn me unheard. Not having time to investigate he returned me to duty without a reprimand.

Lawton now headed into the Terrace Mountains; Lieutenant Gatewood, Tom Horn, the interpreter, and the two hostile Indians accompanying him. On the third day's march we came up to where Geronimo's band was encamped — intrenched I might say, as they had rifle pits dug and fortifications thrown up. Lieutenant Gatewood, Tom Horn and the two Indians were all that Geronimo would let come into his camp. President Cleveland had said that nothing but an unconditional surrender would be accepted. The Indians would not surrender under those terms and their lives were promised them. I don't think they would have surrendered even then had they not been short of ammunition. The rest of the tribe had been rounded up and sent to Florida. Geronimo did not know this and expected to be put back on the reservation, and after resting awhile would be ready to start out afresh on another raid as they had often done before.

We gave the hostile Indians provisions and started north for Arizona. We would camp at night in two separate camps. Geronimo's braves were not disarmed until we reached Fort Bowie.[18] Skeleton Canyon in Arizona was finally reached. There we halted and waited for General Miles to come to us. At the expiration of three days Miles came with an escort. Geronimo, Natchez, Chappo and Captain Lawton returned to Bowie with General Miles. The remaining Indians and our troop started for Fort Bowie and on the third day arrived there at ten o'clock in the morning, marched onto the parade ground. Then for the first time the hostile Indians were disarmed. The Indians were loaded into wagons and hauled to Bowie Station, on the railroad, fourteen miles distant from the fort. There a train was waiting them, and by four o'clock that afternoon the hostile Indians were aboard the cars, on their way to Florida, never to return to Arizona. Since their departure, in 1886, there has been no Indian outbreak.[19]

General Miles was presented with a sword mounted with diamonds by the grateful citizens, and promoted to a major-generalship soon afterward by the President. A controversy rose as to who was entitled to the credit of the surrender — Lawton or Gatewood. It was decided in Lawton's favor, and he was promoted from captain to major, remaining a major but a short time when he was advanced to be lieutenant colonel and acting inspector general of the department of the southwest.[20] When war was declared with Spain, Lawton went to Cuba as a brigadier general. He was promoted to be major general while serving in the Philippines, and when Major General Harry W. Lawton, one of the few major generals ever killed in action, fell, there fell one of the truest, bravest men on God's green earth. An appreciative and grateful public [was] to raise a generous fund for his needy widow and family, as Lawton died a poor man.

LAWRENCE VINTON (Lawrence R. Jerome)

Ex-soldier of B Troop, Fourth United States Cavalry.

NOTES

1. George Crook was born on a farm near Taylorsville, Ohio, on September 8, 1828, graduated from West Point in 1852, and was assigned to duty in California. During the Civil war he rose quickly to brevet major general of volunteers; however, after hostilities ceased in 1865, he reverted to the rank of lieutenant colonel. He served in Idaho Territory before assuming command of the Department of Arizona in 1871. There he discarded standard Army tactics, hiring Indian scouts while seeking to improve relations between whites and Indians. For more information, see Martin F. Schmitt (ed.), GENERAL GEORGE CROOK: *His Autobiography* (Norman: University of Oklahoma Press, 1946).
2. Nelson A Miles was born on August 8, 1839, at Westminster, Massachusetts. He ended his public school career at seventeen, but attended night school and read extensively. In 1860 he took instructions in military drill from a French Army veteran. During the Civil War he served in several major battles, and at the end of the war held the rank of major general of volunteers. He lost both his stars after the war, reverting to the rank of colonel. As commander of the Fifth Infantry Regiment, he fought the Plains Indians in 1874-1875 and the Sioux and Nez Percé shortly thereafter. He made national news when he marched his troop 160 miles through impossible terrain and extreme cold to capture Chief Joseph of the Nez Percé. For this action Miles received one coveted star, in 1880 when he was promoted to brigadier general. In the spring of 1886, he was sent to command the Department of Arizona. For additional information, see Newton F. Tolman, THE SEARCH FOR GENERAL MILES (New York, 1968); Nelson A. Miles, PERSONAL RECOLLECTIONS AND OBSERVATIONS (Chicago: The Werner Company, 1897) and SERVING THE REPUBLIC (New York, 1911).
3. General Miles appointed Captain Henry Ware Lawton, an officer in the Fourth Cavalry, to pursue the Indians south of the Mexican border. Miles admired the captain for Lawton also was a non-West Pointer who had risen by initiative. Lawton was born in 1843 in Toledo, Ohio. He served with distinction during the Civil War, rising from sergeant to brevet colonel of volunteers. In 1866 he was comissioned a second lieutenant of the Forty-first Infantry. After twenty years' service and numerous battles with the Indians, he was made a captain. Both Lawton and Miles agreed that the Apaches could be worn down by constant pursuit and eventually forced to accept Army terms. See Miles, *Personal Recollections and Observations.*
4. Fort Huachuca is located in Southeastern Arizona. It was established in 1877 and used periodically until the present. For information, see Will C. Barnes, ARIZONA PLACE NAMES (The University of Arizona Press, Tucson, 1960), p. 40; and Ray Brandes, FRONTIER MILITARY POSTS OF ARIZONA (Globe Arizona: Dale Stewart King, 1960), pp. 40-45.
5. Peck operated a small ranch just across the border in the Santa Cruz Valley of Arizona Territory. Peck may have been temporarily insane. The Apaches, fearing this as an evil sign or a contagious disease, freed him whereupon Peck made his way to Nogales. See Odie B. Faulk, THE GERONIMO CAMPAIGN (New York: Oxford University Press, 1969).
6. Captain T. C. Lebo was in command of Company K of the Tenth Cavalry, a company made up of many veterans of the Victorio Campaign of six years earlier. Lebo pursued the Indians with instructions from Miles to capture them at all costs. The Army caught the hostiles in the Piñito Mountains, but after a brief encounter the Indians fled. Lebo and his company were relieved shortly afterwards. For details see William H. Leckie, THE BUFFALO SOLDIERS (Norman: University of Oklahoma Press, 1967), pp. 243-244.
7. La Noria was located near the present town of Lochiel, Arizona. The name was changed to Lochiel in 1884. See, Barnes', *Arizona Place Names.*
8. For C. A. P. Hatfield's account of the Geronimo campaign, see "Expeditions against the Chiricahua Apaches, 1882 and 1883, and the Geronimo Campaign of 1885 and 1886," Gatewood Collection, Arizona Historical Society, Tucson.
9. Leonard Wood was a contract surgeon assigned to Lawton's command. Wood was born in Winchester, New Hampshire, on October 9, 1860, and, although he always wanted a

223

military career, he attended Harvard Medical School. After graduating in 1884, he practiced medicine in Boston for awhile, but soon tired of this dull life. In 1885 he took the Army examination for medical surgeons and was appointed an assistant contract surgeon on January 5, 1886. He was sent to Fort Huachuca, Arizona, where he joined Lawton's expedition. For information on Wood, see Jack S. Lane (ed.), CHASING GERONIMO: *The Journal of Leonard Wood May-September, 1886* (Albuquerque: University of New Mexico Press, 1970). See also Henry Creelman, "Leonard Wood — The Doctor who Became a General," *Pearson's Magazine*, Vol. XXI (April, 1909), pp. 361-383.

10. The Sierra Azul are located about seventy-five miles southeast of Fort Huachuca. See Hatfield, "Expeditions Against the Chiricahua."

11. For a description of recovery of the Peck child, see Lane (ed.), *Chasing Geronimo*, pp. 55-56.

12. Although Natchez became chief of the Chiricahua tribe in 1876, it was Geronimo who generally exercised the most influence and ultimately became best known. Geronimo was born in Arizona in 1829. His grandfather had been chief of the Mimbreño Apaches, but as his father had forfeited hereditary rights by marrying outside the tribe, the family became members of the Bedonkohe Apaches. In 1858, while trading with the Mexican village of Janos, this tribe was attacked by Mexican irregular troops and his wife, children, and mother were killed. Seeking vengeance, Geronimo allied his group with the Chiricahuas for war on Mexico. In April, 1877, he was arrested by Indian agent John Clum and taken to the San Carlos Reservation, and in 1881 he fled the reservation and eluded capture for almost two and one-half years. For general information of the Apaches, see Will C. Barnes, APACHES AND LONGHORNS (Los Angeles: Ward Ritchie Press, 1941). For the Geronimo Campaign, see Odie B. Faulk, *The Geronimo Campaign*.

13. General Miles sent Lieutenant H. C. Benson, in command of Troop B of the Fourth Cavalry, to pursue the Apaches. Benson was ordered to Fort Huachuca, and from there he traveled to Nogales where on May 2 he learned of Lebo's fight with the Indians and set the direction of pursuit. He led his men into Mexico and on May 5, relieved Lebo. Benson and his troops followed the hostiles day after day, deeper into the Sierra of Sonora, before they finally lost the trail. Benson and his company remained in the field for four months as part of a larger force tracking the fleeing Apaches. For information, see H. C. Benson, "The Geronimo Campaign," *Army and Navy Journal* (July 3, 1909), copy in the Gatewood Collection.

14. Río Haros, about 250 miles below the border, was the campsite of Lawton and his men for a short time. While camped at the river, Lawton was visited by Lieutenant Charles B. Gatewood, whom General Miles had sent to find Geronimo and convince the Indians to surrender. Charles Baehr Gatewood was born in Woodstock, Virginia, in 1853. He graduated from the Military Academy in 1877, whereupon he was assigned to the Sixth Cavalry. He served in New Mexico and Arizona until the fall of 1886. Although he had seen duty in the Victorio campaign of 1879 and several other expeditions, he had not been promoted beyond lieutenant. See Biographical File, Gatewood Collection, Arizona Historical Society. See also T. J. Clay to C. B. Gatewood, Jr., GOVERNMENT SCOUT AND INTERPRETER (Norman: University of Oklahoma Press, 1964).

15. Billy Long was a civilian courier for the expedition. For information, see Lane, *Chasing Geronimo*, p. 38.

16. Robert Woodward made a fortune in the gold fields during the early rush. He bought land and created a private park of great charm and beauty, in the area now bounded by Mission and Valencia, Thirteenth and Fifteenth Streets, San Francisco.

17. For information, see Torres, Decree to all Prefects, October 2, 1885, "Apache Folder, 1856-1886." Archives of Sonora (microfilm in Arizona Historical Society, Tucson). The treaty of July 29, 1882, ended after two years. Crook therefore had no treaty rights to enter Mexico and had to make a private agreement with Governor Torres.

18. Fort Bowie was established in 1862 and abandoned in 1894. From this fort in southwestern Arizona many expeditions were launched against the Indians. For information on the history of this fort, see Brandes, *Frontier Military Posts of Arizona*, pp. 14-21.

19. Contrary to the agreement Gatewood made with the Indians, they were held prisoners in Florida until 1888, then moved to Mount Vernon Barracks in Alabama until 1894 when they were moved to Fort Sill, Oklahoma. The Indians were held as prisoners of war until 1913, and never were allowed to return to Arizona. See Odie B. Faulk, *The Geronimo Campaign*.

20. Gatewood received nothing for his services — even a belated attempt in 1895 to award him the Medal of Honor failed because he had never come under hostile fire. Yet, he had fearlessly risked death by going into Geronimo's camp, unprotected by troops and had served his country tirelessly. Gatewood had every reason to be bitter when he saw others receiving promotions and rewards for services less significant than his. When he died in 1896, he was senior lieutenant in the Sixth Cavalry and eighth ranking lieutenant in the entire Army. For additional information, see Biographical File, Gatewood Collection.

Index

A

Adobe Walls, battle of, 119-124, 139, 147 nn.[5], [10]
Albee, Lt. George E., 141
Allin, Erskine S., 152
American Horse (Sioux), 188
Anadarko, 131
Anthony, Maj. Scott J., 25-31, 35, 38-40, 44
Apache Canyon, 23
Apache Indians, 17, 176, 207-210, 217ff.
Appleman, Roy E., 171 n.[22]
Arapaho Indians, 1-2, 7, 17, 20, 22, 25-26, 29, 42, 62, 68, 70, 73ff., 90-91, 100, 103, 106, 119, 125
Arapahoe County, Colorado, 20
Arickaree Fork, 72ff., 89, 92
Armes, Capt. George A., 51-56, 61-64
Armour, Judge Charles Lee, 11
Arnold, Courier Ben, 180
Augur, Gen. Christopher C., 124, 140

B

Bailey, Lt. Hobart K., 145-146
Baker City, Oregon, 202-204
Baldwin, Lt. Frank D., 125-128, 131, 144ff.
Bankhead, Capt. Henry C., 70, 75-76, 79-82, 84
Bannock Indians, 24, 191-205
Bannock-Piute War of 1878, 191-205
Barker, Capt. Edgar A., 54, 61, 63
Barr, Capt. Samuel L., 144 n.[11]
Bartlett, Lt. ――――――, 197
Bear River, 24
Beaumont, Capt. Eugene B., 141-142
Beaver (Cheyenne), 4
Beaver Creek, 64, 66 n.[29], 67 n.[32]
Beckwourth, Jim, 27, 37
Beecher, Lt. Frederick H., 70, 72, 73-75, 79, 83-84
Beecher Island, battle of, 68-84
Benham, H. C., 169
Bennet, Delegate H. P., 9, 42
Benson, Lt. H. C., 217, 219-220, 222, 224 n.[13]
Bent, Charles, 28, 62
Bent, George, 4, 12, 17, 29
Bent, Robert, 27
Bent, William, 1, 4, 7, 32, 62
Bernard, Capt. Rueben F., 192-194, 197-199, 202
Berthrong, Prof. Donald J., 2, 20
Bezold, Charles E., 169
Biddle, Major James, 126
Big Bow (Kiowa), 135
Big Creek station, 51-52
Big Head (Cheyenne), 109
Big Sandy, battle of, 70-71
Big Tree (Kiowa), 131, 135, 139, 149 n.[44]
Big Wolf (Cheyenne), 23
Bijou Basin, 24, 71
Bijou Creek, depredations on, 4
Black Bull (Sioux), 83

Black Hawk, 30
Black Hawk Daily Mining Journal, 11-12, 18-22, 25-26, 30-34, 37, 42
Black Kettle (Cheyenne), 5, 7, 12, 17-19, 26-27, 29, 49, 100, 102
Blinn, Mrs. Clara, 101, 116 nn.[31], [32]
Bluff Creek, 102
Blunt, Gen. James G., 8
Bodamer, Lt. John A., 52, 55
Boise City, 200, 203-205
Boone, A. G., 25
Booneville, 24-25
Bosse (Arapaho), 19
Boulder, 21
Bourke, Lt. John G., 175, 177-180
Bowen, Lt. Col. Leavitt L., 27, 30
Bowie Station, 222
Box Elder Creek, Indian raid on, 8
Bozeman Trail, 151
Bradford, Allen A., 11, 23, 25, 42
Bradley, Lt. Col. Luther P., 79-80
Brewster, D. A., 106, 111
Bridger, Jim, 90
Brisbin, Maj. James S., 80
Brooks, Bugler, 194
Brown, Scout George W., 115 n.[19]
Browne, District Attorney S. E., 36, 42
Buell, Lt. Col. George P., 125, 140, 143-144
Buffalo slaughter, a cause of the Red River War, 119
Buffalo Tank, 90
Buffalo Wallow, battle of, 135ff.
Bull Bear (Cheyenne), 17, 19, 73
Bunker Hill station, 50
Burlingame, 93
Burton, ――――――, 200
Butler, Capt. Edmond, 83-84
Byers, Editor William N., 11, 18, 22

C

Cadero, Charlie, 62
California Joe, 101
Camas Meadow, fight at, 194
Camas Prairie, 198-199
Camp, W. M., 169-170
Camp Baxter, 24
Camp Beecher, 93-94, 99
Camp Bernard, 197
Camp Cloud Peak, Gen. Crook at, 175-188
Camp Collins, 9
Camp Crawford, 91-93
Camp Curry, 192, 194
Camp Duncan, 197
Camp Elbert, 24
Camp Evans, 21-22, 24
Camp Hackberry Point, 99
Camp Harney, 194
Camp Lawrence Babbitt, 194, 197
Camp Lyon, 204
Camp Sanborn, 4-6
Camp Starvation, 99

225

Index

U

Umatilla Indians, 202
Umatilla Reservation, 192-193
Union Administration Party, of Colorado, 11, 43
Union Pacific Railroad, Eastern Division, 50
Unrau, Professor William E., 44 n.[1]
Upper Arkansas Indian Reservation, 1-2
Upper Platte Indian Agency, 1-2
Upper Washita, battle of, 148 n.[24]
Ute Indians, 1

V

Valley Station, 21-22
Vancouver, 202, 205
Van Wormer, Isaac P., 8
Vestal, Stanley, 171 nn.[2,28], 172 n.[71]
Viele, Capt. Charles D., 146
Vinton, Lawrence (Trooper Lawrence R. Jerome), account of Geronimo Campaign, 206-223

W

Wade, Senator Ben, 40
Wagon Box corral, 156ff.
Wagon Box fight, 151-168; controversy over site, 168-170
Wagon Train Charge, on McClellan Creek, 144-146
Walla Walla, 193, 199-202
Wallula, 200
War Bonnet (Cheyenne), 29
Washakie (Shoshone), 182, 187
Washita, battle and battleground, 100-103, 107, 113
Watson, Thomas, 209-210
West, Lt. Frank, 131, 132, 135
Wheaton, Gen. _____, 198-202

Whiskey, illegal trade in, effect on Indians, 119
White Antelope (Cheyenne), 28-29
White Fish Creek, 128
White Horse (Cheyenne), 73
White Rock stage station, 53
White, Sarah C., 108-111, 118 n.[58]
Whiteley, Agent Simeon, 19
Whitney, Scout Chauncey B., 75, 81
Wichita, 93
Wichita Agency, 131
Wichita Mountains, 104
Wilder, Maj. William F., 21
Wilkinson, Lt. Melville C., 192, 203
Wilson, Lt. Luther, 27
Wilson, Scout William, 75, 83
Wilson Creek station, 50
Winnemucca, Sarah (Piute), 193, 197-198, 201 203-204
Winnemucca Stage Road, 204
Winters, Capt. _____, 199
Wisconsin Ranch, 22
Woman's Heart (Kiowa), 139
Wood, _____, 197-198
Wood, Dr. Leonard, 211, 219, 223 n.[9]
Woodall, Sgt. Zachariah T., 135ff.
Woodward, George, 219, 221
Woodward, Robert, 224 n.[16]
Woodward's Gardens, in San Francisco, 219
Worrall, Dr. Thomas D., 11
Wright, Jack W., 34, 42
Wyck's party of engineers, 53
Wynkoop, Maj. Edward W., 6, 12, 17-20, 24-26, 35-36, 41, 44

Y

Yellow Bear (Arapaho), 106
Yellow Shield (Cheyenne), 29
Yellow Wolf (Cheyenne), 29

231